Children:
To Have or Have Not?

CHILDREN:
TO HAVE OR HAVE NOT?

A Guide to Making and Living
With Your Decision

Diane C. Elvenstar, Ph.D.

**Published in San Francisco by
HARBOR PUBLISHING**

Distributed by G. P. Putnam's Sons

For information contact Harbor Publishing, 1668 Lombard Street, San Francisco,
CA 94123.

Printed in the United States of America.

Composition and interior design: Printed Page Graphics
Copyeditor: Julie Segedy
Text printer & binder: Fairfield Graphics
Cover illustration and design: Lynn Hollyn Associates

ISBN: 0-936602-39-2

To Elvie and Raccoon.

Acknowledgements

I would like to thank Professor Alexander W. Astin of the UCLA Graduate School of Education for his willingness to support a determined graduate student foolish enough to take on an enormous task. His patience in helping me shape the counseling treatments which became the basis of this book, and in making sense of computer printouts which to me were only baffling columns of numbers, deserves considerable praise.

I would also like to thank Chris Conrad for seeing the possibilities of this book, and easing my transition from magazine and newspaper writer to author. She deserves additional kudos for putting me in touch with the most upbeat and supportive literary agent around, Mike Hamilburg of the Mitchell Hamilburg Agency. His warmth has carried me through some frustrating times.

Jack Jennings, President and Publisher of Harbor Publishing, Inc. is due many thanks for his vision and confidence in the importance of this book. His enthusiasm, encouragement and diplomacy are deeply appreciated.

Finally, I could never leave out my husband, Mickey, who keeps my spirits from sagging and proof-reads on short notice, even when he's busy.

Contents

Introduction

The decision of whether or not to have a child has never been more difficult. Suddenly, it seems, books, newspaper articles, and college courses everywhere are bubbling over the childbearing dilemma. Magazine covers blare teasers of case studies sure to intrigue every passerby. Housewives discuss the pitfalls of their status—how little Susie kept them awake or how prowling Sam trampled a neighbor's garden. Most everyone agrees that parenthood is not to be entered into hastily—that the responsibilities are many and the importance of the job enormous—but nobody has described how to make the crucial decision easier. This book arose out of a need for tools to help make that decision.

Of course, there are a few things most people do on their own to help the process along. It's typical to mull over pros and cons and then talk about them with your partner. Many people whip out legal pads and write down their reasons to parent or to delay. It's also common to consult other people: cousins who successfully oversee their own broods, parents who enjoyed raising you, co-workers who now joyfully or warily await delivery due-dates. Scads of books tell how to be a fantastic parent and have control of your developing charge, how to whip colic and mend a scraped shin. Others tell how to live the life of the model nonparent, investing surplus cash wisely, taking off for romantic spontaneous soirees in foreign climes, preparing that candlelight tete-a-tete for two.

But no one addresses the transition. How do you go from happy couple to untraumatized threesome without trepidation? How do you handle the misgivings that accompany any change—the "buyer's remorse" of both parenthood and a childfree choice?

Few researchers had tackled this question in the early '70s when I first began to follow the parenting issue. After I made my own choice, I saw that others had also discovered there were options and had begun to consider alternatives. They examined the issues rationally and asked, "Are these good reasons to have a child?" They listed things *every* parent would deny were motivations—even if, underneath, the reasons figured heavily in the choice. Then they capped off all their information by stating the only reason for childbearing they considered valid: "Because you want one."

But what exactly *is* this "want," potential parents wondered. How do I decide, when everyone around me has his own idea of what's best? If all these are wrong reasons, and if I admit to any of them, does that automatically disqualify me from being a good parent? All these questions were usually accompanied by the sinking feeling of being all alone, the only freak who can't make what everyone says is such a natural decision.

This gap encouraged me to do a little pioneering—to devise a format to bring together the best of the lists, questionnaires, and forms to really get a grip on elusive emotions; a way to systematically pay attention to both the logical and the emotional side of the decision. As more and more people seemed to be grappling with this decision, its potential grew.

Most of us would agree that pregnancy shouldn't happen without prior knowledge that the child will be cared for and loved. People need to become fully aware of the ramifications of parenthood so that the child's life can be as rewarding as possible. Perhaps, I thought, they need a clearly outlined *process,* which could serve as both a prerequisite to parenthood as well as a decision-making device for those unsure about their desire for children.

When I began tackling this task, I was able to address some of my own conflicts, and I realized that despite my openness to new attitudes, I was in transition.

Like most people, I was raised to think having children was an accepted part of life. I remember challenging my father about his reasons for punishing me, to which he'd respond with all the soft-hearted authoritarianism he could summon: "Because I'm your father, that's why! When you have children, then you can tell *them* what to do!" Indisputable logic. It was his right to tell me what to do; I'd get mine when it was my natural turn.

There were other subtle proparenthood messages. My parents had me and two younger siblings late in life after years of trying and often commented how we "kept them young." My mother gladly followed the fashion of the 1950s, putting aside her secretarial career and joining her peers in baking contributions to PTA fund-raisers. With this kind of model (and an ingrained need to achieve and please) I knew my role in life.

At least part of it. There were contradictions in the messages my conventional parents sent me. On one hand, it was women's destiny to raise progeny. On the other, they told their firstborn she could be anything she wanted in life—I could grow up to be the first lady president, they assured me.

One of their hopes I did fulfill was finding a suitable mate. I remember the women clucking around me at my fancy bridal shower. As I broke the ribbon on one gift, the guests took pleasure in chorusing, "Oh, you'll have a *pink* baby!" Or on a package of another hue, "You'll have a *blue* baby!"

"I'm not having *any* babies!" I retorted, still planning on parenthood but feeling resentful. I felt openly committed to doing my bit to end the population problem; unconsciously, though, I think I was afraid to confront the changes of parenthood.

The elderly women clicked their tongues, winked at each other, and nodded, "Oh, you'll change your mind!" I collected dishtowels, and the ladies left smugly satisfied.

The term "optional parenthood" was in no one's vocabulary when my husband and I discovered there was a choice. It hit him first. One day as he waited for me while I picked up some documents at City Hall, a young woman passed by battling with three screaming children. One whined, clutching at her skirt. Another trailed behind, wailing. A baby blasted from a stroller. The noise echoed in the formal Spanish rotunda. When I emerged from my business, my husband shared his new revelation: we didn't *have* to have any children!

As time passed, nonparenthood began to be accepted in wider circles. The National Organization for Non-Parents (now the National Alliance for Optional Parenthood), for instance, provided support for people choosing this new lifestyle. Though the notion that childlessness can be desirable was still deviant, at least it was suddenly being discussed.

My husband and I didn't talk about it much, however. We were too busy with midterms and part-time jobs, and more existential issues crowded our thoughts as we prolonged our formal educations. Deciding about children is important and scary. We wanted to be sure to consider everything.

Later, while groping for a dissertation topic for my doctorate in counseling at UCLA, a psychology professor encouraged me to do a term project on nonparenthood. I compiled the limited research available in 1976, but I didn't care who decided what. The outcome, choosing to become a parent or nonparent, did not fascinate me as much as the crucial questions of *why* and *how* the decision was made. I found there was little available information about the decision-making process and no method to evaluate the decision systematically.

So that became my task. I incorporated existing research into questionnaires, and devised a personalized scoring system. I defined and specified what's involved in the choice and what the goals of the new method would be. I talked with experts for suggestions. I laid out ways to measure change.

The result was a study of 65 couples, each one spending a week trying out one of the two approaches I'd developed. I wanted to find out demographic characteristics of people who grappled with the childbearing question and whether or not my procedures could help them. I was pleased to find that distress over the decision was significantly reduced after couples completed the newborn decision-making processes.

Soon couples who had heard about my method began to come to me asking to try it. The workshops I developed in answer to this need have grown increasingly popular. But not everyone has time to attend; not every couple feels comfortable asking for help or sharing private feelings with others. This book was intended for such an audience. It is a personalized series of case studies, exercises, and ideas to help you probe and define your own values, expectations, and feelings—your own life.

What Will You Get Out of This Book?

The goal of this book is to help you feel better about the childbearing issue by resolving your own inner conflicts and those of your partner. There are several benefits and also drawbacks of tackling the process. First the drawbacks:

1. *Decision making can be emotionally difficult.* If your own childhood wasn't a collage of pleasant memories, your vision of parenthood may be colored blue. It hurts to know the parenting you'd give would be a far cry from the kind you got or that you might perpetuate the same physical or emotional abuse you may have suffered. It is frightening to realize that you're responsible for the decision or that you're alienating your friends by your feelings. It is crushing to think there's an imbalance of love in your relationship, especially if you're the one who's willing to bend.

2. *You have to work at it.* It would be great if this book could solve all your problems about having a child. You could twirl a spinner marked with "baby," "baby in five years," or "childfree life." No such luck. You've got to invest time and effort—reading, thinking, talking to friends and experts, reading supplementary material, watching your family, children at the park—while your own feelings constantly change hue. You might want to copy the questionnaires in this book and do each one twice, on different days to compare moods and perspectives. You might want to talk to your friends who backpacked through Europe with 8-month-old Amy, or browse a few Sunday afternoons in the infants' section of a department store.

Any project that is time consuming and not always painless is likely to be put off. That's when these two drawbacks surface, when you'll be tempted to set the book on the shelf. Procrastination potential can be a drawback in itself— and you *must* want to resolve the issue or you wouldn't be reading this now.

Don't get too distressed, though—there are bountiful benefits:

1. *You'll gain information to help make a clear choice.* For example, many couples feeling pinched for time are relieved to discover that they have far longer biologically than they first suspected. They're often afraid that postponing parenthood will mean they'll face high risk of a Down's syndrome (Mongoloid) child—but in fact at age 30, the chances are only one in 885; at age 35, they're one in 365; and at age 40, there's still only an 8-percent risk, or one in 109. And amniocentesis, a test where fluid is drawn from the sack surrounding the fetus and then examined, can allow older parents the option of abortion if their child does have a chromosomal abnormality.

Others benefit by learning about new childcare alternatives or hearing that the percentage of childless couples is steadily rising, up to 11 percent of all women 18–34 in 1978. Knowing, first, that you're not alone and, second, that there are abundant resources for new parents can cinch an inclination or let you relax about the decision for a while.

2. *You'll have a definite, structured framework for making the decision.* You may have talked about having a child for hours, written "pro and con" lists, and read every motherhood story in the library. But here's a method you can personalize to your own needs. All the ingredients for the decision are presented so you can digest them bit by bit, at your own convenience. If there's anything you might have overlooked, here is a source for new areas of insight.

3. *You'll gain understanding of your partner's feelings and your own.* You can array your own values, expectations, and feelings from a variety of perspectives. Which values are important enough to remain firm? Which expectations of the future are realistic and which are daydreams? You can refer to written thoughts and noted comments, rearranging and revising them in a context of exchange with your partner.

4. *You'll strengthen your relationship with your partner.* If there are deeply rooted problems in a relationship, people often gain the strength to face them and go their separate ways. But most people report that focusing their feelings and beliefs, and taking the time to share them, brings them warmly together. "Oh, I didn't know you felt that way!" starts new discoveries of taken-for-granted thoughts.

5. *You'll find new strategies for solving problems.* By reading cases of others like yourself, talking to others, and pondering the choices in your future, you'll glean new possibilities. Maybe you'll see how to mesh childcare with a busy professional schedule or discover ways to deal with critics of the childfree lifestyle. You might see how three can get by as cheaply as two (and for how long they manage it) or how professionally working with children can serve as a replacement for parenthood without all the fuss. The forms in this book are designed to help you think up ways around roadblocks.

6. *You'll have tools you can use over and over.* If you "decide not to decide," you'll have a record of how you feel now for reference when you return to the issues later. If circumstances change or you feel ready to confirm your choice, you'll have the tools and the method to try the process again.

Children:
To Have or Have Not?

1

A Most Important Decision

Barbara and Mark have been married eight years, a period that has sped by as they each completed graduate school and started their careers. Barbara is the director of public relations for a large hospital, and enjoys lunches with local editors, staging receptions for visiting physicians, and writing press releases. Mark is a speech pathologist for the local school district, now supervising two dozen therapists on the school level.

"I can't believe I'm 35," Barbara muses, sitting in my office. "I feel so energetic, like I always have, though I do feel entitled to the responsibility I've earned. It's as though I'm just getting started; finally my career's falling into place. And our relationship has become better too—we're so close that often we'll be thinking the same thing at the same time."

Barbara's only real problem was her reluctance to trade the life she and Mark now had for the child she was finding herself desiring more and more. "Mark's on the fence, too—we're so possessive of what we've got that we hate to lose it, yet it comes down to asking the fundamental question of what life's about. Somehow, the answer keeps reducing to love, for each other, for life, and for something

1

more, which I think is family and continuity through generations. I find myself looking at children now, and I never paid them any attention before. I listen when the pregnant women in my office talk, and I fantasize about what I'd name my own child."

Barbara was talking softly, intensely. It was clear that the issue exposed a serious nerve. When her husband Mark joined us, the concerns he expressed were equally serious.

"It's enough trying to share Barbara with her career. She's often at official functions two or three nights a week, and I really like to have her to myself. We're so free in the time we have together. Sometimes we'll just take off to dinner and a movie, and last year I surprised her with a weekend at a cabin I rented in the mountains."

What about his own desire for a child? "It's funny, but I've been thinking along those lines, too," Mark admitted, looking off in slight embarassment. "I'd heard of the mothering instinct before, but I feel a fathering urge. Last week in the park we both saw an adorable 4-year-old boy, and we just looked at each other, feeling the same longing. It was somewhat painful, because we're both so conflicted.

"And then there's the financial issue," Mark continued. "Barb's salary is not far from mine, and for her to take even a year off would really make it tight for us, especially since we're committed to a mortgage. I'd feel a lot of pressure, and we'd have to give up a lot of the extras we've become used to."

Barbara and Mark are typical of couples facing the childbearing dilemma. They know what they'd have to give up, not what they would gain, by having a baby. If your answer to any of the following questions is "yes," you share commonly expressed concerns.

Do You Share These Common Concerns?

1. Do you want the love and family closeness a child could bring, but wonder how you can fit it in with your advancing career?

2. Do you have doubts that daycare, a hired "nanny," or other childcare arrangements will be loving and educational enough to give your child the best start in life?

3. Are you worried that having a child would interfere with your professional competence, and the way others at work view you (or your partner)?

4. Are you afraid that the expense of a child will mean a decline in the standard of living you've achieved, or that such costs will keep you from reaching a standard of living you want?

5. Do you treasure the closeness you now share with your partner and worry that a child might change that?

6. Do you wonder if your life would lose excitement if you settle into parental responsibilities?

7. Do you feel unsure about the kind of parent you'd be or wonder if you and your partner will have conflicts over childrearing?

8. Are you happy with your circle of friends and worry that a child might change the way you fit in?

9. Do you wonder if, deep inside, you really want a child or if you're just listening to pressures of family or friends?

10. Do you wonder how a new baby will fit into your existing family— children from a previous marriage, brothers' or sisters' families, others with whom you are close?

11. Is it hard to imagine yourself as a parent, instead of the free and independent person you are now?

12. Are you afraid that having a child will tie you down and give you feelings of heavy responsibility?

13. Do you think you might resent being unable to take off spontaneously?

14. Do you value quiet, private times and wonder how you could retain them with a child?

15. Are you unsure you "want" a child enough to go ahead and have one?

16. Do you have fears about the processes of pregnancy and birth?

17. Do you generally dislike babies and wonder how you'd relate to your infant and all the baby-connected chores?

18. Do you worry that your teenager might be hard to talk with or control?

19. Do you worry that your child will have some kind of defect or problem?

20. Do you wonder if this is the best time to have a child—and if it isn't, are you concerned that you'll be unable to tell when the time *is* right?

21. Do you worry that you might regret your decision later on?

22. Do you think you're strange for feeling conflicted over a decision that is natural for most people?

The last question is included to show you that you're not alone in pondering the childbearing dilemma. In fact, you are in the forefront of an issue that every couple must confront.

The Childbearing Dilemma:
A Problem Now and in the Future

The parenthood question is a new problem, born out of recent technological advances and attitudes about family and women's roles which make childbearing a conflicting option.

Throughout the history of humankind, children have always been prized because they were so necessary. When famine or disease regularly wiped out half a mother's yield, extra children were needed as insurance that there'd be enough labor to maintain the family. Each child was another planter, harvester, or hunter to aid the survival of the family. Customs, codes, and laws were raised to holy writ to guarantee that no one hedged on the responsibility to procreate. The Bible's "be fruitful and multiply" command was backed up by warnings of sin and denial of the ultimate reward.

Having hosts of children was also associated with social benefits; the respected man had many sons to help him accumulate wealth. Though daughters were usually seen as burdens to feed and eventually sell, most cultures and religions acknowledged, and sometimes respected, women's child-producing accomplishments.

Policymakers in the United States have traditionally encouraged parenthood. "We're proud to announce another tax deduction!" headlines a popular baby announcement. Mother's Day advertisements play on our guilt by hinting that we're not honoring our worthy creators enough during the rest of the year. The term "sanctity of the family" usually doesn't refer to a childless couple—in fact, many marriage licenses are secured in order to have a family with the blessing of the state.

These encouragements to parenthood are called *pronatalism*. And nowhere else is pronatalism more prevalent than in the media, partly because advertisers cater to their audience's existing attitudes to sell their products. Consumerism naturally extends to buying the "best for baby," just as associating youthful motherhood with hair coloring plays on ingrained positive feelings. It's a circle that perpetuates itself. People grow up to revere parenthood, and advertisers grab this to encourage further exhaltation. Yet the same ones who tout baby cosmetics also realize the profits in products for singles ("soup for one"; single-serving packaging) and will appeal to child-free couples when their numbers become sizable enough to be lucrative.

Why Deciding About Childbearing Seems Suddenly Important

1. Reliable Contraception

The birth control revolution made parenthood a real option for the first time. Many of our own mothers can attest to the unreliability of pregnancy-prevention methods prior to the pill, many other mothers to more recent unreliability as well. The fact that the diaphram isn't foolproof was less critical in an age when a full family was desired.

Reliable contraception has allowed prospective parents to plan *when* to have children, but while the siblings' age difference became a matter of choice, it took the availability of failsafe contraception *and* a new set of attitudes to change the question from "when" to "if."

2. New Options for Women

The feminist movement also influenced the childbearing decision by allowing women viable and often economically essential alternatives to motherhood. As the 1960s crested, the idea that women's talents could be used in management as well as mothering caught on. "Equal opportunity" in education and work was extended beyond minorities to the feminine 51 percent of the population. Suddenly alternatives to tradition became available.

Some women who tried them found that entering newly opened fields required specialized preparation, so they filled training programs and colleges. Once prepared for new careers, female graduates have moved forward, enjoying accompanying psychological and economic rewards which they now hesitate to relinquish.

3. Women's Economic Importance

The dollars married women contribute have become increasingly necessary as inflation has edged the cost of living steadily upward. Even if staying home with Baby seemed an attractive use of time, many women felt compelled to work just to survive. This conflict created a pressure that has not existed since Depression days, when the birthrate was the lowest in America's history. Fertility records show that many women who reached childbearing age during the 1930s never got around to having children.

4. Changing Ideas About Families

New attitudes about parenthood, family size, and childcare surfaced in the 1970s. The threat of overpopulation led some couples to limit their reproduction, adopt, or forego parenthood altogether.

Smaller families have also become popular because of economics, a reversal from times when the traditional means of generating prosperity was a large brood. While more field hands previously meant greater yield and more wealth, farms began to become smaller and more automated during mid-century—and more bodies crowded into urban condominiums just don't bring added advantages.

The meaning and status of staying home with a child in the sedate 1950s and much of the 1960s has changed. Mothering was then an end in itself—and women often prepared for this laudable goal by majoring in home economics (perhaps learning to type or teach as something to "fall back on"). It was universally considered a privilege to be a homemaker, nurturing and caring for the breadwinner and wee ones. The idea was to give selflessly for the good of toothpaste-white smiles and a strong America.

But retrospectives of the 1970s tell a tale altogether different from earlier years. Dubbed the "Me Decade," people became more assertive about what they wanted for themselves. Values shifted; it became less fashionable to be devoted solely to the children and the home, more stylish to think of career, self-potential, and body—via jogging, tanning, and thinning—and not be ashamed of any of it.

Children even metamorphosed, on occasion, into millstones. "I love my children but . . ." became a common sentiment, as a child-support-free divorce became, for many, a goal. Admittedly, raising children may never have been a continuous tickle, but the "Me Decade" graduates refused to underplay the bad stuff any longer. Grinning and enduring the trials of parenthood, as many earlier parents had done, became passé.

Falling into Postponement

The World War II crop of children has been most affected by these changes, but the dilemma continues for their successors. Many products of the baby boom period fell into a postponement pattern identified by sociologist Jane Veevers in 1973. Caught in a crossfire of traditional promotherhood upbringing, exploring new career options, needing both incomes, pressuring from grandparent-aspirants, and encountering confusion over values and priorities, they often chose to put off dealing with the problem.

This procrastination pattern usually starts with the postponement of parenthood to a definite date. Couples who are sincere in their desire for children retain every intention of purchasing that layette— just not *yet*. The second stage begins when the deadline approaches and they realize the circumstances for a family are *still* not ideal. They need more time, until some sort of goal is reached: that new house, a promotion, a secure income level, something within grasp but still not quite attainable. In the meantime, of course, the postponers are getting older, becoming used to their childfree life and investments in their careers. So the reasons to remain childfree mount—after all, everything just seems so *comfortable*.

The third stage in the postponement process is when enlightenment strikes, and the couple finally acknowledges the benefits of the life they've been leading. They consider for the first time the possibility of permanent nonparenthood.

Eventually the issue of when to start having a family is seldom even discussed. The layette reserved by the grandparents for their firstborn is bequeathed to younger siblings. The hints have stopped coming, and well-intentioned friends and relatives—and the couple— begin to get on with other aspects of their lives.

The postponers usually believe that having children is desirable. Rather than bucking these feelings—as well as all their socialization—by announcing the intention to stay childfree, they simply "fall into" nonparenthood passively; circumstances rather than intentions get in their way. When the time available to procreate skims away, these couples are often consumed with flashes of regret or uncertainty that they've done the right thing. To avoid this remorse, many couples in this third stage choose to make their own decision before Mother Nature steals it away.

Who Struggles?

I composed a portrait of childbearing decision makers by sampling 65 volunteer couples. The average attendee was 30 years old, married just over five years, income over $20,000, well educated, and holding down a responsible job in management, the professions, or a creative, self-directed field. Of course, the fictional "average" person described above doesn't fairly represent the wide range of individuals who are confronted with the problem. Some couples are more invested in the decision than others. Some don't really have a problem at all, but just want to proceed with their lives cautiously. Others play the baby game for their parents and friends rather than for themselves.

In the following chapters, you'll meet some representative couples pondering the baby dilemma. Because I noticed certain recurrent patterns among couples, I classified decisionmakers into three major groups. Sometimes people see themselves in two of the groups—each individual faces the dilemma with a personal level of commitment, a unique background, and a special interpretation of values, expectations, and feelings. Discovering your uniqueness is the essence of the decision-making process.

While the process in this book will most frequently be used by couples in a solid relationship, I've also discovered three other groups who grapple with the decision. First there are *single people,* usually women, who wonder whether or not to have children. Many choose adoption, and more agencies are placing children in the custody of singles. When single people have attended my workshop, they've usually had two concerns.

Leslie, an independent, confident public relations woman, wanted to have a child. She was nearing 30, had no strong prospects for marriage, and did not want to wait for the fulfillment she knew motherhood would bring. She planned to either be artificially inseminated or simply to "forget" birth control when with a partner who had traits desirable to pass on to her child.

But Leslie didn't want to enter motherhood blindly either. She was aware of social stigmas attached to single parenthood. She knew that her chances of finding a mate—and a father for her child— would diminish if she gave birth. She also wasn't entirely sure that taking the drastic step was right for her now. She wanted to sort it all out.

Marsha also wanted to look at parenthood's considerations before taking an irreversible step—sterilization. She too had never been married, and at age 32 was realizing that she may never find a spouse. She had recently decided that her life could be full and rewarding as a single person, and felt she would never want any children.

But before undergoing sterilization, Marsha also wanted to be sure that there weren't any deeply seated yearnings for motherhood she was sweeping into the closet. She wanted her decision to be as rational as possible.

Homosexuals have also become increasingly concerned with parenthood. Many have the stability of a gay marriage and consider children a logical addition to a strong relationship. Gay men have asked about the prospects of adoption—which are not very good if the gay relationship is acknowledged. But they don't want to give up the chance to parent just because their sexual preference happens to be atypical.

Gay women have used the services of male friends or relatives to conceive children. Many gay women choose long-term relationships, and the traditional training girls receive as youngsters often inclines them toward parenthood. But gays ponder the effects of their unions on their offspring and wonder if social disapproval will mean permanent scars on the children for whom they wish only the best.

A third group of people deciding about parenthood are teenagers. Unfortunately, they seldom take the time to really ponder all the issues but feel they are aware and capable of choosing for themselves. "Contraceptive neglect" is one theory offered to explain the more than 1 million annual teenage pregnancies in the United States. Some researchers suggest contraception implies "planning" for an act that teenagers are told is wrong. Another explanation, sometimes offered by young mothers themselves, is that they *want* a child to love, and to prove their adulthood.

The point is that teenagers do contemplate the possibility of pregnancy. But if they were to consider all aspects of parenthood presented in this book, perhaps they could plan their lives to benefit both themselves and their children.

The Process

This book will provide information and tools to use in your own decision about becoming a parent. You'll find there are three typical dilemmas—and chances are you'll see yourself in at least one of them. Through case studies, you'll discover ways to work with your partner to approach the question. You'll practice recognizing your own feelings, values, and expectations, and see how pressures of family, friends, and the media influence them. You'll be able to make the decision equipped with information on financial concerns, genetic considerations, childcare facts, and parents' and nonparents' reactions. In short, you'll be able to make the most well-informed and thoughtful decision possible.

And you'll probably feel good about it. That's the most important goal, remember—to help *you feel good* about the childbearing decision. Even if you "decide not to decide" until circumstances change, you'll still have the tools to make a satisfying final choice.

2

Now-or-Never:
Time-Pressured Quandary

I first thought the crux of the childbearing dilemma was uncertainty,
that people would approach me with puzzled expressions and hesitation. But I was wrong. Not everyone faces the same choice, and
I started to see how my clients' problems fell into three categories:
couples deciding about having a child "now or never," those in conflict with their partners, and those who want to look at all the ramifications of an existing choice.

The case studies to follow present couples in each of these three
groups. Rebecca and John are typical of "Now-or-Never" couples,
those who hear the clangs of the biological time clock and realize
that they can't remain indecisive forever. If they are going to have
a child, they've got to do it relatively soon, before the choice is made
for them through the passage of time. These couples are full of conflicts and worries about regrets they may have later. They like the
lives they have now and don't know if a child would be a blessing
or a burden.

Rebecca and John – Choosing Now or Never

Rebecca hollered through the screen, welcoming me to the rambling San Fernando Valley home she shared with her husband, John. "C'mon in!" she yelled from the kitchen. "I'll be right there!" I entered an immense living room dominated by a massive stone fireplace in the corner. A traditional-styled flowered sofa, at least 10 feet long, was backed up against a wall of windows looking out to their jungly back yard. Flanking the sofa were straight-backed antique chairs.

As I gazed at the surroundings, I nearly tripped on two Sheltie dogs that silently trotted into the room just before their master. John smiled easily as he strode into the room, his rugged, square-jawed face framed by straight blond strands. He was lean and agile, with a presence greater than his 5-foot 10-inch stature would suggest. Rebecca carried a tray of brunch appetizers from the kitchen.

As the three of us sat down, one of the Shelties, Joey, jumped onto Rebecca's—his "mommy's"—lap. She gave him a tidbit from the appetizer tray as the dog snuggled down to caresses. "*These* are our babies," Rebecca insisted, "but they don't cry and they don't need baby-sitters. They're always so grateful. I find myself looking forward to greeting them when I come home from the office."

John and Rebecca's dedication to their dogs was evident from the line of trophies along their mantel. I recalled last Christmas, when they had placed a handmade stocking with each of the dog's names above the fireplace next to their own. And yet, the couple didn't really seem to look at their "children" unrealistically.

"I know they don't understand a lot of what's going on," Rebecca continued. "And it's always in the back of my mind that dogs just don't live as long as people." She looked down at Joey, curled in an oval on her lap. "But we do teach them things, and they give their love unconditionally. And best of all," she grinned, "they don't talk back, take drugs, or hang around with motorcycle gangs."

John nodded and tamped tobacco into his pipe. Their home was dustless and orderly, showing methodical attention. And just as carefully, John now set up a row of pipes, a fancy lighter, pouches of tobacco, and a pipe rack on the antique table next to the wing chair. The pair were proud of their home and gave me a tour. The rooms were all enormous, and each had beamed ceilings. The master bed-room was set off by an antique quilt bedspread. The den, with its own stone fireplace and mantel crowned with pipe racks, sported deep-cushioned chairs placed just so. Sliding doors from the kitchen led to a patio and a huge backyard. Rebecca bubbled about their plans for building a brick barbeque. John chimed in with his dreams of training areas and hurdles for the dogs. They'd already turned a part of the garage into a workroom, where John's tools and Rebecca's handicraft materials were organized on wooden built-in shelves.

As we stood under a drooping avocado tree, Rebecca returned to the topic of children. "As you can see, we're just now getting everything together. We're planning for what *we* want to do, though, and not for a possible child." John slowly shook his head as Rebecca spoke, as if just the thought of a child turned him off. "But you see, most of what we do is centered around our home. Sure, we galli-vant off to dog shows occasionally. But we love our dogs like our babies—" she knelt next to Mollie, sitting patiently at her feet— "Don't we baby? Huh?" We all laughed and returned inside for some eggs benedict.

"Aunt Penny's, sure, it's Aunt Penny's," Rebecca announced when I oohed at the smoothness of the hollandaise. "Why not use canned sauce when it looks and tastes as good as homemade?" That was Rebecca's style. She unabashedly announces the truth and her feelings with pride. She's no retiring or sophisticated type. She knows what she wants and pursues it.

Just like she does in her work. Rebecca is the supervisor of 18 employees in an office that processes insurance claims for a univer-sity hospital. She efficiently manages thousands of pieces of paper and millions of dollars, and wins the respect of everyone around her. When I visited her at work once, she handled questions quickly and calmly, sharing other workers' frustration with problems.

The Xerox machine outside her office broke down, and instead of delegating the chore of fixing it or calling a repairman, she simply snapped open the side of the machine and fished around for a gnarled piece of paper caught in the innards. Rebecca could handle most anything and was never afraid to try.

That's why she was so distressed over the decision about having a child. At age 36, she knew she couldn't avoid the question much longer, and yet there were far fewer clear-cut solutions to this problem than to the practical ones at home or work. One of her main sources of concern was that a child would change the smooth and comfortable life she and John had constructed for themselves over the past three years.

"John was married before," Rebecca explained when asked about their road to current bliss. "He and his wife lived in the midwest. He was a mechanic and she a housewife. All their family is back there and they were somewhat ensconced in the traditional lifestyle."

John picked up the tale. "Rebecca had some friends in the same town where my ex-wife and I lived who she visited one summer." He drew a long breath on his pipe and grinned at his wife. "She actually stole me away from my marriage." I raised my eyebrows in surprise. "That's right," John confirmed. "You might say Rebecca was a home-wrecker. But it really wasn't much of a home in the first place."

In fact, Rebecca had given up her job and apartment in Los Angeles to be with John during his separation and divorce. They married soon thereafter and returned to the West Coast. Just a year ago they purchased their home and are now enjoying a secure life style. Until now, they were just too involved in getting their lives together to consider having a child.

"I don't think we'll have one," John confessed as Rebecca prepared fruit and cheese in the kitchen. "I'm perfectly satisfied right now, and I don't think a child would significantly improve our lives. We're at the point where we're getting older, more settled, and, yes, perhaps more selfish. I was doing for my parents, then my first wife, and then struggling to find a good job. Now I'm happy with Rebecca. We have some time to travel to show the dogs, take long weekends here and there—and I can't imagine giving them up to powder some baby's bottom."

John always amazed me in the inconsistency between his job and outward trappings and his true personality. He is an incredibly quiet and patient man and respects Rebecca's strong-willed notions. They are almost opposites in personality, yet very compatible. Rebecca talks an entertaining streak, while John relaxes in his wing-backed chair and doesn't mind one bit that attention is showered on his wife. Rather than leaving all the housework to her, John does more than half of it. The home is his domain, and he gingerly returns curios to their positions on tables after proudly showing them off to visitors.

When John and Rebecca completed the workshop, they were still perplexed about the childbearing decision. John was clearer on his reasons for believing they would never be parents. Rebecca conceded that perhaps John was right—they might just keep postponing pregnancy indefinitely. But she refused to give up the idea that they could still change their minds. "I want all those warm cuddly feelings!" she lamented after the workshop ended. "I want all those goodies that cooing babies bring. It's delightful to hold my niece's infant. I don't want to put her down until I go home. But I realize then that I don't want to take the baby home with me either. I like coming home to the two dogs, always running around in circles in glee. But I'm just not ready to come home to diaper pails and 2 AM feedings.

"And yet," she continued to muse, "I know these inconveniences are just temporary. I know that in a few years I'll have a real person to talk to, someone who will develop independently—and I can marvel that I created that life!" She looked down, her face sombering.

"And also, the child will be mine forever. I do think about that— a child will be there to give me warm family feelings always, into my old age. That part is selfish, I think." Rebecca could honestly evaluate most of her feelings and reasons, but she was still undecided. She was glad to know that with amniocentisis, she had a couple more years to debate. The extra time was like a reprieve from a visit to the dentist, though, instead of an aid to planning her life with a longer-range perspective.

At least she didn't need to leave time to have a large brood. "If we did have a child, just one would be perfect, no more," Rebecca said resolutely. She had spent days daydreaming about what her child would be like and how she would juggle all her responsibilities. As a deliberate, conscientious person, she knew she could do it all. "We'd be darn good parents," she admitted, raising her head suddenly. "We'd give our child everything—I'm sure he or she would be spoiled rotten. But there'd be discipline, there'd be responsibility for small household tasks from the time he or she could do them."

Meanwhile, John leaned back in his chair and shook his head once more. "Sure, we'd be fantastic parents. If we did have one, we'd be devoted all the way. But I can't see us intentionally deciding to take a dozen years—and the rest of our lives, too, for that matter—to tend to the many chores that accompany parenthood. We're just too wrapped up in a hassle-free existence. I would only want a child if Rebecca and I became really *enthusiastic* about the proposition. I don't want any child of mine ever feeling like a burden to his parents."

Rebecca had pinpointed their concerns fairly easily. Financial worries didn't exist. Their relationship was sublime. Pressures from parents and friends were easily recognized and dismissed. Career interruptions could be arranged.

"The problem's inside me," Rebecca reflected. "I just don't know what I want, and I'm too scared to go ahead and make a commitment."

The next time I saw Rebecca she was as unsure as ever. "People keep asking us if we've made up our minds about having a child," she told me. "Well, the truth is, *I* haven't. John still thinks we'll just coast along without having one, and I guess he's probably right. But since I have so much control in every other area of my life, I want to make a conscious choice. After going through the workshop, all my reasons and feelings are clear. And yet I somehow just can't let go of one of life's most treasured experiences." Rebecca's voice, normally booming, had sunk to a whisper.

In the six months since that conversation, Rebecca has moved on to a better job running a public relations office. John still enjoys tinkering with transmissions. Their house now boasts two recently purchased antique hutches. Mollie has been bred and has a litter of puppies—and Rebecca is thrilled.

She's not so pleased with her continuing indecision about having a baby. The fact that she's letting time go by without making a firm choice sticks in the back of her consciousness, she tells me, though she tries not to notice its disturbing effects.

John and Rebecca are typical of "Now-or-Never" couples, confronting the childbearing question after years of achievement. They've excelled in careers, waded through first marriages, and postponed material things while educations were prolonged. Before they realize it, they're into their thirties, experiencing the "good life" they've waited for.

External pressures from family and pronatalist media push couples into now-or-never distress. But much of the anxiety comes from inside, from psychological forces that first germinated during childhood. These feelings are especially strong in women. After all, little girls play with dolls and receive praise for acting "just like a little lady." Little boys, on the other hand, aren't expected to think about such things as eventual fatherhood; they're too busy playing with miniature tool kits and doctors' stethoscopes.

When women eventually confront the realities of motherhood, they often feel conflict. They may be enjoying growth in a fantastic career or their financial contributions to the household. Women who face the now-or-never choice often feel like Rebecca—even thinking about the urgency of the decision sends them into anxious fits of up-again-down-again ambivalence. It's an excruciating choice. Having a child is a crisis and many of the ramifications are unknown. The insecurity is enough to upset even the strongest, most organized person.

Men making the now-or-never choice are often as uncertain as their partners, but biologically and emotionally have far less investment in the decision. Like John, they may offer to assume half of the responsibility for the child, and sometimes are even willing to accommodate fatherhood by altering their career schedules. Too often, however, the accommodations don't last. After all, most men argue indisputably, adjusting their lives *too* much would mean an untenable reduction in income. And, heaven confirms, *they* know considerably less than their wives about baby related chores anyway. While Rebecca was pleased by John's willingness to be a participatory parent, she had underlying feelings of distrust, having seen too many cases where well-intentioned fathers end up coasting along as their wives take up the slack.

"That's what I'm afraid of," Rebecca confided one day. "John will be the perfect, unselfish daddy when we're both around to do the chores. But when the chips are down, his transmission will need repairing more than my meeting needs attending."

Rebecca also knew that she had a need to command; to do every-thing *right*. Rather than let John fumble through the bath-giving, fin-gernail clipping, and endless cleaning, she'd want to simplify matters by doing the jobs herself. Yet she was afraid it would soon become a habit hard to shake.

Much as now-or-never women like Rebecca assert that they want to continue their jobs, that they'll delegate tasks to their husbands, that it's *desirable* to leave the child in the hands of competent day care and continue working—somehow there's a nagging tug to stay home, forsake the career (at least temporarily), and raise the child *right*. Rebecca was torn by this conflict, at one point confessing that the decision scared her because, once made, she could never change her mind and go back to the career status she held before. She felt that the dual roles of mother and career woman were compatible, but to pursue them both she'd have to give up something of each.

As a mother, she'd be concerned about her child's development in her absence; yet leaving work to raise a child would suggest to her employer that her family took priority over her career. This double bind kept Rebecca from confronting the issue. And because she was 36 and had few childbearing years left, the psychological consequences of putting off the decision were magnified.

As time passed, her guilt about ignoring the question grew. Her terror of making the choice increased. Subsequently, she became more and more involved in a career, life-style, and marriage that afforded security and comfort.

John didn't help the situation either. His passivity and silence panicked Rebecca even more. He said he'd go along with her choice, but he voiced only vague predictions of slipping into a decision by default, which put more pressure on Rebecca to take responsibility for making a conscious decision and, in turn, added to her strong anxiety.

In a sense, John dangled a carrot in front of Rebecca, teasing her and then avoiding any constructive determination. He said he'd gladly be a great daddy, if that was what Rebecca wanted—so she had a promise with a contingency. If she asked John to come through and take on the father role, only to find for herself that motherhood was *not* what she wanted, then she'd have to bear the additional guilt of imposing parenthood on a partner originally willing to settle for a childfree life.

There are three outcomes for now-or-never couples. About half of them reluctantly admit that they'll probably end up without taking the plunge. They may hate to let go of an option, just as Rebecca did, but they're honest enough to admit that they're set and comfortable in their ways. They also realize there are other outlets for their parenting tendencies. Some realize they simply aren't parent types and don't want to be encumbered by the responsibilities of raising children—or perhaps that they don't even like children at all.

Many other now-or-never couples share a sinking boat with Rebecca. When they discover amniocentisis, it's as if more hours have been added to their biological time clocks. They deliberately take this new-found time to rethink and reevaluate their choices, sometimes setting deadlines—often one or two years away—for resolving to come to a final decision. Like Rebecca, they just don't want to face the decision now, and because the urgency of the choice is temporarily postponed, feel they have a respite before dealing with the difficult decision again.

Still other now-or-never couples examine their motives and decide to have a child within a year—many whom begin as soon as possible. These are often methodical problem-solvers who see parenthood as a series of specific steps, and want to predict the precise impact a child would have on their lives. Working through the decision-making phase has turned vague options into concrete acts and consequences. Although some of the results are, of course, unpredictable, parenthood becomes manageable by dividing it into component influences.

To identify your own type of now-or-never behavior, take a look at your life. You can learn the most about your future from past behavior patterns. Here are a few common patterns.

Couples who decide to *forego parenthood* usually have entered into romantic relationships relatively late in life—often without previous marriages or children. They've become respected in their professions and have held the same job for several years. They like to travel and value their independence. Their lives are filled with outings and adventures. They are also realistic about their unwilling-ness to change and want to keep what they've got with few com-promises. They almost invariably have very satisfying relationships with their partners.

Women like Rebecca who postpone the final choice even further often feel the weight of the decision on themselves, even though their partners claim they're equally involved. In many cases, the male will defer the final decision to his mate, which is generous and accom-modating but also presents the woman with an albatross of respon-sibility. These women have often had difficulty making decisions in the past and have sought others' advice when making important choices. Their partners might have been willing to provide direction on other matters, but refrain from doing so now. These women enter the decision-making process hoping that a decision will magically appear; they hesitate to confront the conflicting feelings, values, and expectations that are the root of the problem. They are efficient achievers, but procrastination might be their middle names.

Now-or-never choosers who decide *in favor of parenthood* are quite different. They are well-organized and stick to their plans on schedule. They are prompt in paying bills, on time for appointments, and observe deadlines for reports and other assignments. Yet they're flexible. If an unforeseen event pops up, they'll deal with it effec-tively. An exterior of efficiency masks strong underlying emotionality, however; their feelings are openly and honestly expressed. Women who decide to go ahead and have a child *know* they want one and have a workable plan to make it happen. While there still may be uncertainties about what the future holds, there's an inherent confi-dence that it will work out. Moreover, their spouses are supportive and in full accord with their decision.

In every case, time forces a decision. Most couples who have been together more than five years have fallen into the four-step post-ponement process described earlier. They just never found the right time to have children. First there was preparation—an extended education, the "dues-paying" of lower-level jobs, the search for a mate. A few years of stabilization followed. Then came a dreamed-of vacation perhaps, or a few expensive possessions, or maybe even a house. As obligations at work increased, dinners out became a habit.

And the scramble continued. New career goals became tempting. There was more dependence on that paycheck. A better position appeared, or business required hours of overtime. Nothing slowed down, but the worry about deciding started to nag. As time unmercifully slithered by, the anxiety increased until it fell in the lap like a pie sinking from its mark.

That's the nature of the now-or-never choice. Its weight is strong and constant: either act now and have a child, or give up parenthood forever.

Donna and Matthew — Deciding to Have a Child

One now-or-never couple who made the decision to have a child fit into the typical pattern. Donna, a social worker, was not sure that she wanted the responsibility of motherhood and was afraid of the alterations she would have to make to accommodate her child. She telephoned me as soon as she heard about the workshops, relieved that she could find other couples who suffered a similar distress.

After the first session was over, Donna, Matthew, and I had lunch. As we slid into the booth at a deli, she murmured, "Even as simple a thing as having lunch out would be a problem."

"What do you mean?" I wanted to know.

As she dipped into the bowl of pickles on our table, she replied, "Right now I'd probably be fussing with some sort of high chair contraption instead of munching. I'd be taking a bib out of a bulky bag of diapers and bottles and tying it around an uncooperative baby's neck. I'd be ordering pureed peas or mashed banana, or unpacking a carton of it I'd prepared earlier. In other words, what might have been a conversation in peace would be a series of actions directed at my child. It seems too complex to me."

Donna, an attractive woman very involved in the social service agency for whom she worked, was rational at all times. She was trained to analyze situations clearly, and the decision about her future was to receive no less care. She supervised several community service programs and a staff of five in an organized, orderly fashion. But her background in psychology also let her recognize her feelings and verbalize them clearly.

"I just don't know if having the child will be worth all the effort I know the parenting job will require," she said calmly. "But I know that Matthew wants a child very much." She picked at the top button of the plaid shirt she wore tucked into blue jeans. "I've worked very hard on our relationship. I never would've thought, ten years ago, that I would be happily married. But despite my hesitations, we got married, and now I wouldn't have it any other way. I can't help thinking that while I'm so unsure now, after we had our child, I would work to make sure that was a satisfying experience, too."

Matthew, normally quite reserved, nodded. "I *know* you'd be a fantastic mother, and even though there'd be a slew of normal problems, you'd end up very glad—"

"But the issue is not the kind of mother I'd make," Donna cut in.

"I know, I know," Matthew answered calmly. It seemed like he was used to handling Donna's quick responses and provided a tranquil balance to their relationship. Matthew, 33, carried his tall, slim body with a smooth assurance. His bearded face smiled easily. "But you're not going to be doing this parenting thing alone, you know."

Donna stroked Matthew's arm and smiled weakly. She had earlier lamented that Matthew's enthusiasm about a child had made her feel all the worse about her reluctance to provide him with one. Matthew had proudly announced that he actually *looked forward* to bathing the baby, taking his turn watching it so Donna could have some time to herself each week. He had admitted that he would not rearrange his job schedule—as a junior high school assistant principal his hours weren't flexible—but he didn't think Donna should feel tied to the child. His solution was to let eager relatives care for the child or else hire daytime help. Matthew seemed able to assess his feelings and desires without being blinded by emotions; his wife did not share that facility.

"I know that sometimes my fears get out of hand," she admitted. "And that scares me all the more. I want too many things, and I want them all to go smoothly," Donna paused. Then she became more insistent. "But I don't think that all my fears about the future with a child are unwarranted. They're based on what I see around me. And what I see happening to my friends often is *not* what I want for myself." Donna's closest girlfriend, she explained, had had her first child two years before. "She went from a competent professional— a buyer for a department store chain—to a simpering stay-at-home whose greatest venture is to drive to Penney's for a sale on rompers. All she ever does is talk about her child. I understand that, but there's so much more to life that's passing her by." Donna nervously combed her fingers through her shoulder-length dark hair. "I can see us both in four or five years, ogling each other's wallet photographs as we wait outside the kindergarten for school to get out. I really worry that I'll lose my professional identity. And what's worse, I think I might just let it happen when it becomes apparent that the world will go on without me, that I'm not indispensable."

She'd told me that when she hinted that she was contemplating having a baby, her boss had begged her to return after a short maternity leave. He said he could never replace her; that she was the most efficient, understanding, organized, and valuable employee the agency had ever hired. He said he'd hold her job for her for as long as she liked—but the shorter the time out, the better. After all, he had said, it would take *two* social workers to even approach the job she did. We finished our corned beef sandwiches and headed for separate cars. As Matthew and Donna turned with their workshop materials in hand, Donna suddenly seemed struck with renewed fear. "How much would you take to silently steal this stuff so I don't have to deal with it?" she asked in feigned seriousness.

During the next week I got a call. "It really makes me mad that women have to take the brunt of this whole childbearing thing!" Donna fumed. "Here I am suffering with all these monstrous decisions, and Matthew just takes it all so calmly. Why *should* I have to have my body all distorted and then suffer in delivery? No wonder he's so enthusiastic. He only gets the good parts!" She wanted some references and referrals on natural childbirth. She also asked if some parents could come to the next workshop session to share their experiences. I was glad that Donna called—she gave me feedback on her reactions to the decision-making process—but I was also sad-dened by her obvious frustration. She told me that Matthew's coop-eration and good humor during an emotionally trying week compounded her misery, reinforcing the dichotomy between the roles of mother and father, and emphasizing the mother's greater investment in the child.

I saw Donna and Matthew again a week later, after the work-shop's second session. Since they lived just a few minutes away from where it was held, I stopped by to pick up a magazine article Donna thought I'd find interesting. Children noisily chased each other on the sidewalk in front of their house. In the quiet street nearby, two teenage boys played catch. Their home was a typical California tract house built after World War II, but they had added personal touches to make it distinctive.

A wall-hanging Donna had macramed hung over the couch in their small living room. Watercolor paintings from arts-and-crafts fairs were clustered on another wall above a bookcase jammed with texts on education and psychology. I followed Donna into her study, piled with manila files, more books, and a file cabinet. The television faced a loveseat covered with newspapers and magazines. It was apparent that Donna and Matthew spent a good deal of their free time on professional projects, and they were proud of their academic accomplishments; one wall held an artistically arranged cluster of diplomas and certificates, another was a melange of family snap-shots, wedding portraits, and a bulletin board containing clippings about family members.

While Donna sifted through the stacks on her desk, Matthew brought in a tray of cookies and lemonade. The lemons, he remarked, had grown on their backyard tree. Matthew had made the cookies—rich shortbread with tiny chocolate chips—himself.

"I think you'll like this article because it talks about working mothers," Donna said, pulling it from a folder. "It contains concrete steps to take in locating reliable childcare. It talks about the hassles involved in combining childrearing with a professional career. But the bottom line is that with expert planning it can be done. That was the message that was most important to me. You have to really get your priorities straight. It may mean giving up the dustless house you were proud of—" She laughed and shook her head surveying the not-quite-neat home she kept, "but you just rearrange your attitudes and somehow it's not so bad muddling through."

Donna's confidence came as a welcome surprise. During the workshop sessions she had seemed somewhat negative toward all the problems associated with motherhood. Suddenly, it was as if she had broken through her characteristic emotionality and regained her well-developed sense of reason. She was such an efficient organizer at work; she could do the same in her personal life if she so chose.

A week later, after she and Matthew completed the final week of the decision-making process, they returned to the workshop with a new, optimistic perspective. "I think I've got it all figured out," Donna beamed. "If I get pregnant right away, I'll have my child just when the caseloads lighten up and my boss will have a couple summer interns to take over for me." She ticked off on her fingers all the changes she'd planned into her life, as if reading a manual to success. The members of the workshop group were amazed at her change over the three meetings, from unsure to self-assured. I was amazed, too.

At the break I asked her what happened to change her doubts. "I just looked at the situation calmly, after I let my emotions out," she explained, "and I saw that just as I can manage all the other aspects of my life, I can make this fit in, too." What about her feelings that parental responsibilities would be unfair, a burden to her more than to Matthew? "Well," she answered thoughtfully, "the insecurity is still there. But I decided that I do want to be a mother and I've disproved my doubts before. I had a lot of men in my life before Matthew, but our relationship is the best thing that I have going, now. The rewards exceed the problems by a hundred-fold."

I wasn't convinced. "You seemed so reluctant to go through pregnancy and childbirth before," I reminded her.

Donna had thought about this, she admitted. "I'm still scared. I'm afraid it will be a disruptive, painful experience. But I've psyched myself into bearing the pain as a necessary precursor to motherhood, which I really do want. I could never forgive myself for foregoing parenthood just because I was afraid of some temporary pain. The pain of childbirth lasts maybe one day; the child is with you the rest of your life."

Matthew, grinning broadly as he listened, added, "If I could go through it for you, you know I would. You know that I'll be the most attentive, sympathetic prospective father in the world." Donna smiled and they sealed the bargain with a quick kiss.

Couples like Matthew and Donna, postponing and then deciding to have children, are usually happy with their choice. Their friends and family are initially surprised and then extremely pleased that a couple formerly so wrapped up in themselves have made the decision for parenthood. Women who become mothers relatively late in life have a supportive peer group and are often admired for their choice.

The National Center for Health Statistics in Washington reports that between 1975 and 1979, there was a 37-percent increase in the number of women between 30 and 35 years old having first children. Some call this a "baby echo" resounding a generation-plus after World War II's baby boom. Census figures show a large jump in the number of American women reaching the prime childbearing age of 25–35: in 1970, there were 12.7 million; in 1980 the figure reached 18.2 million.

Deciding to have a child is also made easier for now-or-never couples when the man is willing to contribute time and energy to parenthood. One of the crucial factors in Donna's decision was Matthew's strong, unwavering desire and his realistic assessment of the role he would have in the child's upbringing. Even if the man does not alter his working hours, a commitment to fatherhood will allow him to suggest means for childcare and accompanying responsibilities. It was Matthew's even keel that allowed Donna to work through her fears and face the issue in a more logical way.

It's important to note that underneath it all, Donna and Matthew really *did* want to have a child. The only thing that made them put it off—and almost caused Donna to forego the experience entirely—was Donna's doubt. Her fear of childbirth and pregnancy were probably smokescreens for larger, underlying issues about her identity as a valued career woman. Donna's career was extremely important to her. Each day she received reinforcement as a needed, valued individual. While she knew her work role was rewarding, she couldn't be sure that the benefits of motherhood would be as fulfilling. Donna finally realized that less praise in her professional life was inevitable and recognized that this was a trade-off for the love she would receive from her family.

No wonder people put off the decision until it's now-or-never. For women especially, parenthood means questioning fundamental assumptions about sources of daily rewards. It means giving up a core of identity—the umbilical cord to complete identity through work. The scariest element of the process is realizing that a new aspect to your life cannot be added without rearranging what's left. There's no way to have a child and not give up a lot of the heart and soul you may have plunged into your work: heart and soul now belong to baby.

About a third of the now-or-never couples who complete the decision-making process decide *not* to have children. It is often with reluctance that they admit they'll not experience such a positive part of life. The reason they're now-or-never couples, after all, is because they've kept the door open to childbearing, letting time slip away without making any final decision. For these couples, the decision-making process is a slow realization that they have actually already made choices and priorities so that a child would not fit into the pattern of their lives.

A Conversation with Jo and Marty — Deciding "Never"

After they completed the workshop, I spent some time with Jo and Marty, an unmarried couple who had lived together for eight years. Jo wore her dark hair pulled back into a soft bun, so that the wisps of gray at her temples graced her cheeks. At 38, crows feet were visible and worry lines lightly etched her forehead, yet she was youthful in appearance.

Her partner, Marty, 43, also showed physical signs of age. Gray strands sprinkled through his closely cropped wavy hair and dominated his dark beard. We sat on the grass in a park near the workshop. As Jo unwrapped a sandwich, her sadness unraveled.

"Throughout the whole two weeks we grappled with this decision, I kind of wished I could take back ten years," Jo lamented, carefully folding the used paper. "I looked at the patterns in our lives and realized that we were deliberately making choices that excluded the possibility of children—choices that protected our freedom."

Marty nodded and enumerated. "For example, we never got married, though I feel a genuine, permanent commitment to Jo."

"But I'd come out of a short-lived, unhappy marriage," Jo explained, "and I guess that was Marty's way of not hemming me in or scaring me that it might happen again. Not getting married was an out for those suffocating feelings at first, I guess," she said, "but truthfully, as time went on, I knew that our relationship was secure. I knew it was different and warm. So there was really no need to avoid marriage. Avoiding it just kept us from having to make further choices."

"Like having a child," Marty reflected. "We did all we could *not* to have to face that decision. We set up barriers to it by our whole style of living. We bought a condominium that didn't allow kids, and that was a very conscious decision. We each have tiny two-seater sportscars, hardly conducive to infant seats. We belong to a gourmet club where once a month we fly to a special restaurant within a 400-mile radius. And when we have quiet weekends at home, we get hostile if we hear the voice of a child outside for five minutes."

"And it's so ironic," Jo added. "Because I spend all my days working with children. I place foster children, and that means meeting them, finding a perfect match with a foster parent, and following up to ensure their welfare. I get to know some of these children pretty well, and I really do fall in love sometimes. Some of them are infants of mothers on drugs or in prison. Others have been scarred by some horrible experience in their parents' homes, like incest or alcoholism. I weep for these children. I want so badly to make them whole. And yet I scream out the window at children playing in the alley on Sunday mornings." She fiddled with her paper napkin and seemed to be fighting back tears. A katydid alighted on her arm, and she was motionless. I felt very sad for her. She must have believed she was selfish. Yet she neglected to see how much good she did for the children she served. Marty put his arm around her comfortingly.

"Come on, Jo," he cheered. "Maybe we *are* giving up something, but you've also got to look at what we're gaining." Marty was a computer specialist, and he consulted with major corporations in designing and maintaining their computer systems. Because his clients were international, he often took off for three or four days at a time. "We're gaining our freedom to express ourselves in other ways," he continued, "and you know we've always treasured that. You work sometimes till seven or eight at night. And I jet all over the world. We couldn't continue our lives like that if we were continuously responsible for another human being."

Jo perked up and nodded as she passed both Marty and me an apple. "I know. Of course I know what you're saying. Not only have we said it to ourselves about a thousand times, but I keep repeating it to myself every day, especially when I see babies being raised by teenagers who have no thoughts of the future. I say it when I see bruised toddlers, and I want to take them home and cuddle them until their tears stop. But I also have in the back of my mind that if I were truly a good, decent person, I would want to care permanently for someone else. The truth is, I don't, and I have to stop thinking I'm an ogre for having my true feelings."

She looked at me solemnly. "That's why we had to make time to sit down and bring our unconscious choice out in the open. That's why I had to stop saying 'someday I'll have a child' without meaning it."

Marty added, "And that's why we were so glad there was a workshop. It gave us a chance to plan our lives so there wouldn't be a cloud hanging over the future. We could admit that what we were afraid to say was true."

Jo and Marty had clarified their priorities. Jo's upbringing was such that she placed a huge value on the role of motherhood and the security of a family. She felt isolated when she deviated from this script; her inclinations battled with her emotions. At 38, she felt she had postponed the decision as long as she could. Now-or-never was not even the question, since "never" had been her unconscious choice for years.

Jo and Marty were pleased with the outcome of the workshop and took it upon themselves to plan a "reunion" for the group members eight months later. I saw them there, busily checking with the wine steward of the restaurant they had selected. Their interest in gourmet food benefited all who attended.

Jo looked radiant in a sea green dress and discussed her promotion to area supervisor. She was happy to see that two group members were pregnant, and she shared with them facts about maternity leave laws. I asked her if she regretted her decision not to have children. "Not one bit," she responded immediately. "The decision was hardest on me at first, when I mourned the loss of the child I wasn't destined to have. As time went on, I felt somehow smugly satisfied to have swept that corner of my life clean. I didn't feel guilty working late after that, thinking I should devote more time to my 'family.' It had finally gotten into my mind that all I have to do, from here on out, is satisfy *me*."

Later in the evening, as Marty poured another round of wine, I asked him the same question. "Sometimes I think about what I'd be doing if I had a child," he confessed, "and sometimes I'm a bit melancholy about what might have been. But I have no more regrets about that than over not going to graduate school in journalism, my secret passion, or my regrets over not going to bed with my college sweetheart. I'll never know what would have happened, but since I'm so satisfied with what I have, those fantasies really don't count for much." He swallowed the last drops in his glass with a grin.

3

Clashing Choices

The second group of decision-making couples also suffers. Their conflict is that one partner wants a child—preferably soon—while the other disagrees. Maybe the woman wants a baby, and her husband's just not ready yet. Or perhaps it's the wife who's unsure she wants to set aside her career to accommodate her husband's desire. Each partner is staunch in their choice, and both realize there's no such thing as compromise on this life-long commitment. Couples often squabble for months over this issue. Or they might avoid the topic, sensing their conflict and hating to disturb an otherwise tranquil relationship.

Barry and Michele: In Conflict

Barry and Michele knew they definitely needed help. "I'm almost desperate to have a child," Michele told me over the phone, "and my husband is just as stubborn about not wanting to have any." Her cool, sing-song voice was edged with immediacy. "We've been arguing back and forth for four years now. I've been willing to put it off, but I'm 30 now, and that is my deadline. I wanted to have a child by the time I was 30, but with Barry's attitude, there's no way it will happen even in the next ten years." I talked with her awhile longer and could tell that the issue was threatening their seven-year marriage.

When I met Barry and Michele in my office, Michele wore a perfectly coordinated cobalt blue silk skirt and blouse. Her dark hair flowed in waves around her strikingly attractive face. Brown eyes contrasted with milky clear skin. I thought that she easily could have been a model rather than a teacher of 5-year-olds in a community experimental school.

Barry was equally attractive. His excellent physique was not hidden by his French-cut three-piece suit. His blond hair, blue eyes, and even suntan reminded me of a California surfer gone straight to success in the financial world. He strode in with an air of confidence, aware that he would soon have to defend himself. He sat on the opposite end of the couch from Michele. He crossed his legs, and with his ankle resting on his knee assumed the body language stance of competition.

Michele took great care to appear composed. "I simply don't think he's being fair about it," she began. "When we got married, we talked about having children, and Barry agreed to it. He knew very well just how much they meant to me. I'd always wanted to have my own children—it was something I have never doubted. My own home life was very happy, and I want that warm closeness for myself."

"You agreed to have children before?" I asked Barry. He nodded, wearing a grin that might have been confused with a smirk. "Then what happened?"

His smile faded fast. "Over the years, I just changed my mind, that's all," he shrugged. "When we first got married, all I knew was that I loved Michele. She's beautiful and vivacious and intelligent. We'd gone together since we were freshmen in college—I'm three years older but had a hitch in the military during the Vietnam years. I figured I'd enlist for a noncombat position and then go to school on the benefits, which I did. So when I found her, it was like heaven.

She was so accommodating to me, I thought I'd go along with her desires. Anyway, I never really thought about it. In those days getting married was automatically followed by children. And having them in the future is somehow just not the same as reality. I suppose I thought that when the time came, I'd be ready for them."

"But the time never came," interjected Michele ruefully. "He kept putting it off. I'm not saying I raised the issue in the first three or four years of our marriage. I was getting my B.A. and then starting my training at the experimental school. I've been working there two-and-a-half years now, and I truly love it. And it really wears me out. But work was always a stop-gap for me. I never doubted that someday I'd have my own child to escort to school, and that parenting would then become the major thrust of my life. I want to be a mother, not a teacher."

Michele's message was clear, but Barry's seemed confused. I turned to him. "So you're saying that you never really wanted children at all?" I asked.

"No, I'm not saying that," Barry frowned. "I was sincere in saying I wanted them. But different things happened in my life, and the more I saw friends of ours becoming parents, the more I didn't want to be like them. I simply changed my mind. I now feel very strongly—I absolutely don't want children in my life."

It was an impasse. Michele definitely wanted children; Barry refused. I raised the possibility that if neither one gave in, they would become filled with resentment until their marriage broke up.

"I've thought about it a lot," Michele replied. "I've pleaded with Barry, spent afternoons crying, and even fantasized about leaving him. It's been like hell, and the hell has been surrounding me for over a year. That was when I started bringing up my desire for a child regularly. And regularly, I was rebuffed."

"I certainly want Michele to stay with me," Barry said. "I think we have a great relationship, a strong one. I don't see why she wouldn't be happy with it continuing just as it is. It's a great life, really. We're free to go anytime we please—out to dinner, off for the weekend in Palm Springs, whatever. And I have to work late most nights, until 8 P.M. or so at the ad agency, so I don't have enough energy to come home to a houseful of kids."

Michele turned to her husband, her anger growing. "There's nothing wrong with our life now, and you know it. We've been over this a hundred times. You know darn well that I just don't think my life is complete as it is. You know I want to be a mother. Why can't I just do it?"

"Go ahead!" Barry challenged. His irritation pierced Michele. Tears overflowed her eyes. She began to sob.

After a few minutes, she continued, explaining to me and not Barry: "I want my child to have a willing father. I can't say I haven't been tempted to just forget my diaphragm. In fact, I think I should tell you that I had an abortion two years ago. Barry wanted me to have it, saying we just couldn't handle a child financially. I went along with him. Now I wake up nights wishing to God I hadn't killed that child."

Barry's venom returned. "What do you mean, 'kill that child'? It wasn't a child to you then. You know it was the only move we could make."

"But it might have been my only chance to have a baby with you," Michele answered quietly. "Now we may break up, and I might have to find another man to be the father of my child." Barry sat expressionless.

As a first strategy, I suggested both Barry and Michele try to accept the other's point of view—try it on for size rather than remain planted in opposite corners of the boxing ring. So Michele agreed to go for career counseling at her graduate school to try to find a career that could provide substitute fulfillment. In return, Barry said he'd spend a couple weekends with children Michele brought for visits from her school. At the next session they gave me a progress report.

"My interest tests showed I should be a teacher or YWCA worker," Michele laughed, "and it did get me thinking that perhaps I'd like to to be in charge of a school. I think I put so much time into my work because it has been like a substitute for motherhood. Sometimes I wish I could take those children home with me every night, they're so cute. But much as I adore the little ones I work with, it's just not the same as having my own child. I tried to imagine having my own school and being in charge instead of having a family. But it just didn't work. I became terribly depressed. The thought that I would never see my own child grow up—like I see those children every day developing into more mature human beings—that thought makes me feel worthless, like I'm not fulfilling my purpose on earth."

"I just don't think Michele got into the positive aspects of a life without children," Barry replied. "All she saw were the negatives. It isn't like she would be depressed all the time. We do a lot of things now. And if she had her own school, there would be a million new things for her to do."

"That's not the point," Michele snapped. "I don't want to clutter my life with distractions. I want to be a mother as an occupation. I want to teach my child, not hundreds of other people's children. I don't want to administer a school with buildings, books, equipment, and payrolls. I want to spend quiet moments with my own child. I want to feel the child growing inside me and know I produced a complete, emotionally healthy individual. How can you expect any career to do that for me?" Barry looked her in the eye, but said nothing.

It was obvious that Michele knew what she wanted. There was no compromise. She was willing to wait a couple years for the child, but would wait no longer for the promise of one. Their weekends with the children borrowed from Michele's class didn't change Barry's mind either.

"We took 6-year-old Danny to the beach," Barry reported. "I actually had a good time. I played frisbee with him on the sand, and we had hot dogs and soda walking along the boardwalk."

"Actually, Barry was very good with Danny," Michele nodded. "They really seemed to have fun. Then we brought Danny back to our apartment, just three blocks from the beach. Barry was worried that he'd get his hands on our collection of antique glass. So I just 'child-proofed' a little. There were no problems at all."

"But there is a big difference in having a guest and having your own kid 24 hours a day," Barry noted. "Do you really think Danny is as polite around his own parents? We were a treat, a novelty. He was an angel, it's true. But somehow I doubt we got a taste of reality."

"So how do you feel?" I quizzed. Barry's face turned sour.

"I'd be a great uncle. As long as I could drop off the kid at the end of the day. Frankly, a child would impinge on my life too much."

It was another stalemate. Again, it seemed one of them would have to give in, or they would break up. They reiterated that they wanted to work this out. "But I'm willing to leave if I have to," Michele affirmed.

The next tactic was to examine their feelings about having a child more closely, to get at the root of the issue. Also involved was a look at the patterns in their relationship, to discover which of them was more flexible. Several sessions were spent delving into Barry's unhappy background, which was a distressing experience. His father was an alcoholic, a very poor role model. So Barry's brother, 12 years his senior, had early-on become his idol. But the idol, too, failed him, slipping into drugs and eventually stealing household furnishings to support his habit. This turned Barry against him in defense of his mother, who was helpless in the face of the tragedies around her. She finally died without the comfort of her husband or oldest son, leaving Barry bitter. He had not seen either his brother or his father in eight years, intentionally moving across the country to escape them. On his own, he had become a successful advertising director. He saw his zenith just ahead of him, and yet was cautious. "In this business, you're over the hill at 40," he commented, "and you could be out on your ass in one day if a client doesn't like the tie you're wearing." He claimed this insecurity was a major reason why he didn't think having children was appropriate. It was more likely that his insecurity about the stability of families was more important to his choice.

As this was discussed, Barry kept his emotions hidden. "That's one thing that has frustrated me all these years," Michele responded. "He can't cry; he doesn't yell; he never seems to let out his feelings in words. Instead, he just goes off to the gym where he works out regularly. Every evening after work—and that's usually 8 or 9 P.M.— he's there. No wonder he doesn't think he'll have time for children. He's always spending so much time on himself."

That had become the theme of their relationship. I discovered that they had established a pattern over their years together, a pattern where Michele always gave in. When Barry wanted to buy a sailboat Michele felt was too expensive, he persuaded her. When he wanted to indulge a photography hobby by building a darkroom in the garage, Michele ended up moving out the teaching materials she stored there. When Barry wanted to go to Tahiti and Michele preferred backpacking in the Sierras, they spent their entire two weeks on the South Pacific sand. And despite Michele's devotion to her job, she always had a hot meal awaiting Barry when he returned from his nightly routine at the gym. No wonder Barry expected Michele to come around on the baby issue too. He'd even hinted that coming to counseling was a means of assuaging Michele's feelings so that when she finally gave in, she wouldn't be resentful.

But this time it didn't work. Michele spent more and more time each session in tears. She realized that she'd have to break out of her pattern if she wanted to have a child. She couldn't just threaten to leave; she'd have to do it. Michele and I spent a few sessions alone discussing the practical side of independence. We talked about the singles scene and her prospects for finding a man to father her child. She knew that her first choice would always be Barry. But if he refused to cooperate, she'd have to strike out on her own.

Fortunately, the chances for finding a new mate for a woman of Michele's intelligence and looks seemed good. She said she would never have a child alone as a single woman—"That would be unfair. Every child deserves both a mother and a father." She talked with her friends about the planned move. She began psychologically separating herself from Barry, though he tried to prevent it. When Barry bought tickets for a summer vacation in Canada, Michele immediately made plans to visit her family in Oregon. When Barry ordered the livingroom couch she'd been raving about, Michele called the store to have it returned. She began to think in terms of his items versus her items. She listened to the advice of divorced friends. And her sorrow grew, because she realized that she was destroying what had been the most precious thing in her life.

One night she telephoned me. Sobs punctuated her speech. "I've got to move tonight," she whimpered. "I gave him one last chance to change his mind. He said he didn't believe I would do it. He said he loved me, tried all his old tricks. He's daring me. I'm afraid I'll give in to him again." I felt my throat tighten. Barry had left the house for the gym, sure that he had "cured" Michele of her threat. Barry didn't believe that Michele had grown in past years and was no longer dependent on him. She could make it on her own. That night she packed two suitcases and drove to a girlfriend's apartment in North Hollywood. When Barry came home, he called me in a rage. He had been crossed, and for the first time, his emotions were plain.

"Where did she go?" he demanded. "I know you put her up to this!" I tried to calm him but his anger pushed my words aside. "She thinks she can get away with this nonsense! That bitch! What is she trying to do to me?" His screams didn't wait for answers. He had never been hit like this before. When the screams stopped, I told him that Michele had chosen to go out of her own will. He started to cry. I could only hear short chokes, but his hurt was apparent. I waited in silence, never telling him where Michele was. He finally slammed the receiver, and I felt numb, realizing human fragility.

I didn't hear anything from Barry or Michele for five days. Michele had left a message on my answering machine canceling our appointment two days earlier. I worried that she was in psychological distress, but knew that her girlfriend was supportive and would be available to her. Michele's call came as a surprise.

"I just wanted you to know that I'm all right," she said. "In fact, I'm back home with Barry now." I was stunned. I immediately thought that he had charmed her back home on his terms. I was wrong. "I stayed with Nancy for two nights," she explained, "and it scared the hell out of Barry." She giggled. "He never thought I had it in me to make good on any of my threats. He tried to find me at the school, but I took a couple days off. Nancy and I drove up the coast and I talked and cried and got everything out. I'm really lucky to have so good a friend. When I got back, Barry had figured out where I was staying. He was camped on the doorstep with a copy of Dr. Spock and a jar of pickles. He said we could have the baby. He gave in. He said we could start trying to get pregnant right away, but now I'm the one who's delaying. I want us to have more exposure to children together. He says now he wants a child, but I'm hoping to get him downright enthused." She sounded bright and hopeful. I worried that her optimism was premature, but I expressed my happiness for her.

I saw Michele and Barry a few times after that. I was surprised to find that Barry had truly changed his stance. He'd realized that his fear of losing Michele was stronger than his desire not to have children. He stopped taking Michele and her ideas for granted and even rearranged his gym schedule so he could come home earlier to be with her.

"Our relationship will never be the same," Michele later confided. "I'll never trust Barry like I did before all this happened. I'll always have in the back of my mind how he hurt me, how he put me through so much pain and agony just to call my bluff. But on the other hand," she brightened, "I also know that I have far more inner strength than I realized. I know I can leave. It's a new kind of freedom. I'm staying with Barry now because I want to, and he respects that. I think it's strengthened our relationship, because now we're much more equal than we were. He doesn't expect me to wait on him. In fact, he even makes dinner as often as I do. That's a real switch. He's become very appreciative of me."

In Barry and Michele's case, their marriage was more important than other concerns to one of the partners. If Barry's breaking point not been reached, the ending of the story might have been different: Michele might be sharing Nancy's flat and entering the singles scene. Perhaps a quarter of couples in conflict dissolve their marriages over this issue.

Despite traditional socialization, women as often as men don't want children. Women are beginning to realize they have a choice. They don't want to be tied to traditional roles when their careers are taking off in nontraditional directions. Similarly, men are discovering that the home is not only a woman's domain. They are participating more fully in all aspects of family life, and many don't want to be deprived of having a child—or two or three.

In quite a few conflict cases, one partner wants a child and the other, while basically in favor of the proposition, just doesn't want to have one now. But if the proparenthood partner is staunch, the reluctant one often concedes. It's a matter of realizing the importance that having a child holds for the other partner. Here are two examples of couples in this situation.

Wayne and Susan—Second Marriage Jitters

Wayne had been married once before and had two children, ages 9 and 11. He and Susan were married two years, and they agreed

that their relationship was "heavenly." I interviewed them one afternoon at their Marina del Rey condominium overlooking bobbing sailboat masts. Wayne, a heavy-set man with a salt-and-pepper mustache,
welcomed me. Their home showed expensive, sophisticated taste.
Danish teak furniture mixed well with an occasional antique. He led
me to their large balcony, laid out with white wine and sandwiches.

Susan, short but slim at 34, joined us. "What do you want to
know about our conflict?" she grinned, floating into a chaise. "It's
really very simple: I want a child right away. I know I'm ready to be
a mother and that Wayne is the man I want to father my children.
The conflict is entirely in him."

Wayne nodded and sipped his wine. "I just don't think we should
tamper with our relationship. Having been through the fathering routine, admittedly at quite an unready age, I know what it's like. Parenting means disruptions, plain and simple. It's impossible to devote
as much time to each other when there's a screaming infant in the
other room. Even with live-in help, your nerves are on edge waiting
for your baby's cry. I'm frankly ecstatic with Susan, and I don't want
to give up any of her."

"I'm flattered, honey," Susan smiled, reaching over to squeeze
Wayne's arm, "but I think having a child would enrich the relationship we have. It's a natural extension of a great love and affection."

"So she says," Wayne teased, waving his wine glass. "She has
her arguments in favor of children; I have mine against. But *she* was
never married before, and *I'm* speaking from experience. Don't get
me wrong; I love my children fiercely. They've both turned out great.
In fact, I don't see why Susan can't just get the pleasures of mothering
when they're around on weekends and in the summer."

"Because it's just not the same," Susan countered. "Those children are already shaped by your ex-wife, not by me. And anyway,
they have to go home. Visiting us is like a vacation, not like reality
to them. I want the whole enchilada. I want to feel the baby growing
inside me; I want to give birth; I want to gripe at the 4 A.M. feedings
and when it says that first word, I want the 'Mama' to mean me."

Susan was used to getting her way. As a film producer, she had
command of million-dollar budgets and creative control of writers,
directors, and editors. She held power in her professional life and

was frustrated that her husband had not seen the same light that illuminated her life script. But Wayne was used to wielding power, too, and he sincerely felt he had the upper hand based on his past experience.

"We're both Leos," he chuckled, "and you know what *that* means. We both have to be the center of attention. We both have to have our own way."

"And *that's* exactly why I have to have this baby—and the sooner the better!" Susan exclaimed with finality. "You've already had this experience, and how many times have you said you wouldn't trade it for anything? So now that you've had your way, it's only fair that I have mine." She popped a grape in her mouth and looked out toward the harbor: end of debate.

"It's as if having a child were a beachball we toss back and forth," Wayne said, "but every time I write out a child support check, I confirm what a lifetime commitment it is. It's damned serious business. I've already paid my dues that way once, and of course I'll never stop loving my children. But Susan just won't listen when I warn her about all the ways children impinge on your life. I just don't think I should have to go through it again."

We chatted about a new film idea Susan was toying with. The telephone rang, and she excused herself to snarl loudly at somebody's agent. In the meantime, Wayne told me how much he appreciated his life. "My company's been in the black—lots of black, in fact—for the past five years. I'm earning a very decent living and enjoying life. See that yacht?" He handed me a pair of binoculars and pointed to the slips for the larger boats about a mile away. "I own that yacht. Not 25 percent of it, not 50 percent of it, but the whole thing. Do you know that Susan and I took off for Tokyo two weeks ago on the spur of the moment? We only had three days over Memorial Day weekend, but we flew to Tokyo. Most of it was spent having jet lag, but at least we felt hungover in Japan. That's what I call freedom.

And that's what I want to preserve."

I nodded in admiration of his life style. Susan drifted back into the room in her theatrical way. "Those damn agents. Think they can screw a deal over a percentage. Who needs them?" Susan was so independent, defiant, charmingly unreal. That's why it was hard to believe she was sincere about her craving for a child. We talked about show business, then about the workshops. Susan gave her opinion of everyone who had attended it with her. Wayne chuckled and shook his head with amusement at her audacity. I found myself entertained by her sense of humor and skills of observation—but frivolity only lasts so long; eventually our giggles subsided, and we returned to the interview.

"Do you feel pressured to have a child right away?" I asked Susan.

"Yes, I do," she answered simply. Prodded, she continued, "I'm 34 years old—a very successful 34, I realize, but ingrained in me is the notion that if I don't have a child, I won't be a complete person. I have it in my mind that the real purpose we're here is not film or Hollywood hype but family—good, solid family—spanning the generations, and all that. Because in the end, what else is there? When the stock market crashes and you lose your millions; when there's a warehouse fire and all your prints burn; when even your beloved partner dies, heaven forbid, what's left?" Her eyebrows raised expectantly. "Your children—your family—that's what's left, and I don't want to be without it."

"But what are you depending on them for?" Wayne asked her. "Do you expect them to comfort you, serve you, be there all the time?"

Susan nodded. "Well, forget it!" Wayne declared. "They'll be off to college, or earning their own millions, and won't have time to visit you in your elegant rest home. You have to depend on yourself, and you have to have your own interests."

"That's not what I meant," Susan corrected. "What I'm talking about is continuity. I'm talking about the human race and the meaning of life—not just some selfish desire to be listened to when I'm babbling out of senility."

This conversation with Wayne and Susan took place after the first workshop meeting. Two weeks later the scene at their home was more serious as Wayne told me that he'd changed his mind. "Over the past couple weeks we've taken the time to hash and rehash out the pros and cons to this baby thing," he told me, "and I discovered that I married a pretty miraculous woman. She may seem flighty on the surface, but she really takes it all quite seriously. I saw her cry. I'd never seen her cry before. She always wore a smile, and when things went badly she usually got angry. She never cried until I cruelly mentioned the possibility that perhaps she *couldn't* physically have any children. Then the decision was out of her hands, and I saw how much having one meant." He looked down as his tone dropped. "It moved me to see such a strong woman vulnerable. I love her so much. How could I deny her such an important part of life? I must be incredibly selfish."

Susan leaned over and hugged him. "This man is fabulous," she said. "I think part of our problem before was that I simply didn't know how to communicate. I treat everything like it's a script rather than my feelings, and I confuse facade with fact. I learned that I don't have to be that way around my husband. It's a wonderful feeling to realize you're loved no matter what you think."

Just six weeks later I got a note in the mail from Susan. In it she scribbled, "I think I'm pregnant—it's an unmistakable bloat." Her singular prediction was correct, and I'm now the proud recipient of a splashy Hollywood-style personalized birth announcement. Her child is a boy, pictured in the hospital with his glowing mommy and daddy.

Wayne and Susan's case shows that hesitancy can be overcome. The important ingredient in the transition is that both partners place their highest priority on the relationship. Pleasing and caring for the other partner must be more important than work or a personal role. Wayne and Susan never got to the point of break-up because if the situation became severe, both were willing to change to preserve their relationship.

Danielle and Arthur — Hesitant About the Future

Danielle and Arthur were neither rich nor powerful, but they did share Susan and Wayne's regard for their relationship. Married six years, they both wanted children. The conflict arose a year ago when Danielle asserted that now was the perfect time to have their first child, while Arthur pleaded that they wait just three or four years until his career picked up.

Arthur was an artist, able to capture likenesses in photographic detail. But his work had a twist a whimsy; a cowlick on the distinguished professor; a run in the stocking of the dignitary's wife. I first started chatting with Arthur and Danielle at a local art show where I admired his work. When I mentioned that I ran workshops for couples making the childbearing decision, they eagerly confided the problem they'd been arguing.

"Danielle doesn't see how insecure my life is right now," Arthur began, tipping his tooled-leather cowboy hat back over his straight brown hair. "I go to one of these shows and never know if I'll even make back the entry fees. Today I happened to sell a couple larger pieces, so I'll make out all right. But sometimes months go by without a sale, and I'm in the doldrums. I don't think we should start our family until I've at least got something going with a major gallery."

Danielle, a petite woman whose long blond hair hung to the middle of her back, frowned. "That's what he's been saying for three years. My job with the travel agency won't go away. We've been living on my salary for the six years we've been together. If we wait for everything to be perfect, we'll never have a child."

Danielle and Arthur were in agreement on the decision but at odds on the schedule. I came to their Studio City home to pick up a small portrait, and Arthur elaborated on their dilemma. As he led me through his garage-studio, Arthur expressed the first hints of insecurity about his direction in life. "I know I'm a damned good artist," he said, "but I'm beginning to think that I just can't make a career of it. I've been struggling for too long. By now I should have more reviews to show, more connections. I keep wondering if I should go out and get some kind of straight job."

He carried my new acquisition into their living room so I could say hello to Danielle. She was rehanging plants she had doused with the garden hose. Their living room was like a jungle, dominated by a huge ficus tree. The walls displayed a couple of Arthur's commentaries—a tipsy doctor and a teacher writing a misspelled comment on a pupil's paper—as well as the work of other artists.

I jokingly mentioned Arthur's comment that maybe art wasn't his calling. I was taken aback by Danielle's reply. "Maybe it's not," she shrugged. "Maybe if he got into a secure field we could start to live like normal people and have the family we both want. I think he'd be good in a more commercial art-related field—maybe in advertising or even with the studios. He just seems to take so long on his work. We'll never make any real money until he speeds things up."

Arthur scowled. "What's the goal of life anyway? I just want to express myself through my work. I just want to do what I *want*—who wants to live to make money?"

"The goal of life is to be happy," Danielle responded, "but in creeping toward your own happiness, you've overlooked mine. I want a child *now*. I've waited long enough. My youth won't last forever, even if you *do* think you're Superman!" Her words made us all smile, but underneath the grin was an awareness of the seriousness of their conflict.

Rather than attending a workshop, Danielle and Arthur wanted to use the materials in private consultation. At our first meeting, Danielle reemphasized her impatience to have a child. "It's getting so that Arthur won't even have sex with me anymore because he's afraid our contraceptive will fail," she whispered, leaning back in the plush chair in my office.

"It's not what you think," Arthur hastened to explain. "About five months ago, Danielle went off the pill on the advice of her doctor. It seems that she has a chance of dangerous blood clotting. A vein in her leg broke, and the doctor told her to stop taking the pill immediately. Since then we tried the diaphragm, but she says that hurts her and that sex isn't as pleasurable as it was. Condoms weren't as good either. So we're using those suppositories, and I'm really afraid they just won't work. I think Danielle's secretly hoping they fail. I have to remind her to insert the damn things, because she would never remember on her own." He glanced threateningly to his wife, and then quickly turned to me.

"I think she believes that if I don't remind her about the suppository, then I'm giving my consent for her to get pregnant. It's like I have to be a watchdog, and that thought really turns me off. I just haven't wanted to make love to her when we have this psychological battle."

Hearing this shook Danielle. Her eyes brimmed with tears and she looked away suddenly. After a heavy silence she retorted, "I don't want this baby to be conceived out of trickery. I want it to be our mutual choice. I don't understand why Arthur has to resist! He says he wants a child; why can't he just let me have one now?"

"I'm feeling pushed into a corner," Arthur said calmly. "I don't think it's fair to have one unless we both feel ready. When I *am* ready, I'll want to take the role of nurturer. I'll want to stay home with my child and help him develop. I'll want to do it right. But why should I enter into that kind of thing before I'm ready?"

I could tell that Arthur and Danielle were no strangers to therapy. They'd picked up the tricks of "owning their feelings" and were quite astute at observing their motivations and influences. Their power was equally matched in the relationship; it was clear that neither of them was frequently pushed around. I tried to explore why Arthur was so hesitant about becoming a father at this stage of his life.

"I'm hesitant because I want more time to get established. When my career is solid, then I'll definitely want to go ahead."

"When will that be?" I queried.

"Maybe two or three years, I don't know. But it could take longer."

"How will you know when that point comes?" I asked, hoping he'd indicate a date. But he refused to be pinned down, and Danielle exploded.

"You don't know how many times I've tried to get him to just say *when* I can get pregnant. I've told him how frustrated this waiting makes me. I've cried and cajoled. But he keeps saying that 'he'll know' when the time comes. For me the time was a year ago. I can wait a little longer, but not without the assurance that I'll have a child by a specific date."

I suggested that there was something frightening about parenthood for Arthur, and that he try desensitizing himself to it by spending a lot of time with children. I also suggested he fantasize about his own child. The following week he gave this report:

"I played magician with our next door neighbor. When I asked his mother if I could 'borrow' him, she was ecstatic! I thought the experience was a lot of fun. But I never had any problem being around kids. I've always loved it. In fact, I'm like a kid myself." A very telling remark, it turned out, and Danielle caught it.

"That's your problem!" She clapped her hands in recognition as I nodded a confirmation. "You just can't fancy yourself a grown-up. After all, you can't be a father and a child at the same time. And until now, I've been the support for the family—almost like your mother." She paused, realizing her own contribution to Arthur's behavior.

It took several sessions for Arthur to see the many ways he had resisted assuming the roles of adulthood. He'd never had a "nine-to-five" career, preferring instead to move from being a student and relying on his family, to having a string of part-time menial jobs during art school, to his final financial dependence on Danielle. He'd even made a few moves to ensure that his artistic success was limited—"forgetting" to call back important contacts, letting deadlines for projects go by, and even once getting ill—a 24 hour virus—for a crucial show.

On the other hand, as much as Danielle swore she wanted a child right away, she also fostered Arthur's childlike role. She was willing to take on a traditional job with its financial security to protect him from the world. In a sense, Danielle's acts were unselfish gifts of love, but after six years of sheltering Arthur, her role had become almost masochistic. She began to see herself as a martyr, and one way to emphasize the martyr position was to add Arthur's refusal to accept parenthood to her burden.

Both Danielle and Arthur realized their symbiotic relationship with tears. After five minutes of weeping, hugging, renewed crying, and nose-blowing, there was new resolve. But there was no change in Danielle's position.

"I still want that child," she decided. "It's more than an urge to make Arthur feel guilty. We've always wanted children and I'd still like one as soon as possible—call it the mothering instinct, if you want. When I see a child, I long to hold it. After six years of marriage and living like impoverished students, I want some permanence, some stability in my home life. And I want to know when I'll have it." We talked further about Arthur's ambivalence over success in his career, and we agreed it was time to set some deadlines. This would give both of them a renegotiable framework for their plans. It would set out projections for the next five years and ten years in several areas of their lives: career, family, travel, life-style. Then they could look for milestones that would show them they were achieving those goals.

Arthur decided that earning a decent living—his figure was at least $24,000 per year—was a high priority goal for the coming year. He plotted ways to make that money, and he listed the steps he would have to take to pursue those ways. Danielle decided she would be willing to wait two years before having a baby—which gave her just over a year to reach her own interim goals of losing ten pounds, using her travel agency benefits to see Africa and South America, and preparing mentally and physically for the pregnancy.

The planning process took several weeks of discussion and fantasizing, but there were some immediate benefits. "Our sex life has picked up considerably," Arthur noted. "We know we don't want to make a baby for 15 months, so we're both willing to take better precautions now, using contraception that won't hurt our potential for a healthy baby."

"It's been very satisfying, actually," Danielle said in her open style. "We've been experimenting with oral sex on my fertile days to play it safe, and we've discovered some aspects to sensuality we've overlooked for years."

Conflict couples *can* have a happy ending. When both partners are basically in favor of having a child, but differ on the appropriate time, they usually do come to agreement. And because one of the partners wants a baby soon, resolving the conflict usually makes them parents within two years.

There are a few common characteristics that accompany conflict. Some conflict couples also belong in the "now-or-never" category. Usually one of the partners in these cases feels a growing awareness that time is slipping away. Often there's a desire to "be young with my child," indicating a negative image of any wide age gap between generations.

In some cases, a tolerant partner has waited until the biological clock threatens all hope of childbearing before menopause. In this way, the reluctant partner may silently say that he or she chooses not to have any children but doesn't want to spoil the relationship by voicing that preference.

Arthur and Danielle's case illustrates how conflict between partners over the baby issue can be symptomatic of other underlying problems. Arthur was afraid to grow up; Danielle fed on this by getting maternal satisfaction from pacifying Arthur. From another angle, Arthur was afraid of success in his career, and he felt internal conflict over the validity of art as a steady, profitable endeavor. Each person has to look at past behavior patterns to see how the childbearing dilemma fits into personal history. She or he also has to look for satisfaction with the direction life is taking. Sometimes dissatisfaction with a boring career can be enough to make parenting attractive. When the job conflict is resolved—sometimes by finding another field or position, sometimes by finding outlets for creative urges— then the desire for a baby to fill a void in life diminishes. Conversely, a career can also be used as an excuse to avoid confronting the responsibilities of parenthood.

4

Acting On an Inclination

The third group of decision-makers has really made up its mind. "Planners" know in their "heart of hearts" what they really want to do. Before they go ahead and either have a child or become surgically sterilized, however, they want to be reassured that they're making the right choice and have fully considered all the ramifications of their proposed move. It's a matter of confirmation for them, so that when they take the important step, they will know they made the most considered, well thought-out move possible.

I call them "planners" because they're always very rational, logical people. When they make decisions, like buying a house, selecting a wine, getting married, or making an investment, they shop around. They compare pros and cons and arrive at a reasoned conclusion. Having a child is an emotional decision, and in the end it's "gut feelings" that determine behavior. Planners like to back up their emotions with as much evidence and support data as possible.

51

Brenda and Dick – Planners

I knew Brenda from my graduate training. She worked as the assistant to a professor in the psychology department, coordinating a massive study on marijuana use. I first met her when I took a class on psychological testing taught by the professor. As part of the course, we were supposed to give certain tests to our peers. In order to check out the tests, though, we had to sign in and out through the office where Brenda worked.

A zaftig woman of 35, Brenda loved to talk. Whenever I'd come into the office, she'd chat about the students in her study or the latest activity of the Women's Resource Center. Her long natural hair would shake as she spoke, and she looked much younger than her years. Part of the reason was her curly hair, which pirouetted out from her round cheeks like matted corkscrews. Another reason was her dress—jeans with patches at the knees and T-shirts or embroidered workshirts left over from the 1960s. The most likely reason for her youthful appearance was her manner—"California laid-back." She was the perfect stereotype to participate in marijuana research, but it was hard to believe she was the University official running it.

One afternoon as I returned a test manual, she asked me about my dissertation study. I told her I was testing materials to help couples decide about having children. She immediately told me how she and her husband Dick had decided long ago that they wanted to be parents. "In fact, we think we'd like to go ahead and have a baby right away, but—" she glanced at the punk rock poster taped to the wall above her gray steel desk—"we want to make sure we know what we're getting into. So many of my friends went ahead and had a child before thinking it through. We want to know how the baby will affect all areas of our lives."

I suggested that my materials might help clarify her values, expectations, and feelings about parenthood. It didn't take much persuading; she and Dick were early for the first group meeting.

Dick, a tall string-bean of a fellow, also 35, was congenial and, like his wife, quite mellow. Since they were the first ones in the classroom, we talked. He told me he was a sales representative for an office supplies firm. "I have to hustle people," he chuckled, "so it's always a pleasure to come home and let Brenda hustle me for awhile." He put his arm around her and squeezed. "It'll be even more fun coming home to a baby," he grinned, "because then I can regress with someone who'll understand my ga-gas and goo-goos."

"You both seem so positive about wanting a child," I noted.

"We are, but this is such a big step," Brenda answered. "After all, you can quit your job, move from your house, and, God forbid, divorce your spouse. But you can never get rid of your own kid. Once you're a parent, you're a parent forever."

"So why take chances?" Dick asked. "Anyway, I do have some fears about parenthood. I wonder if I'm up to the task. I get scared of all the responsibility. I wonder if a baby will change me into some kind of authority figure, or if the child will tie us down. I don't think these conflicts are very serious," he qualified, "but I need some way to judge just how important they are."

Their comments sounded good to me. In fact, they made a lot of sense. If every couple contemplating parenthood took a couple of weeks to seriously consider all the ramifications, there would be a lot fewer unwanted children. And those who were created would be conceived with a plan for their lifetime welfare.

"And also," Brenda added, "if we go through the motions of looking at everything, when we do go ahead and get pregnant, we won't have any lingering doubts. We'll enter into it confident that we've made the best decision we could. We'll know we're psychologically prepared. When I told my mother about this class, she immediately said, 'I wish there was something like that around when I was having you and your brother.' Of course *I* don't wish that because I'd probably not be here today, but I know she regrets not living more of her own life before getting into motherhood."

Brenda and Dick were different from most of the other couples in the workshop. Others would emphasize the negative side of parenthood—fears about financial obligations, responsibility, loss of spontaneity, and freedom. Then Brenda or Dick would pipe up with the *good* side of the story. They provided a counterpoint that allowed the other couples to contemplate more than their own insecurities. When I saw Brenda in the department office after the first workshop meeting, I commented on this.

"I was glad they focused on the bad side," she said, "because it gave me something with which to contrast my own feelings. Now

I'm starting to see how insignificant a role the negative side has in my decision." She told me that she and Dick were filling out the questionnaires almost identically. "The whole process is really an upper. After eight years of marriage, we're finding more and more we have in common."

Brenda and Dick exemplify the most common type of planners, eager to confirm an inclination before acting on it. At the last workshop meeting, they happily announced they'd already started trying for their child. The process let them clearly lay out all the elements of parenthood. Brenda could plan every detail of the proposed move in an orderly way so that the transition into parenthood could be smooth and trauma-free.

"I'm going to take two years off from my work life," she reported, "and then go to graduate school in psychology. I want to stay home with my child for the early formative period. I know from my work in the field that I would be the most effective teacher for this crucial stage. Then I think that it's best my child develop social skills with others, and I could choose my classes so that I could be available when needed." Brenda assumed that she would enroll locally, and the colleges she was considering had daycare centers for student use.

"I can take off periods of one to three hours during the day," Dick noted, "so I can play an active role in the child's upbringing. As a salesman, I can schedule my meetings as I choose. And we've looked at childcare alternatives as well—my mother has volunteered to help out as often as we need her. There's a licensed daycare center within two blocks at a price about 25 percent more than the university daycare, but still affordable. I feel more confident about having this baby now because we have so many desirable options."

Brenda and Dick were holding hands and beaming as they left the meeting room. It's been several years since then, and still smiling from the bulletin board in the psychology office is a somewhat faded color snapshot of their toothless, hairless infant boy.

Of course, planners don't all want children, though probably two-thirds do seek confirmation of that choice. The remaining third want to make sure they *don't* want any before going through with sterilization. While the decision to either have a child and to forego having one are both permanent steps, somehow the prospect of surgery carries with it a more serious connotation. And there are some unique considerations in the decision to be sterilized that are not faced by others making the choice.

Christine and Don — Committing to a Life Without Children

At first, I was surprised by Christine's physical appearance. She dressed neatly, but in fashions at least five years old. Her mousy brown hair fell to her collar, and the lack of makeup on her pale face aged her beyond her 33 years. When I started talking with her, however, I saw how her priorities were far from appearance.

Christine was the psychologist in charge of a clinic for the terminally ill. I interviewed her for a newspaper story I was doing on the loneliness of illness, and her compassion and humanity projected clearly through her outward appearance.

After an educational and moving interview, she told me that she recognized my name from announcements about the workshops. "My husband Don and I have made up our minds that we don't want children," she said matter-of-factly, "but my intellectual decision just hasn't filtered down to my emotions yet. Somehow I can't quite close that door without working this whole thing out in my mind."

Christine explained that Don had already had mandatory pre-vasectomy counseling. Though not legally required, his doctor had asked her to sign an acknowledgement form, stating that she understood the ramifications of the step her husband was about to take. "I put it on my desk, and I've been meaning to sign it," she said, shaking her head slowly. "I don't know why I can't. The possibility that I might regret this decision keeps recurring. Then I argue to myself that I *know* I don't like children. I *know* I don't want the 24-hour-per-day responsibility of raising them. I tell my hand to pick up the pen and sign my name to the form. I don't understand why my fingers won't obey my commands."

She and Don showed up at the next workshop session. Like his wife, Don seemed to care little about outward trappings. He worked alone as a real estate loan trustee in a private office all day. Over-weight and clad in bell-bottom pants falling midcalf over rubber-tire-soled sandals, he approached the topic of parenthood casually. "I'm perfectly content with our present life-style. We spend our weekends working on the house, lying around reading the paper. I like a slower paced life than Christine does, and I don't want the financial pressures that would make me work very hard. Frankly, having a vasectomy was not a hard decision for me to make. I've been willing to do it for the whole four years we've been married. In fact, I've never wanted children. One of the reasons my first marriage broke up was because my ex-wife wanted me to get enthusiastic about fatherhood. I just couldn't, and I really don't think I ever can." He turned to his wife, seated next to him on the couch. "I don't really have a problem, but I know Chris is having a hard time, and I do care about her. If she really wanted a child, I'd probably go along with it. I admire and love her in a way quite different from how I loved my first wife. Chris doesn't need me. She's self-sufficient. I know that I'd do anything to see her happy, and that's the only reason why I'm here."

During the next week, Christine came down to the newspaper where I worked to drop off some materials about her clinic's programs, and we had lunch. We talked about buying homes, publicizing workshops, and traveling around the world. She had many external interests, but family was not among them.

"My parents were both professional people," she explained, "and I was their only child. I remember my mother always hurrying out the door with her briefcase, and I guess in many ways I ended up emulating her. I married late, after graduate school in psychology. I actually didn't look for a husband, preferring instead to earn scholarly acclaim by publishing journal articles. After we were introduced at a charity fundraiser, it was Don who pursued me, although I still don't know why. I never did much to encourage him. In fact, it was shortly after my mother died from a tormenting battle with cancer that we got married. I realized I needed some ongoing comfort in my life, and he provided it. I just don't think I need children." She crunched on her chef's salad. "But maybe I do," she continued.

"What do you mean?" I asked.

"Well, it could be that I'm afraid to let go of my link with family support. I was my mother's main comfort during her illness. In fact, it was her ordeal that led me into this aspect of psychology. I think I could be unconsciously afraid that if the time ever came when I needed help, there would be no one there."

"What about your father? Wasn't he supportive to your mother before she died?" I was curious to know. "And you have Don to lean on."

"No, my father actually went to pieces over my mother's death," Christine replied. "She had always been so competent, always there for him to depend on. Suddenly she was vulnerable, helpless. I ended up picking up the pieces for them both. Now Dad's retired and really kind of pathetic. He lives in one of those retirement hotels. He was a dentist, and he has some money, but he's listless and thinks more about the past than his potential for the present and future."

"It sounds like you feel responsible for him now," I noted.

"I guess I do. That could be another factor in my decision not to have children. I'm getting to the point in life where my father is something like my child. It's very disheartening to me. He was dependent on my mother, and now he's dependent on me. It's likely that somewhere in my subconscious I'm hoping that I'll never be dependent on anyone like that. If I don't have a child, and if I keep working and feel competent, than I'll avoid my father's fate."

Christine proved her sensitivity by recognizing the complexity of her feelings. "I'm an organized person," she said as she wiped her mouth and placed her napkin on the table. "I want to sort out all these considerations once and for all. It's really a formality I have to go through before I make the irrevocable decision to sign Don's vasectomy acknowledgement form."

By the final workshop meeting, the form was signed. "I went through the questionnaires and took the time to analyze my fears," Christine reported. "I focused on my priorities." She ticked off her choices. "First, I care about my image of myself as a competent professional. My work is important and helps me understand the value of life, because I have to deal with death every day. I get innumerable rewards from my work, and that's what I want to devote myself to most. Then there's Don." She paused. "This may seem twisted, placing my career before my husband. But it's only because I feel independent and valuable in work that I can let myself take his emotional support. And also, because I feel worthwhile away from him, I feel confident I can give him love and attention without being vulnerable or reliant."

Don put his arm around Christine as she talked, and kissed her temple.

In Don and Christine's case, one partner was more distressed by the childbearing decision than the other. Don's first concern was his wife, rather than whether or not to have a child. He had a clear preference but understood the importance of the choice for her and was willing to accommodate her needs. Christine focused her attention on resolution of her own severe conflicts.

Women contemplating a future without children often have doubts about their inclinations. Traditionally, women were raised to expect motherhood to be the central feature of their lives. Women without children were pitied, and it was assumed that their condition was involuntary. When women made a conscious choice to remain child-free, they were scorned for selfishly avoiding an accepted responsibility. Christine observed this social attitude, and also realized how others saw her own mother, a career woman. All this combined with a resistance to the traditional feminine submissive role. Signing Don's vasectomy form brought out all these conflicts, and it also reminded her that she was closing off the potential to share parenthood with him.

Don had much less to lose by getting a vasectomy. "I never expected to deal with children," he reported at the workshop reunion eight months later. "So I never took much of an interest in them." Don obviously felt comfortable with himself. "We've been doing some woodworking in our spare time lately and have refinished our kitchen cabinets. After the vasectomy, the topic of children hasn't even been mentioned once."

"I did the tile work for the kitchen counters," Christine added proudly, "and I organized a conference on hospice care for the terminally ill. I think I dealt with the childbearing possibility like I deal with most aspects of my life: I confront the issue, analyze my feelings about it along with objective considerations, and then I stick by my decision. We don't have friends with children, so I've simply moved on to other things in my life. I suppose I'll think about my choice again when I get near 40 or 45 and my reproductive years end, but I honestly don't think I'll regret it. I simply haven't got time to. And I have the confidence of knowing I took the effort to be sure of my feelings before I went ahead."

In gathering materials for this book, I talked to a well-known doctor who does vasectomies. "Couples who go ahead with the procedure have thought long and hard," he said. "Why would any man subject himself to pain and probable embarrassment if he weren't sure that he didn't want any children?" Couples like Christine and Don, who are contemplating sterilization, share this attitude. They're firm in their choice, but because they are organized people, they don't want to take the final step without fully considering their move.

Some couples who choose vasectomy or tubal ligation are stuck on the "what ifs." What if my partner dies and I remarry? What if I change my mind? What if I go ahead and regret my decision? But they share Christine's mental process: they answer the "what ifs" by setting up priorities for their lives. If they are immersed in enough activities and interests so they feel occupied and secure, the inclination to be sterilized is confirmed. Only a tiny number of couples decide *not* to go ahead with their childfree plan.

Christine and Don are representative of "planners" who enter the decision-making process with an inclination to remain childfree. Brenda and Dick exemplify "planners" confirming a choice in favor of having a child. There is a third group of planners, though, who are inclined toward parenthood but who have physical problems that make their choice one between natural childbearing and adoption. Here's a brief glimpse at the concerns of one such couple.

Kathy and Lou — Adoption Blues

Their home was a decorator's dream. Nestled in the Hollywood hills above a jeweled city, Kathy and Lou's home revealed their affluence. Kathy was a model, one of the up-and-coming black faces. At 27, she had appeared in several magazines, whirled in status jeans for a series of television commercials, and even played minor roles in two feature films. Lou was a promoter of rock concerts, handling familiar names in disco and soul. Despite their glamour occupations, they enjoyed a stable home life and were deeply religious.

I drove to their hilltop retreat to interview them on the problems surrounding adoption. It turned out that the problem was far more complex than I'd been led to believe. Kathy greeted me, a tall vision in a flowing caftan, and led me to the livingroom, suspended from the mountain with a wall of glass.

"The question isn't just how to go about adopting," Kathy explained. "It's whether adopting a child is worth the emotional turmoil." Lou quietly entered the room, put a classical record on the stereo, and took a seat in an off-white upholstered chair near the brick fireplace across from her.

"You see, we've been trying for a child for three years," he continued, "and that was after waiting four years before that. Our infertility after postponing all that time led us to several doctors and a string of tests. It turns out that all these expensive specialists still don't know why we haven't conceived, but they did find that Kathy has a medical problem that makes childbirth especially risky."

"Here we've been praying for a child," Kathy said quietly, folding her long fingers onto her lap. "We ask the Lord every night to complete our family. He has his own reasons for saying no, but it's brought me a lot of tears."

"Since we found out about Kathy's physical problem, we've looked into adoption," Lou went on, "but it's so discouraging. We really want an infant—and a healthy one at that. You'd think there would be a black baby somewhere for us, but we found out that most teenage mothers are keeping their babies to raise themselves." He sounded annoyed. "None of them could give a child what we could—the best education, sound nutrition, decent moral values. Sure, we run with the Hollywood crowd. But only a few run with us on Sundays—to church. So many are getting divorced and remarried and then divorced again. They marvel at our solid relationship. It's no wonder to us because we have God to keep us together. But lately this problem of finding a child is giving us new strains to overcome."

"First we went to the public adoption agencies. They told us right off that if we passed their scrutiny, we'd have to wait at least four years for a healthy infant. When I heard that, I wanted to scream."

Kathy did not raise her voice. In fact, her voice was velvet-smooth at all times, and she looked straight into my eyes as she spoke.

Lou picked up the story. "The adoption agency said that we shouldn't have to wait as long if we would accept a handicapped child, an older child, or one of mixed ancestry. Hearing this increased our heartache, because we both knew inside that we wanted to raise a healthy child from the start. We wanted one who would fit in with us perfectly, and that realization made us feel selfish. Why didn't we have room in our hearts for one of these unfortunate children, the ones with scars still open, waiting for the medicine to heal them? We wrestled with ourselves and God over that one. But the answer was still the same," he lowered his eyes to the glass of wine in his hand. "Even adopting a child was a step down for us from having our own. We thought a child deserved to feel he was our first choice, not a leftover accepted reluctantly or out of pity."

"So we filled out all the forms for an infant, and went to interviews with social workers," Kathy whispered. "All those questions— as if we were suspects in some crime. 'Will your friends in show business provide a bad example?' 'How would you feel if your child wanted to contact his natural mother?' They asked so many questions, my emotions bounced from hopeful to angry to sad. I know the agencies weren't intentionally hurtful; they were just doing their jobs—but now that children are in short supply, they can afford to be picky. They don't just judge you on sincerity. You have to be sincere and wealthy and available to the child and downright average. Maybe it's my imagination," she looked up resolutely, "but I got the feeling that they'd rather give our baby to some insurance salesman and his housewife from middle America than to us. I was too beautiful and my husband too high-powered."

All this talk was a prelude to discussing the act about which they felt guilty: arranging a private adoption. "I'm 27 and Lou is 34," Kathy said. "And to many people that's quite young. They don't understand our frustration and desperation. I felt inadequate because I was barren and because I was built with a pelvic abnormality that would endanger myself and our child. I didn't want to wait four more years to adopt a child."

So now they were dealing with a baby broker. For the mother's expenses and the lawyer's fee, they were to get a baby girl in just four months. It was all legal, but somehow clandestine. "This has been a great source of conflict," Kathy admitted. "There were many points when we debated going through with it. We still question whether it's right for us to pay $20,000 for a child. It's like buying happiness." Her cool facade began to break, and she put her manicured hand to her face and looked out to the lights below. As if to distract from his wife's vulnerability, Lou went on.

"But if we don't take this child, someone else will pay the price. The mother, we're told, got pregnant by a man other than her husband. He's in the military, out of the country. The child would suffer emotionally if we didn't step in."

Kathy looked across the room to her husband. At first she nodded, and then demanded, her voice cracking, "How do we know this isn't all a story? Maybe this child was sold in someplace like Haiti! Maybe she is being imported to order! Is my selfish desire for a baby fostering the separation of a family for money?" The question could not be answered. I froze in awkward silence.

Lou got up and moved to the couch next to his wife. They looked at each other and he lifted a dark strand off her forehead in a gesture of comfort. "As you can see, this is a very emotional topic for us," he said to me. "We do know what we want, but acting on that choice has been difficult." I talked with Kathy and Lou for awhile, but many of their concerns could not be resolved easily.

The question of adoption arises more and more frequently, since obtaining a child has become a waiting or paying game. Those who in the past blithely would've said "We'll adopt" when asked about a child are now considering fulfilling parenting needs in other ways. Adoption has become a grueling process, and even when couples are positive of their desire for a child, they may not be willing or able to withstand the process to adoptive parenthood.

I never found out whether or not Kathy and Lou received their daughter. I still see Kathy's smiling face and svelte body in magazine ads for cosmetics, clothes, and perfumes. Since my interview with them, however, I have met about a dozen other couples with a similar desire to adopt, facing the same bleak prospects through agencies and the expensive discreet process of private adoption. One of these couples recently held their own baby shower at the six-month milestone after which the natural mother cannot reclaim her baby. Another couple decided they did not have either the wherewithall to pay for a private adoption or the determination to wade through years of waiting for a healthy white infant from an agency. They sold their house at the beach and went on a year-long vagabond through Europe.

So now you have become acquainted with three types of planners: Brenda and Dick, anxious to have a baby; Christine and Don, ready to take steps to remain childfree; and Kathy and Lou, debating the merits of adoption. You've also met the now-or-never couples: Rebecca and John, whose indecision continues; Donna and Matthew, determined to make a child fit into their lives; and Jo and Marty, reluctantly realizing that their lives will remain childfree. Finally, you've discovered three couples in conflict: Barry and Michele, whose brief separation led to greater understanding; Wayne and Susan, overcoming his second-marriage jitters; and lastly, Danielle and Arthur, grappling with career and personal conflicts that formed barriers to having a child.

These three types of couples are all willing to face the decision. But there is one more type of couple that I must mention. If you and your partner fit into this pattern, be prepared for frustration. These are the "dropouts," people for whom the investment in the childbearing decision is so different that only one partner carries the brunt of the problem. And a problem it is.

Laura and Michael – She Cares, He Doesn't

This is a rather short story. And it is, unfortunately, a predictable one for me, because it occurs for as many as one out of every fifteen couples with whom I have contact.

Laura first reached me by phone. Her shrill voice seemed edged with urgency. "I'm so glad somebody is helping people decide about having a child. I'm certainly going crazy trying to make the decision." She was calling from her job as manager of a franchise florist's. "Some days I'm so depressed, I wake up and simply start to cry. I have no one to talk to about it, and I just can't decide what to do."

"How about your husband?" I asked. "How does he feel about having a baby?"

"He doesn't care what I do, doesn't even want to discuss it. He says that having a child is a woman's decision, and he's too busy to think about it."

That's a danger sign. Laura was staggering under the weight of an albatross that should be lifted jointly by two people. Instead, she recognized severe negative consequences either way she decided: if she had a baby, she knew that all responsibility for its care would be hers; if she let the opportunity go by, she would forego her family's—and Michael's—acceptance and praise, and she would never know an experience she desired.

"I don't know if I can get Michael to come with me to the workshop," she worried aloud. "Why should he come when he's already left the whole decision to me? What would he get out of it except to lose three Saturday mornings?" Of course, Laura had assessed her situation well. She suffered both the gravity of the choice as well as the pain of knowing that her husband did not care about her distress.

Laura did cajole Michael into accompanying her to the group. She was a strikingly attractive 28-year-old brunette who obviously took great care to present a finished appearance. Not a hair strayed from a bun curved at the back of her head; her makeup was applied delicately. She wore expensive status shoes, quality label jeans, and a silk blouse accented with gold that showed she cared about other people's impressions. I had the feeling that she relied on others for direction and recognition—but in this decision, she floundered all alone.

Michael was a swarthy but handsome man, muscular and powerful. He was somewhat quiet, but did not seem hostile. "I'll let her do whatever she wants," he shrugged. "If she wants a baby, fine. If she doesn't, that's fine too. I work for the state as a personnel payroll clerk. Frankly, my work's boring now, but I'm in line for a promotion within the system. I took the state test, and advancement is a matter of a small amount of time. I'm also studying law at night through a nonaccredited school, which means I have to take the 'baby bar exam' in just a couple months. I haven't got time to worry about domestic affairs."

"You *ought* to worry!" Laura snapped. "And not just for financial reasons, either! You know I've wanted a child for a couple of years, ever since we got married. But you keep pushing the problem off onto me. Well, I want to take this opportunity to discuss it with you!"

Michael was annoyed. "We *have* discussed it! What more do you want? You can do anything you want. If you want a baby, go ahead!"

"I want your cooperation!" Laura replied, equally irritated. Michael crossed his arms on his chest and grunted. Laura turned to me. "Some days I want to get pregnant right away. I see a baby in a stroller and can't wait to make baby talk and stroke his soft little cheek. On the other hand, I think I'd be bored as a mother at home— and yet that's where I'd want to be, raising my child right. I think the mother ought to be with her child. But it's no good if you feel trapped."

Laura shared many concerns with now-or-never couples like Rebecca and John. She couldn't make up her mind about her future, seeing both advantages and disadvantages to having a child. But unlike Rebecca, she had no partner with whom to share her fears and anxieties. Her dilemma was made all the more frustrating because Michael refused to admit that he was not supportive. In fact, he thought he was actually being helpful; he felt that his responsibility was to provide economic security, and in exchange his wife would take care of the family. Accompanying this traditional view was the expectation that his wife would accede to all his wishes. He wished to spend his Saturday mornings playing basketball. He did not wish to fill out questionnaires and checklists.

So he didn't. My telephone rang just two days later. An exasperated Laura apologized for being unable to continue the decision-making process. "Michael's in this basketball group," she said. "Every Saturday morning at the time when the workshops meet, they're out playing. He said that he gave up one game to come with me, and he didn't get very much out of it." I'd heard this tale before. "He didn't even want to look at my questionnaires."

Laura was caught between a rock and a hard place. She was used to firmly supporting her husband and catering to his desires, but in a situation as important as this, she could expect no reciprocal respect.

There are millions of Lauras grappling with the decision about getting pregnant. All of them feel isolated. They think they're the only ones considering that maybe it's not worth it to have a child. They feel that their partners love them but simply don't understand all aspects of the choice. And they know that if they do choose to have a child, the responsibility for its care won't be shared. Daddy will get the credit and the clean, smiling moments. Mommy will get the rest. The rest may not be all that bad—in fact it's appealing—but . . . it's such a lonely decision.

Now you've met them all: the now-or-nevers, the conflict couples, the planners, and the dropouts. You've probably recognized elements in these couples' stories that apply to you. And now that you're familiar with the problems, you're ready for the solutions. Read on.

5

Skills For a Crucial Choice

T his chapter offers some basic know-how for approaching the child-bearing decision with confidence.

Working as a Team

Just as it takes two to play frisbee, devour a chateaubriand, or conceive a child, two people are involved in the continued state of parenthood. Some single women may strongly disagree, feeling they could independently and admirably give a child a loving, well-rounded history. In fact, growing number of women are realizing that they can handle motherhood without the help of a man. More power to them. They undertake a difficult and rewarding task.

Despite progress by the women's movement and society's changing attitudes toward single parenthood, single women are not the primary group involved in the childbearing decision. Couples are. And when there *is* a two-partner relationship, the decision should not rest with only one of them. With motherhood comes fatherhood.

Even if Daddy stays home with Baby, Mommy always returns from the executive suite at the end of the day. Adequate childcare doesn't preclude emotional responsibility, even if one parent departs the scene entirely. Recognize this.

Also recognize that while, optimally, both partners are equally invested in the decision, this is rarely the case. "Marriage should be 50/50," say the new egalitarians. "Parental responsibilities should be evenly split. Fathers can share the same intimacy with a child, the same close bonding that mothers traditionaly have had. This is the age of equality."

And so it is. Now's the time when sexist myths are being exposed for what they are, and new generations are gradually trained to sift shibbolith from reality. But the fact is that most people who make this decision weren't raised in such enlightened times and find it hard to shake ingrained values. It may not, in fact, be the woman who wants most to be a parent, although she may feel the most anxiety about the choice. The uniqueness of each individual's background and personality determines his or her investment in the parenthood role.

When you're holding down the lower end of the teeter-totter—feeling that it's *you* making the weightier decision—the space between you and your partner, way up with head in the trees, seems enormous.

Women's Problem

Commonly, women feel more overwhelmed by the childbearing decision than men. My studies of couples who used the materials in this book confirmed that women *do* feel greater distress than men about the choice. Perhaps it's because they're more physically involved.

Men can't physically bear children—there's no getting around it (except in the fantasies of filmmakers and authors). Women's bodies respond in personalized, unique ways to a child's development inside them. Hormones surge, triggering lactation, shape change, and maternal bonding with the child. True, men can have sympathetic physical reactions and undergo profound psychological changes as part of the birthing process, but they'll never feel the womb ripening toward fruition.

So women are usually more invested in the outcome of the childbearing decision. An imbalance doesn't have to be a problem if it's recognized and discussed. This is much easier said than done, of course.

Remember Michelle, who was willing to leave Barry to find a father for her desperately desired child? Her investment was much deeper than Barry's until a dramatic act—leaving him—finally evened the score. It was finally when Danielle told Arthur she was fed up with his dependence on her and his hesitancy to follow through on his promise of parenthood that he changed his mind. And there certainly was a difference in investment between Laura and Michael—he was the husband who abdicated all responsibility for the decision and eventually dropped out of the childbearing workshop.

How to Equalize the Decision

All of these women were more involved in the decision than their partners. That in itself is not a problem; the problem begins with each person's own indecision or frustration. If the less-concerned spouse is supportive—like Don who was willing to work through Christine's doubts about his vasectomy—then slowly distress unravels.

If not, there's still hope. To approach a difference in concern about having a baby, first check to see if your partner uses any of these diversionary tactics, which should clue you to a potential problem. Does she or he:

Reach for the TV remote control, willing to endure a game show rather than talk about children? (change the subject)

Stroke your hair and sympathize but never concede the dilemma is his or hers too? (deny responsibility)

Ask you to quit nagging? (on the offensive; make you a villain)

Say he or she will leave it all to you, satisfied with whatever you choose?

Start discussing having a child—until a more important chore interrupts?

To equalize the choice, you need to talk about what's going on between you aside from the baby issue. Point out how the avoider changes the subject, turns on the TV, or remembers a golf appointment. Be honest, admit that this is frustrating, perplexing, and hurtful. Say explicitly how you feel about the interruptions and the import of the decision, and why his or her willingness to talk and give input is so crucial.

If your partner denies all, make verbal note of his behavior whenever the topic is introduced. Keep a record of patterns of behavior so you can present proof of your partner's reactions. Point out that it's okay to feel upset, worried, confused, or ambivalent about this subject. Sometimes an unwillingness not to confront childbearing is really a fear of what the issue might trigger emotionally. Be understanding of this—someone abused as a child may be frightened of his fatherhood; a person dissatisfied with her career might not want to admit she's using the child as a way out.

If your partner still won't cooperate, you can use the questionnaires and materials in this book by yourself. But in that case, decide if your relationship is on solid ground before introducing a child.

Using the Materials Alone

If you are a single person deciding whether or not to have a child on your own, or if your partner staunchly refuses to approach the topic, or if your schedules or travels make it impossible to agree on the decision-making process, you can use these materials alone. They were designed to help you probe your own feelings, motivations, values, and expectations so you can be clear on them before adding the additional consideration of your partner's views.

If there is no one you can talk with daily, it helps to get feedback from friends, family members, a clergyperson, or counselor. It's also valuable to keep a journal of your feelings and reactions to the whole process. It's often startling to put your journal aside and then return to it later for reevaluation from a new perspective. Even perusing what you've written on the questionnaires and forms at a different time can reveal how your feelings change or can let you discover insights from a more objective position.

Communicating About Having a Child

Each couple evolves special patterns for communication reflecting each partner's experiences since childhood. Each child discovers the most effective ways to get a desired reaction from his parents, and later from his mate, taking cues from the mood (anger, tenderness) of each particular situation. Partners can usually predict how a conversation around a topic will go.

For example,

He: "Ahh, a few quiet minutes at the end of a hectic weekend."

She: "You know, I'd like to talk about when we can have a baby. I think now would be the perfect time. I've got a career I can return to after a year at home, our financial state is secure, certainly everything's going great between us . . ."

He: "Well, I just don't think that's true. I don't have that promotion I've wanted and we're going to have to pay off your student loan. Now is not the time!"

She: "Why do you want to deprive me of this?"

He: "Why do you want to force me into it?"

She: "Because if I left it up to you, you'd never accomplish anything in life!"

He: "If it were up to you, we'd be in complete financial ruin!"

That night they make passionate love on the bear rug in front of leaping flames in their fireplace.

This illustrates one "interaction style"—the habit this couple falls into when they talk. They sound, at various points in their discussion, like logical thinkers, arguers, and accusers. Some would swear they were on the brink of divorce. But *they wouldn't* say that. Fighting gives them an excuse for an exciting reunion; their volatile explosions are ingrained preludes to a pendulum swing into passionate love.

Six Styles of Communicating

Think about how you interact with your partner—especially the way you've handled the childbearing decision. The possibilities are endless, but there are six basic ways couples approach the subject: three are characteristic of people with a more rational outlook to problems;

the rest reflect an emphasis on feelings. Decide which are most applicable to you.

1. Weigh pros and cons calmly. Almost everyone uses the rational approach some of the time. Maybe you have pulled out a piece of notebook paper and slashed a vertical line on it. One half of the page is dubbed "pros"; the other "cons." You might stare at that black-and-white analysis of reasons and know deep down there's something missing from the equation. It's easy to verbalize all the negatives, and less easy to mark down those intangibles that make parenting attractive.

2. Mind changing. Rebecca told me one day that she had firmly resolved not to have any children. Her husband concurred. After all, their lives were just about perfect. She feared being tied down to a child as well as other potential negative possibilities such as having a handicapped child. Her resolve strengthened. They decided that John would get the vasectomy they'd been talking about for years. The debate was over—until two days later. Rebecca's girlfriend announced she was pregnant, and Rebecca felt an uncontrollable longing stab her, and realized she was jealous of her friend. Maybe in a couple of years, she reconsidered, she might change her mind about John's vasectomy and want a child. The more she talked with her girlfriend, the more she thought that a child could bring an exciting new dimension to her life.

And so it goes. At one point all the pros and cons add up to a "no" answer to parenthood. Then another reason in favor of children suddenly looms large, and that definite "no" becomes a "maybe" and then a "probably." It's resolved again—until the next reason barges through. One famous publicist summed up the predicament: "The greatest cause of unhappiness is indecision." Mind-changers know he's right.

Mind-changing occurs within couples as well as within individuals. If both partners look at things rationally, their pro-and-con list fluctuates with different reasons at different times. Trying to gain consensus between two ambivalent people can double the unhappiness that wise publicist predicted.

3. Arguing for your point. A third interaction style rational people use is to take a stand and then use every argument possible to persuade the other partner that your position is the best. The stand might be for or against having a child. Or it might be to defer a decision until particular circumstances occur. This interaction often involves outsiders, such as parents and friends; Dr. Spock, population statistics, and layette brochures may all be called into testimony.

For example, Michele wanted a child. She stated her reasons and reinforced them as best as she could. She invited some of her elementary-school pupils over for the weekend to show how darling they were and how she had developed a rapport with them. She encouraged her husband to play with them and earn some of those loving smiles she cherished. She pointed out toy sales, father–son activities, and illustrations of happy relationships as she scanned the daily newspapers.

Her husband Barry resisted. He drew up lists of ways in which their lives would change if a child were present. He pointed out that every time they went out to dinner, they would have to find a babysitter. He emphasized the insecure aspects of his job as an advertising executive whenever a co-worker moved on or an ad campaign flopped. Barry and Michele didn't hear each other because they were were so involved in making their own points.

Some interaction styles reflect a more emotional response to the question:

4. *Clamming up or avoiding the subject.* When all the feelings about a baby become too overwhelming, the simplest thing may be not to face it. In a sense, this is dealing with the issue by postponing any action, and it usually means continuing with birth control and not having a child. Even people who do want children often avoid direct discussion about it, because the idea that "tonight's the night we try for a child" is too scary to confront.

When a couple is facing the decision about a child, one of the partners may tend to clam up whenever asked about the future, or say whatever seems the most placating at that moment and then change the subject. This can happen when men, particularly, want to divorce themselves from the experience of parenthood: they want their wives to handle it so their self-image as the carefree, independent guy doesn't have to change. "Why become involved with your wife's occupation, anyway?" they might shrug.

5. Becoming depressed or moody. Confronting the desire for or against a child calls up all sorts of feelings about losing your own childhood, taking responsibility, beginning a new life. Just thinking about all this—even if you're really committed to having a child—can cause depression and moodiness. Sometimes people like to attribute these feelings to anything *but* the childbearing decision. Other times they know just what's causing their feelings, and they wallow in it—which may not be such a bad thing, because least they're addressing their conflicts.

When one partner brings up the question, the other may suddenly shift from a sunny mood to morosity. The trigger is pulled and the victim falls. After this happened to Suzanne a few times, she realized that her ever-and-ever plan of motherhood may not coincide with her real feelings. She then told her husband that maybe she wasn't "parent material" after all, and they began to discuss this possibility.

6. Becoming happy and enthusiastic. If you yearn, smile, and urge when talking about starting a family, you can be pretty sure your partner's going to realize your goal. If the enthusiasm is for all the travel plans you can make without a child, then it's pretty obvious that parenthood isn't your greatest desire. Pure enthusiasm by one of the partners, however, can stall any constructive debate or expression of *all* feelings. Such fervor can dominate the conversation, and more negative ideas may then be avoided. This type of emotional response may become a sneaky way to avoid realistically looking at the parenthood issue.

Rules for Talking About Having a Child

Analyze your usual patterns for discussing a child. Think about how they might be roadblocks to the decision. People who rely on pros and cons might try to talk about their feelings; those who clam up might let themselves cry or shout their normally unexpressed emotions.

The following are some common-sense rules that can be used in any discussion. People who stick by them report improved quality in their communication. For now, you might just consider them ground rules for making this one important decision together.

1. *Plan your time for talking.* Set aside a time for discussions a day in advance—or a week in advance if you have hectic schedules—and keep your appointment with each other.

2. *When you're talking together, divide the time fairly.* One person may have more to say, but don't let enthusiasm, more research, or even a facility with words interfere. Set aside 2–5 minutes for each person to talk without interruption at the beginning of the conversation. After each person's feelings, reasons, experiences, ideas, and complaints are expressed, then allow responses and give-and-take.

3. *Respect your partner's answers and feelings.* "Your're wrong!" can be a very hurtful phrase. Remember that each person's view is unique—no one else comes to this issue with the same experiences and emotions. If there's misinformation, show evidence to the contrary. If there's a prediction you feel is off base, gently say why you feel your view is more accurate.

For example, Donna predicted she'd have to stay home with her child. Matthew reminded her that the neighborhood childcare center would be opening the following year. Donna countered that she wouldn't feel right leaving her child there until he was at least aged 2 or 3—all those germs and no guarantee of the kind of care she felt would be essential. Matthew then suggested that his mother might be able to help out part-time.

4. *Take credit for your own feelings.* This refers to *how* you say things, not *what* you say. Try to say "*I* feel . . ." rather than "You make me feel . . .". (This approach will help keep tempers under control so you and your partner can keep communication open.)

Here's an example. Donna said she really didn't want to go through pregnancy—that the idea of having her body distorted and out of control for nine months scared her. This hit her husband hard. He felt she did not have the right to deprive him of his own child just because she didn't want to go through nine months of pregnancy. "You make me so angry!" he fumed. "You're taking away my child! You think you're so powerful! Well, I think you're just selfish!"

Sparks begin to fly. Donna could reply with more of the same: "You're the selfish one! All you want is a little Matthew doll! You don't care about me!" The conversation might halt right there with doors slamming and wedding rings hurled.

Or Matthew could have phrased his expression of anger in more personal, accurate terms, when Donna said she didn't want to be pregnant. "I feel like a part of me has been taken away. I really want a child—I feel frustrated that *I* can't have one unless *you're* willing to go through a pregnancy. I'm angry because I want you to have and want this child and, in truth, you're not giving me what I want."

This may be an extreme example. Few people are as reasonable as Matthew, and few have the presence of mind to see that they're angry because they just don't get what they want. But at least if you scream, *"I'm* angry!" you're not blaming anyone for it.

5. *Ask questions.* Don't make assumptions. Opinions that seem wrong to you may simply be based on inaccurate information. Perhaps you just didn't understand what your partner was trying to say. Questions can also be useful ways to probe unexplored areas. For example, a "what if . . ." question can lead to fantasizing about new alternatives to the problem. "What if we became foster parents instead of having our own?" "What if I became a big brother rather than a Daddy?" "What if we buy a duplex instead of a house for less cost?" "What if that job doesn't work out and we have a little one to feed?"

"Why?" is a good clarifier. A series of "why" questions can cause rethinking of long-held beliefs (but could end you up in a tither, so don't overuse).

6. *Recognize problems.* Sometimes people just can't agree. Make note of these problem areas. Also jot down how strongly each of you feels. Try a scale from one to ten, with ten being the strongest feelings. Then go away and discuss the problem the next day. Write out things you can do to change the situation. Having ideas on paper makes your thoughts clear and keeps important things out in the open. Keep a legal pad or notebook handy all the time to write down new concepts or questions.

7. *Compromise when you can.* Even in the most severe of conflicts, there are *some* areas of agreement. Start with those, then carefully approach topics or predications on which you're willing to compromise. For example, Danielle wanted a baby right away. She had been postponing her desire for a child because her partner, Arthur, kept saying he "just wasn't ready." She'd already passed age 30, the age by which she'd always planned to have a child, because

Arthur wanted to be more secure in his free-lance art career. The time had come, she insisted, that he come through on his promises.

As you recall, Arthur truly liked kids. He loved playing magician with neighbor children, and really did want to be a permanent playmate and teacher to his own. He just wanted more time to get a few regular clients so his income wouldn't be erratic; more time to feel secure about himself and his own direction.

Danielle asked how much time Arthur needed. He didn't know. She ranted. He whimpered, argued, relented. As a compromise in this deadlock, they decided that Arthur would have more time, but the amount of time would be set—two years.

Remember, you're on the same team. Only rarely does the issue come down to whether your relationship means more to you than your desire to have or not have a child. This small group of couples are the only ones who find minor compromises just can't overcome a major conflict.

Recognizing Your Feelings, Values, and Expectations

Values, expectations, and feelings all influence the decision-making process. Values and expectations are the "tangibles"—the notions that arise from your logical brain. It's no easy task to find them, but when you do, values and expectations can be written rationally and calmly.

Values

A value is a rule about what is bad and good gleaned from upbringing and experience. Peoples' values are extremely individual—what's marvelous to you may be shameful to someone else. Cliches about one man's meat as another's poison, "vive la difference," and beauty being in the eye of the beholder sum up the idea.

Many people agree about what's bad and good. For example, it's good to obey the law; bad to break it. Individuals with values that conflict with this idea are sternly told that their view is not acceptable.

Society traditionally valued having children as both good and necessary. Churches called deviants who intentionally chose non-parenthood "sinners," governments called them "unpatriotic," relatives called them "selfish."

Personal values are held on all sorts of subjects. Is it wrong to swipe a towel from a hotel room? Is it right to give a quarter to a beggar who might be able to work for a living? One value holds that Mother's Day is the time to honor a dedicated person; another suggests the same holiday is a commercial means of glorifying what should be an optional condition.

When considering parenthood, your own values will be important in answering just about every question. For example, some say a daycare center is "bad" and stifles development; others say it is "good" and promotes socializing skills. If you believe it's bad, you might interrupt your career to stay with the child and provide a "better" environment. If you think daycare is a blessed innovation, you may decide to make that career move into responsibility without misgivings about your child's welfare.

Expectations

Expectations are based on experience and projection. Expectations of yourself as a parent are based on what you know about yourself and how you act around children, how you adapt to new situations, and how tolerant you are. You then project these existing behaviors into the future to predict your reactions to your own child—who, by the way, is also a projection based on your experience with children.

Feelings

The third ingredient in the childbearing decision is feelings. They're the most difficult to pin down. Some people like to smother their feelings with more rational values and expectations to avoid emotional pain. Others don't know how to confront them or incorporate them into a rational choice.

Research on the childbearing decision shows people can identify reasons for and against having a child. But no one has tried to harness emotions—the factor researchers *and* parents concur is the most important determinant. Magazine quizzes that ask you to list reasons or check off preferences don't get at them; peers asking "why" you had a child don't touch on them. Yet everyone agrees that, after the lists are made and the reasons explained, the real clincher of the choice is how much *you want* a child.

Practice Catching Feelings

Here's an exercise for sharpening your self-observation skills, specifically your awareness of feelings. Look at each of the pictures below and quickly check off the feelings that arise. Then go through and decide what about the picture or yourself makes you feel that way. Remember, don't censor; just catch whatever you feel.

Sad _____	Disciplined _____
Angry _____	Enthused _____
Free _____	Tired _____
Embarrassed _____	Guilty _____

Proud _____	Angry _____
Detached _____	Afraid _____
Sad _____	Peaceful _____
Content _____	Enthused _____

Angry _____   Envious _____

Disbelieving _____   Joyful _____

Warm _____   Disgusted _____

Guilty _____   Proud _____

Embarrassed _____   Reverent _____

Amused _____   Envious _____

Pitying _____   Guilty _____

Joyful _____   Disgusted _____

Carefree _____   Guilty _____

Jealous _____   Joyful _____

Disbelieving _____   Angry _____

Sad _____   Afraid _____

Whenever you identify feelings, you'll learn more about yourself. Try to be as descriptive as possible. For example, instead of saying the picture of the women dancing makes you "happy," try to use a specific word like "exhilarated," "content," or "lithe." You might using comparisons: "Drinking hot chocolate makes me feel warm and cozy, like snuggling in front of the fire." "Your accusation felt like a blow to my stomach." "Rainy weather makes me feel frustrated, like my shoes are nailed to the floor." Thinking up comparisons forces you to analyze what you're feeling.

It may be difficult at first to really pin down specific feelings that an instant, a sentence, or a glance arouses. Most people were taught to describe events in analytical, objective terms, but since what you're observing is yourself, you've got to reverse this training and eliminate outside noises and influences. Go for the gut reaction, capture it, cage it, and finally label it as a feeling.

"Pronatalism:" It Shapes and Nudges Toward Parenthood

"Pro-what?" most people ask, wrinkling their noses, perhaps wondering if it's another "ism" coined by academics. The term "pronatalism" was born in the early 1970s when psychologist Ellen Peck and others realized that the option of parenthood had been mislabeled a "given"—like death and taxes.

Pronatalism is the push, the influence, the subtle and screamed message traditionally blasted and whispered by family, friends, government, and media. It says "Go out and multiply." It says "A woman is fulfilled by motherhood." It says "A mother is what you want to be." Pronatalism can be indirect, too—the lovingly knitted booties someone gives to newlyweds. It's the Clairol hair dye commercial showing women who have replaced the gray and are surrounded by tots. Pronatalism is the tax deduction parents get and nonparents forfeit. Pronatalism is any policy, law, or portrayal that intimates parenthood is preferable to being childfree.

Here's a way to sharpen your recognition of pronatalistic messages. As you unwind some evening in front of the TV, keep a tally of ideas, apparel, camera poses, and plots that insist children are life's enhancement. Chances are, your tally will run off the page. Take a look at women's magazines with Pampers ads, touted toys, baby-food recipes. It would be easy to see how someone who spends a lot of time in doctors' waiting rooms reading might equate parenthood with euphoria.

For many it *is* euphoric. Magazines run ads that serve a large segment of their audiences. Lots of people think babies mean bliss and that covering their gray hairs will at least make them *feel* like young mothers. There's nothing wrong with that. And there's certainly nothing wrong with enjoying motherhood and being fulfilled by it. The point is that it's *you* who has to decide whether to love it or hate it; whether to embrace it or forego it. With so many proparenthood messages around, there's barely time to realize you have a choice.

Pronatalism has been the norm for at least the last several decades. With the arrival of new consciousnesses of the 1970s, though, some fresh notions have yielded a new consensus of what's right.

Antinatalism: "Mommy" is a No-No

Values have begun to change, and some women are now offering a new slogan: antinatalism. Antinatalism, like any one-sided view, restricts acceptable options by dictating that only one life-style is acceptable. The antinatalistic theme arose from women's new success and is a reaction to traditional thought. This new myth suggests that any well-educated woman who stays home with her child is wasting her time and talent. "Being a homemaker is boring and mundane." "Career should come before family obligations; *I* am more important than *they*."

This dogma can make a mother who enjoys her child feel guilty. It can make a career woman who contemplates parenthood think she must be crazy. It can turn a potentially fabulous mother away from an occupation she might adore.

I remember a business trip I took in the mid-1970s to a little town in Michigan. A professor from the college I was visiting met me at the airport and brought along his wife, a pert red-head, conservatively dressed in a green tweed coat. As we dodged the snowflakes getting into the car for the ride to my hotel, I casually asked what she did.

Instead of a brief, matter-of-fact reply, I received her ire. "Damn it, I *like* being a housewife," the woman of 35 insisted, hostility edging her voice, "and I resent all those women's lib types telling me not to!" She had two children, she explained, and raising them was a handful. I was struck with sympathy, and nodded my agreement with her desires.

"Why should I give away the pleasure of hearing my son form new words, of walking my daughter leisurely to her nursery school? Why should I let some harried teenager in a daycare center have the joy of nurturing my children, the awe of watching them grow and develop? And how do I know that a teenager would be as caring, as loving, as *educating* as I am, giving my children all my attention every day?" she angered. "Why do all those feminists think they have to protect me? Who are they to say a job as a sales rep is more important than fostering the development of two individuals?"

Indeed, that was the problem. She felt pressured into thinking that the career she chose—motherhood—was unimportant; that earning money was a symbol of success. She was a victim of antinatalism, needlessly distressed over otherwise happy events.

At home, she was comfortable with her children and her life. I respected her ability to see the influences in her life so clearly. Yet it's essential to sift out influences that intrude on your own values, expectations, and feelings when making the childbearing decision. It's alright to take other peoples' feelings into account, but it's not alright to confuse them with what you really want.

The Pressure Points

There are four main sources of pro- and antinatalist pressure. The first is the *family*. "Isn't it about time you started a family?" Mom and Dad sweetly and repeatedly ask.

"Oh look, did you notice that your girlfriend from high school has two lovely sons? One of them is having a piano recital!" This is a not-so-subtle reminder that *you* don't have the lovely sons.

Then come the more direct approaches: "You're not getting any younger, you know." "It's not good to get too used to being just the two of you." Or how about the ever-popular "You're selfish!" (There's a section later in this book on how to cope with this kind of pressure; meanwhile, it can drive you crazy.)

Even more progressive types of parents pressure couples. Don recalled his own mother. "She tells us to do whatever we want with our lives," he began. "She doesn't put any direct pressure on us— doesn't even mention that she'd like grandchildren. But I know her. I know I'm disappointing her because she loves children so much— loved having me so much. Not only would she love to be a doting grandmother, but she thinks we're missing a precious experience. I feel badly because I know she wants us to have the joy she did."

Christine, as you recall, didn't think she ever wanted children. But complete cooperation and understanding from Don's mother didn't help the strength of that choice. "She's almost too quiet on the topic," Christine confessed. "If she complained, like my mother does, at least I'd have a reason to hold my ground. As it is, her silence makes me wonder if her underlying positive feelings toward parenthood aren't really right."

Christine and Don needed to stop interpreting his mother's support. They needed to divorce themselves from family influences altogether for just a while, say they don't care at all what others think, and focus on their own lives.

A second type of pro- or antinatalist influence is that of *peers.* When friends become pregnant one-by-one, and conversation most frequently turns from politics to cutting teeth, it's hard to resist the desire to be a part of it all. Who likes to be the only one in the group unfamiliar with brands of infant formula or unable to share in the brag sessions about first burps and forelock curls? We all want to be part of the crowd, expecially when that crowd is a group of people we know and like. That's pronatalist pressure.

Friends and co-workers can exert antinatalist strength, too. The after-work cocktail slogan of successful professional women that business beats diapers is one example.

A third source of pro- and antinatalism is the *media.* Lately, magazines directed toward women in the 20–40 age group have been enamored of the antinatalist message. Magazine racks of "on-the-go, working-woman" reading matter emphasize that "dressing for success" doesn't mean a T-shirt with spit-up on it. They discuss 30 ways to ask for a raise, but give few suggestions for scrutinizing a babysitter.

But television is still stuck in the old pronatalist mold. The title "Eight Is Enough" suggests calling reproduction quits, but the message is of one big, happy family. "Happy Days" recalls the mother-at-home 1950s. Contestants on the widely viewed Miss America pageants want to be pilots and ventriloquists—and then have five children because "the family is the backbone of America."

The fourth pro- or antinatalist influence is our own *socialization*. We're raised to think all our practice with dollies will come to some good use. We're taught that we get married to have babies; that Christmas means nothing without children. Decision makers must sift through their own experiences and discern which memories accurately reflect the past, and which pro- and antiparenthood feelings accurately represent current inclinations.

An interesting study completed in 1980 at UCLA by Drs. Gail Zellman, Jacqueline Goodchilds, and Paula Johnson found that, despite headway by the women's movement to change attitudes about roles for men and women, today's teenagers carry the same old scripts about what boys and girls should do. The study focused on how 14–18-year-olds relate to each other in a dating context and how various cues are interpreted by each sex. Girls are still acting out the old roles—pleasing the male, resisting his advances, never initiating acquaintance or contact—as their counterparts of the 1950s and 1960s. These kinds of roles, learned early in life, can guide actions too much and can camouflage underlying or conflicting desires.

Socialization comes from all sorts of sources: parents, institutions (church, school, and state), textbooks, our early role models. Think, for example, of Miss Jones, the teacher who was called an old maid behind her back because it was considered a disgrace to not have husband and children. Again, it's important to sift through your own past to decide which parts of your socialization you continue to feel comfortable with and which parts are vestiges of the past.

Your Past Colors the Decision-making Process

Your past is important not only for the socialization you received but also for the impact of your own childhood on perceptions of parenthood.

Borrow a Child

Recent experience you may have interacting with children helps mold how you view parenthood. Before you make a final choice, it's helpful to get as much experience around children as you can. Borrow a child or two—not just for a day or even a weekend, when your work routine is set aside to pay attention to this novelty visitor. Borrow a child for an entire regular workweek to see how the responsibilities and rewards accrue.

"But children act differently when they're away from their parents!" "But what if the one I get is unusually angelic? Or a pure terror? Who's to say my own flesh-and-blood will be anywhere near the same?" "How are we supposed to work a child into our set routines?" These are examples of the objections people raise at the idea of a strange human being intruding in their lives.

Yes, borrowing a child provides a real taste of parenthood. You might have to get up a half-hour early to drive Johnny to his usual car pool, or make a few phone calls to make sure he's watched until you get home from work. You may have to be concerned that he finishes the peas on his plate, or that he takes his vitamin pill and doesn't forget his jacket when he goes dashing off to softball practice.

These inconveniences will yield rewards. Johnny will talk with you, respond to you. He may say "thanks" when you give him a cup of hot chocolate. He may fall asleep on your fold-out couch with the most perfect look of tranquility. His response to you is more helpful in your decision than any fantasizing about hassles and drawbacks ever can be.

It's true that the next-door neighbor you borrow may be an exceptional child. She could be the sweetest little cupcake that ever peeked shyly around a doorjamb, or Calamity Jane, hanging precariously from tree limbs and accidentally knocking every crystal paperweight off your coffee table. Each child is different and unique, each child is born with a temperament. Research has shown that within one family there often are a variety of temperaments among siblings. There's the quiet one who slept through the night at two months and the colicky one who hollered no matter what you did. So when you borrow a child, imagine that the one you produce is similarly tempered.

The more experience you have with children, the more realistic and educated your decision about having your own will be. Long-term relationships are best—for example, as a scout troup leader or a Big Brother. Regularly volunteer to baby-sit a variety of neighborhood children. Become an Uncle Bob or Auntie May to a close friend's child. Then you'll be able to witness an individual's development first-hand, with a personal investment in the process.

It's also wise to have contact with children of different ages, especially children of the age you fear most. Do the shrill strains of a baby's cry bring the same spinal shivers as a fingernail on a blackboard? Is the notion of an uncivilized 10-lb. blob traumatic? Do diapers conjure up images of pricked fingers or commercials of unattached arms pouring measuring cups of water through layers of expensive paper sponges? Then borrow an infant and see if your fears are accurate. If you have strong trepidation, approach the feared age in stages—first in the presence of the child's parent, then in the company of other adults and children, then finally one-to-one. (The process is similar to "desensitization," the same technique psychologists use to help patients overcome fear of snakes. At least most children don't bite.)

Quite a few people think they can handle being the parent of a young child, but quiver at the thought of harnessing the energies of an independent teenager. The truth is that not every teenager has had sex before the age of 12; not every adolescent carries a trunkful of drug paraphenalia; not all high schoolers have written the dictionary of obscenity. Each teenager is different, with his or her own vices and charms, just like adults. The dare is to find out about them yourself.

Interview Parents

It's also helpful to enter into the decision-making process armed with as much of other people's experience as possible. This means interviewing just about every parent you see. Don't give them a license to ramble on—you're doing research and want to know specific things. Some sample questions:

- If you had it to do over again, would you have had your child(ren)? Why?
- What have you found to be the worst aspects of parenthood?
- What are the best aspects of parenthood?
- What means do you use to continue with your career and supervise and raise your child? (or, alternately) Since you've taken time from your career to stay with your child, what disadvantages and advantages in doing that have you found?
- I am deciding whether or not to have a child. What do you feel are the most important things for me to consider?
- What turned out to be surprises about parenthood—things you didn't expect?

Add additional questions depending on your relationship with the person you're interviewing, your personal concerns, and what you know about their circumstance. Gather information in a structured way so that you can compare responses from one parent to the next. Be sure to think about how your personality differs from the people you interview. Maybe Beulah feels trapped at home with her baby, but you know you'd welcome a year's respite from your rather ho-hum job.

The experience of professionals is also a good source of information. Read everything you can about parenting, from prepared childbirth books to Dr. Spock's diagnosis of chickenpox. Take a look at parenting guides, like Parenthood Effectiveness Training and even TA for Kids. Telephone a child psychologist about the most frequent problems and joys kids go through; talk to a summer camp counselor to find out the cleverly devious situations fun-loving half-pints can create. Learn about parenthood as much as possible. Then you can get a somewhat better idea of what you may be missing.

On the other hand, take some time to evaluate the rewards of a childfree life-style too. Before you begin this process, you might want to jot down everything you enjoy about your childfree state, plus everything you regret. Pause in travel agency windows and see if descriptions of spur-of-the-moment weekend escapes stir your heart. Pick out Halloween candy and compare your present doorbell-answering evenings with the night-walk you might have as a parent. Evaluate as much as you can on your own—your own experience, others' histories and feelings, professionals' offerings—and then you'll be prepared to systematically make a satisfying choice.

6

Exploration Begins

Many couples come to the childbearing decision after years of discussion, skirting the issue, and writing lists of pros and cons. Others have gingerly avoided the topic, either for fear of their own feelings or fear that their partners' opinions won't coincide with their own.

The only way to find out what's truly going on is to assess where you're standing right now, whether it's a precarious precipice or solid ground. It's essential to look inward first and to disregard pressure from your spouse, your in-laws and family, or your friends. This will afford you an opportunity to approach the decision personally. So, before you become submerged with actually *deciding* about having a child, both you and your partner should each take time to complete the following "Before" questionnaire. After you've completed it, compare your answers.

As you can see, "A Before Questionnaire" zeroes in on your present status in four different areas. First you marked the amount and type of *distress* this issue is causing you. Easing distress over the baby decision is a primary goal of this book—even if you "decide not to decide" (that is, postpone making a final choice about having a child), relieving anxieties about the choice is a major improvement.

Of course, many people just push their discomfort to the back of their minds or blame symptoms of it (headache, overeating, nervousness, lack of sleep, crankiness) on other aspects of life. Maybe it isn't your boss or that horrendous project that's causing your anxiety—think about your feelings when the childbearing issue is raised, and then decide whether or not it *is* impinging on your mental state.

Some people feel distress but don't like to admit to it. This is especially true of men, who've been raised to negate their emotions. Even the ones who like to think of themselves as "liberated" are often stoic. "This is certainly an issue of concern," I remember one man telling me, worry lines creasing his tanned brow. "but I just want to evaluate the issues rationally. I remove myself from emotional bouts. That's my wife's department."

The second area measured by "A Before Questionnaire" is *conflict*. Conflict has two types: the swirling "do-I-or-don't-I?" within yourself, and disagreement between your partner and yourself.

A third area assessed is *communication style*. Questions 7 and 8 ask you to observe your own reaction and that of your partner to the decision. I've heard some amazing disputes about who-does-what when the notion of having a child is raised. Three of the choices—"logically weigh the pros and cons," "argue strongly for my point," and "change my mind a lot"—show a rational perspective. Someone more emotional might choose the other alternatives. Of course, most people change their approach to the issue depending on mood, although many couples never get a chance to discover each others' interaction style because they refuse to let the childbearing topic come up.

The final area assessed by "A Before Questionnaire" is *inclination*. When you are boxed into a corner by those percentages, you're forced to take a position. Probably the most telling question is number 14, which asks if in a decade you see yourself as a parent. If you conclude that yes, you will have had a child, then it's prudent to work backward and decide just when you're going to fit this all in.

About the Decision-making Process

To develop the questionnaires in this book, I first surveyed nearly 100 parents and asked them why they had their children, if they were happy about the choice, what they wished they'd known about parenting before they began (that is, surprises of the parenting experience), and what they'd advise couples making the choice now.

Then I videotaped a panel of parents, nonparents, singles, and experts, which turned into a heated debate. One panelist said she was glad that she had her four children 20 years ago, because now the choice is so hard to make. Now that she knows her brood, she added, she's glad to have done it; but if she had it to do all over again, well, life would be very complex. A younger, single man countered that trends change but values basic to society remain the same—how could she trade the warmth of family for her selfish goals? These comments offered insights no questionnaire could reveal.

Here are some of the reasons why parents said they had their children, condensed from the work of five researchers in the years 1969–1977: status as an adult; expansion of the self toward immortality, morality, and religion; creative accomplishment and competence, power, and influence; the process of having and raising children; social expectations of motherhood; peer pressure; and marriage enhancement. But these very rational reasons for having children barely touch on those warm, cuddly feelings and the spark that can instantly well up from inside and bring an otherwise businesslike career person to tears.

Two Sides to the Issue

Coming up now is a process that exhaults those personal, sometimes embarassing feelings. True, there are rounds of questionnaires that center on logical concerns, but there are also activities that emphasize just doing and observing emotional reactions.

You'll spend time role-playing as the expectant parent, and then consider your life as if you were unable to have any children at all. The experience is analgous to a decision-making process some people

Name: _____   Date: _____

A Before Questionnaire

1. **Distress** is anxiety, being upset, or having other emotions you feel are negative or undesirable. How much has the decision about whether or not to have a child been a source of distress at this stage of your life:

   a. For you?   None   A little   Some   A lot

   b. Between you and your partner?   None   A little   Some   A lot

2. Everyone has more than one thing to think about. Compared to the other concerns you have, how would you rate the childbearing decision in importance to you? (Please circle one)

   Very Important   Important   Somewhat Important   Unimportant

3. How often do you feel these levels of distress about whether or not to have a child?

	Most of the time	Some of the time	A small amount	Never
a. Very strong (crying, depressed)				
b. Moderately strong (upset, angry, defensive)				
c. Not very strong (a worry, bothersome)				

4. Over the past several months, how often have you thought about having a child? (Please circle one)

Once a day or more	Once every few days	Once every week or two	Once every 2–3 weeks	Once a month or less

5. Over the past several months, how often have you and your partner talked together about having a child? (Please circle one)

Once a day or more	Once every few days	Once every week or two	Once every 2–3 weeks	Once a month or less

6. When you think about having a child, how often do you feel each of these?

	Mostly	Some	A little	Never
a. Positive (happy, enthusiastic)				
b. Negative (scared, depressed, distressed)				
c. Confused or conflicted (decide back and forth)				

7. When you and your partner talk together about having a child, which of these things do **you** do? (Put an **X** for the things you do, but put **XX** for the one done **most**.)

_____Logically weigh the pros and cons _____Get happy and enthusiastic
_____Clam up or avoid the subject _____Change my mind a lot
_____Argue strongly for my point _____Get depressed or moody

8. When you and your partner talk together about having a child, which of these things does **your partner** do? (One **X** for what he or she does; **XX** for the one he or she does **most**.)

_____Argue strongly for his/her point _____Get depressed or moody
_____Clam up or avoid the subject _____Change her/his mind a lot
_____Logically weigh the pros and cons _____Get happy and enthusiastic

9. **Conflict** is indecision or deciding back and forth; pitting one decision against the other; a clash of ideas. How much conflict has there been over the childbearing decision over the last month:

a. Within yourself? None A little Some A lot
b. Within your partner? None A little Some A lot
c. Between the two of you? None A little Some A lot

10. What is the percentage you lean **toward** having a child, and the percentage you lean **against** having one:

a. **Within a year**   b. **In the future**   How long? _____

_____% + _____% = 100%   _____% + _____% = 100%
Toward   Against   Toward   Against
having   having   having   having
one   one   one   one

11. What is the percentage **your partner** seems to lean toward having a child, and the percentage he or she seems to lean against having one:

a. **Within a year**   b. **In the future**   How long? _____

_____% + _____% = 100%   _____% + _____% = 100%
Toward   Against   Toward   Against

12. Right now, your own preference is to: (Please check one)

a. _____Have a child within a year   b. _____Postpone having a child
                                                         (How long? _____)

c. _____Not have any children   d. _____Not make any decision yet

13. How certain are you that your present choice (as you checked above) will hold true?

a. _____ Very certain   b. Somewhat certain   c. _____ Uncertain

14. Ten years from now, realistically, do you guess that you will have:

a. _____ Had one or more child   b. _____ Not have had any children use to select one of two equally-appealing choices: flipping a coin. "Heads" stands for one decision, and "tails" signifies another. The coin is flipped, and the emotional reaction analyzed. If you find yourself secretly rooting for "tails," you know you wanted that choice all along. Conversely, if the coin lands on "heads" and you're disappointed, perhaps adding "we'll flip two out of three," your inner inclination is also revealed.

The idea of "living with" pregnancy and permanent nonparenthood is similar. If thinking about having a baby makes you depressed, you know you're not ready to have one. On the other hand, if imagining sterility causes swings of happiness and then depression, parenthood is more important to you than you realize.

A Caveat

Because the baby decision is so emotional, often people who rationally want to make up their minds often find themselves avoiding the issue. The kitchen needs painting, just when they were going to discuss that touchy questionnaire. Or somehow there are endless demands every night at the office, and it's just too tough scheduling time to talk about such a heavy issue. And after sitting at a desk all day, who wants to do more "paperwork?" Just about any task can be less scary than dredging up childhood memories, broaching an "untouchable" topic with a hostile spouse or facing uncomfortable truths about priorities in life.

The caveat is that it's often easy to avoid the issue. If you know your patterns in advance, you can discipline yourself to work through the avoidance into awareness. Assumptions about what you want out of life, your career choice, your happiness with your mate may all be called into question. Facing these issues isn't easy, and you may want to consult a professional counselor for fresh perspectives.

The time it takes to go through the materials in this book doesn't take an enormous chunk out of your life. But the resulting decision just may be the most important one you ever make. You can always change career directions or quit your job; you can sell the house you've mortgaged your soul to afford; you can divorce your husband or wife, but you can never end your fatherhood or motherhood. Even women who place their unwanted babies for adoption wonder about that child over the years. And of course, the responsibility doesn't end when the financial obligation ceases at age 18 or 21. Just as you're probably a "kid" to your parents, your child will always remain central to your life.

If you think too many cobwebbed corners of your personality will disturb your emotional welfare, consider professional counseling. If you find yourself frequently crying or having mood swings that affect your work or homelife, you probably could use a well-trained ear.

7

The Rational Side
of Parenthood

This chapter focuses on rational considerations of parenthood, though of course your decision will always be tinged with emotion and shaped by your underlying values. Several questionnaires and information on crucial areas of the childbearing decision are included. The rational side of the decision is presented before the emotional process because it's often easier to examine pros and cons than delve into murky feelings. Start from the somewhat detached position of thinker and analyzer. If you're rational in making other decisions in your life, you've had practice weighing alternatives—you may compare prices on a new stereo or look at dozens of homes over several months before entering escrow on one. Chapter 8 describes how to zero in on feelings; you can use the information in this chapter to understand *why* those feelings are so strong.

Being rational requires facts, and you should look to several sources: the information provided here, your own history, and outside information sources who add their own experiences to what you've already observed. Counselors, university researchers, and health care professionals can add findings based on large samples of parents, career-minded couples, the medical community, and poli-cymakers. Finally, you can reach out to strangers through college classes, recreation, or work to ask their views on your own issues.

You're on an exploratory mission, discovering a unique entity: yourself at this particular point in time. Naturally, you'll profit more if you invest more energy and thought. Complete all the forms inde-pendently of your partner, but afterwards share and discuss. Then, seek out more information if necessary and *repeat* the forms in light of the new facts. It often helps to complete each form several times, using different frames of reference. For example, you might want to use the "Expectations Questionnaire" as if you were expecting a child in six months, a couple years, and five years in the future. If you're considering adoption as well as natural childbearing, com-plete the forms twice with both possibilities.

Viewpoints Questionnaire

The first questionnaire lays out potential viewpoints in each of ten major areas. Each item is a commonly heard quotation from couples in the workshops I run on making the childbearing decision. There is a value expressed in each one of them, too, so you're bound to disagree with some of them. Check off whether you agree or disagree with each statement. There aren't any "wrong" or "right" responses here.

Viewpoints Questionnaire

Check whether you agree or disagree with the values expressed in the following statements below.

On Career and Education

Agree Disagree

☐ ☐ "I'm just at the difficult part of my education or career. Having a child now would be a perfect reason to put it off."

☐ ☐ "If I have a child now, I'll miss out on my chance for career advancement."

☐ ☐ "When I return from parenthood leave, I'll be right where I am now, while my co-workers will be up a notch in status."

☐ ☐ "I've been a housewife and I enjoy it, even though some people say it's better to be working. Now I feel it's time to extend that role by devoting myself to caring for a child."

☐ ☐ "I want to go for new heights in my career, which would mean taking some risks. But if I had a child, I'd feel financial security would be important, so I'd probably not risk it."

☐ ☐ "I like my job, but the idea of staying home is attractive. It's a desirable alternative to the hassles of employment."

☐ ☐ "If I stay home with a child, I can do all the things I've been meaning to do around the house for years."

☐ ☐ "My partner and I would have to work out some sort of arrangement where both of us would change our careers to accommodate childcare."

☐ ☐ "Neither of us are willing to sacrifice any part of our careers for a child, and we feel the child would benefit knowing its parents were doing what they wanted."

☐ ☐ "Who says you can't have it all—career, marriage, and children? There's definitely more work and exhaustion, but it can be done."

☐ ☐ "Something has to suffer when a woman tries to combine a career with family. Her children just don't get as much contact, which is crucial in the early years."

☐ ☐ "I'm torn between staying home with my child, providing the care and education I know I'd provide best, and returning to work and using childcare. I'm worried that strangers just can't do the job I would with my child."

☐ ☐ "I've been raised to believe that being a mother is a noble profession in itself, and I resent it when others imply that it's less important than holding down a job."

☐ ☐ "I'm afraid that if I stayed home with the child, I'd become a narrower person and lose the spark I get from daily contact with professionals."

☐ ☐ "I'm afraid my wife might become less exciting to me because she'll be concerned only with baby topics and not broader issues."

On Personal Concerns

☐ ☐ "I'm scared of pregnancy because it's such an unknown. I'm afraid of the pain, what it might do to my body, and that my husband won't think I'm attractive anymore."

☐ ☐ "I'm afraid I won't find my wife as attractive after the child. The thought of her body distended and stretched is not appealing."

☐ ☐ "I think having a child is using your body for its intended purpose. It will most likely improve it rather than make it worse."

☐ ☐ "This is a logical time in my life to have a child. We're finally settled, and having a child is the natural progression of things."

☐ ☐ "A child would complete my already satisfying life. It would be a bonus rather than the focus of all my career energy."

☐ ☐ "It would be an extension of myself to be a parent. I'm a good mate, a good friend, and I know I'd be great in this new role."

☐ ☐ "The idea of someone in the world that is uniquely created from my partner and me is very exciting. It's as if there's a piece of me that will be here after I die."

☐ ☐ "I like being free and flexible. I'd have many more responsibilities with a child, and I'm afraid that I just couldn't do as I please."

☐ ☐ "I strongly believe my partner and I should have a child because we have so much to offer."

☐ ☐ "I want to have as many children as we can handle, because I think we were put on this earth to continue the species."

On Parenthood

☐ ☐ "I'm really looking forward to caring for my baby. Feeding and bathing seems so loving and filled with so much nonverbal communication between parent and child."

☐ ☐ "The idea of a baby spitting up, needing formula at proper temperatures, and buying fumbly little booties is revolting. A baby is a blob with no redeeming features that you have to tolerate until it develops into a real person."

☐ ☐ "To me, the early years are fabulous. The rate of development at that stage is fascinating to observe. I want to be part of that miracle."

☐ ☐ "I resent having to get down on children's level and gurgle itsy-bitsy silly words. I think rubber duckies and pull toys are clutters that the child appreciates only minimally."

☐ ☐ "A child 4–9 is really in a great age range. They're growing at an awesome rate, and you can talk with them, reason about what's going on. They're still young enough to hug without them getting embarrassed."

☐ ☐ "I'm not fond of the ages between 4 and 9 because then children are in such a different world from mine. I crack a joke and they don't get it, but if I try to explain slowly, they seem already to know it all."

☐ ☐ "To me, it's least pleasant to deal with the pubescent child aged 10–14. They're neither child nor adult. As a parent, you have to draw strict lines so they don't grow up too fast, even though their peers may be doing things we never thought about until college."

☐ ☐ "Puberty is such a wondrous age. Things are changing fast; that's when the parent has the best opportunity to offer guidance and become really close."

☐ ☐ "The teenage years are probably the worst for a parent because it's so easy to lose control. There are so many temptations for teenagers today, it's hard to guarantee that your child won't succumb."

☐ ☐ "Most teenagers are reasonable people. If you've instilled them with your values, they can evaluate things for themselves. It's not like they're suddenly different, evil people. They can become your friends as well as your children."

☐ ☐ "I'd love to be a parent because then I'd have a real reason to be involved in all sorts of child-related activities I've only watched from the sidelines."

☐ ☐ "I'm leaning toward having a child because then I'll always have someone to care for me and also to give my love to. You can't count on your partner being there when you're old, but you can reasonably assume you'll have contact with your children."

☐ ☐ "I see old people in nursing homes lamenting because they never hear from their children. Children can be either a bonus or a source of anguish in old age."

☐ ☐ "I don't need children because I plan to keep active and be involved in close friendships until I die. Children can't substitute for — or necessarily contribute to — your own life."

On Relationship with My Partner

☐ ☐ "Right now the two of us can devote all our attention to each other. With a child, I might get much less attention and this might later cause me to resent the child."

☐ ☐ "I have the best partner in the world. I know he'd (she'd) be the best parent, too. But I don't think it's possible for him (or her) to be both."

☐ ☐ "Right now we like to do adult things — active sports or spontaneous outings — and I'm afraid that with a child we'd have to focus on activities to accommodate the child. I don't want to give up the things we like to do."

☐ ☐ "Our relationship is so strong that a child would just be an extension of that warmth. I believe that a child is the next logical step for our relationship, an evolution to new heights."

☐ ☐ "My partner and I don't know if we want to stay together. But if we do, then we ought to have a child to renew and extend a too-familiar relationship."

☐ ☐ "I don't want a child, and my partner does. If we had one, I might resent both my partner and the child. It might ruin our relationship as much as if we never fulfilled her (or his) desire."

☐ ☐ "I may not want a child, but I care enough about my partner to go along with whatever he (she) wants. If he (she) wants a child, then I'll do my damndest to be the best parent possible."

☐ ☐ "We've had a hot-and-cold relationship. I'm worried that a child might force us to stay together when we don't want to, or that the child might be psychologically harmed if we fight."

☐ ☐ "Even though I want a child, it's too scary for me to go ahead and get pregnant."

☐ ☐ "I'm a permissive person, but my partner believes in stricter discipline. I can envision lots of disagreements about raising the child."

☐ ☐ "I'm worried that my partner wouldn't be as concerned about creating a good moral climate for our child, and I don't want to be the one left to set rules, discipline, and protect the family."

☐ ☐ "I love my partner, but I'm just not sure he'd (she'd) be the parent type. If not, that would leave a lot of responsibility to me."

☐ ☐ "I want some kind of assurance my partner will share in the parent role as much as he (she) says he (she) will now."

On Economic Factors

☐ ☐ "I think we can handle the costs of a child — I believe that the expense has been overestimated and overpublicized."

☐ ☐ "You get used to the new family size, that's all. You don't think about what you could have done with the money if you didn't have a child. You just manage."

☐ ☐ "I think paying the expenses of a child is one of the best investments you can make. I would pay for everything gladly, willingly."

☐ ☐ "The immediate costs of a child can escalate beyond your wildest fantasies as soon as you find out how many products and comforts are available."

☐ ☐ "The costs of childcare left me agog. It isn't just school fees, but all the accoutrements, like transportation and time to chauffeur the child around."

☐ ☐ "I'd like to provide for my child's college education, but with inflation, it's absurd. The prices will go up so much, it's a losing battle to plan ahead."

☐ ☐ "The costs of a child aren't just in expenses, but in what you could have done with the money if you had it. We are really deciding between spending on a nice house and travel, or having a child."

☐ ☐ "We'd have to get another apartment or preferably a house to have a child. That significantly escalates the cost of the whole deal."

☐ ☐ "Thank heavens we've never gotten used to a fancy life style. If we have a child, we'll just continue in the style to which we're accustomed, instead of moving up to more luxurious environs."

☐ ☐ "We'd be moving downward in our living standard with a child. Because I'd stop working for awhile, our income would be cut drastically."

On Life-Style

☐ ☐ "The idea of having a child with my partner around is exciting. But I don't think I could handle it if he (she) departed the scene. I don't like the idea of being 100-percent responsible for another human being."

☐ ☐ "I'm confident that I'd be a great single parent. I don't like the prospect, but I'm not worried. I can handle myself, and I know it would work out."

☐ ☐ "I'd want to provide a sense of stability for a child. That would preclude our moving a lot."

☐ ☐ "A child is very flexible. There's no need to have it restrict your life-style."

☐ ☐ "I'd want to live where there were good schools, so we'd have to carefully consider the area we live in for its impact on my child more than any other considerations."

☐ ☐ "I remember growing up with many changes. I was never the worse for it. I don't think a child has to restrict your mobility."

☐ ☐ "When we go out to dinner, I often think, 'Gee, we could never have done this if we had a child without first hassling with baby-sitters.'"

☐ ☐ "We like to take off on weekends. We couldn't go on the spur of the moment with a child."

☐ ☐ "We're home-bodies anyway, and having a child wouldn't be any inconvenience."

☐ ☐ "There's nothing like having children around for holidays. And there's such a cozy feeling when you share new adventures with your children. I want to do all those 'family things.'"

☐ ☐ "To me, the disruption of my peaceful home with additional clutter and noise is a real drawback. When I come home from work, I like quiet relaxation. I'm worried I couldn't do that with a child around."

☐ ☐ "I like having children's belongings around. They're a reminder that there's life in the house. I can't stand a home where everything's too perfect; that it doesn't look lived in."

☐ ☐ "The thought of additional chores to do is really awful. I make the bed or clean the shower only when I have to. Taking care of a demanding infant or growing child would make me scream."

☐ ☐ "Though I despise housework, taking care of a child somehow seems different. When you bathe a baby, you receive rewards in the glances and movements of your child."

☐ ☐ "If I were to announce that we were having a baby, my parents would jump up and down with joy. It would make everyone happy if we joined the parent club."

☐ ☐ "All our friends have children. We feel really out of it when they talk about them. We'd fit in so much better with a child."

☐ ☐ "None of our friends have children. I worry that if we did, we'd lose contact with them."

☐ ☐ "Children are an entrée into so many social spheres. Just looking out for their welfare can put you in touch with so many community resources and people you'd never otherwise meet."

☐ ☐ "Children tie you down. You think you'll be able to get out and do things, but half the day goes by and you're still in robe and slippers. Just packing a diaper bag and all the accessories you need takes too much time in itself."

On Family Composition

☐ ☐ "I'd always imagined that I'd have two children, and I feel that's the best number. The children can play together and you're not overburdened."

☐ ☐ "I think having one child has been underrated. Research shows that they perform highly, and having just one will allow us to maintain the closeness we have now."

☐ ☐ "I always thought I should have my children before I turned 30 (or 35). That way I'll have enough energy to keep up with them."

☐ ☐ "It's better to wait until your 30s to have a child. Then you're more mature and aren't worried about finances or making your mark on the world. You've already had time to solidify your marriage and become a stable person."

☐ ☐ "Children wear you out, so you should time them so they're far apart or don't have as many."

☐ ☐ "Children keep you young, so if you have them when you're older, you'll never act like an 'old' person."

☐ ☐ "We have so many things to accomplish. We want to get the baby years over with so we can enjoy life as a family and do all these things over a longer period."

☐ ☐ "My partner has children from a former marriage. We have to consider how having one together would affect them."

☐ ☐ "I resist having a child now, because all our friends are going through it and I'd be part of their competition to see who has the best this or that. If I wait a few years, I can relax and feel less pressure from them."

On Health of the Child

☐ ☐ "We often think about what a child of ours would look like and be like. Would it have our best features or our worst? We'd kind of like to have one to find out."

☐ ☐ "We're exceptions in our families, and the odds are that our child wouldn't be as smart or as good-looking as we are."

☐ ☐ "I have horrible teeth and terrible vision. My partner's dad is bald. I'd hate to stick a kid with all these afflictions!"

☐ ☐ "I came from a family with severe problems. I've read that children from homes like these often turn out to be the same kinds of parents theirs were. I'm afraid that it could happen to me."

☐ ☐ "I'm older and thinking about a first child. I know about amniocentisis, but I don't think I could go through with an abortion if I found out I had a defective baby. On the other hand, I don't know if I could bear the heartbreak of knowing I was carrying an imperfect child."

☐ ☐ "If we were to have a handicapped child, I don't know if I could handle it. I'm afraid to have one just in case the statistics turned against me."

☐ ☐ "Most handicapped children can contribute to my happiness and society too. The possibility I might have one is a risk, but there are risks in everything you do."

On Important Relationships

☐ ☐ "I'm letting my partner decide if we have a child. After all he (she) would be the one to take care of it."

☐ ☐ "My partner wants a child so badly that if I say no, he (she) might leave me."

☐ ☐ "It's not worth risking her health for a child. She's the most important thing to me."

☐ ☐ "I think my partner would be happier than he (she) realizes with a child. Many people think they're against it at first, but end up practically enjoying a second childhood with their children."

☐ ☐ "My parents live far away, and having a child would make me miss them more, because I'd want my child to know his (her) grandparents."

☐ ☐ "My folks would be over a lot to visit if we had a child. We'd probably lose a lot of our privacy."

☐ ☐ "Our child would benefit from lots of doting aunts and uncles, and would enrich our relationships with our relatives."

☐ ☐ "I'm an only child, and it's important to me that I carry on the family name."

☐ ☐ "This stuff about the family name is a sexist, useless tradition."

☐ ☐ "My mother has been saving the family heirloom to give my future child. Tradition is very important in our family."

☐ ☐ "We've been married a long time, and by our age, most folks have had kids. I don't like the feeling of being a freak."

☐ ☐ "This issue about having kids is driving us away from our friends."

☐ ☐ "I really value our friends, and I'm afraid I might tumble into having kids because I want to fit in with them, not because I want the lifetime commitment."

On Society

☐ ☐ "My religion instructs us that couples should have children to carry on our beliefs and traditions."

☐ ☐ "I'm conflicted because while my religion teaches us to have kids, I just don't want any."

☐ ☐ "There are too many people in the world already. It's not right to bring additional people onto a limited earth."

☐ ☐ "I belong to an ethnic group that needs replenishing. I feel it's my duty to continue my people."

☐ ☐ "With water shortages, gasoline shortages, and other resources in demand, the world my child would face may not be a pleasant one."

☐ ☐ "I shouldn't bring a child into the world because he would use up scarce resources that we should try to conserve."

☐ ☐ "Nuclear war is just a push button away, and political skirmishes are happening all over the world. The future for my child looks grim."

☐ ☐ "There will always be problems in the world. They are no reason to avoid having a child."

Interpreting the Viewpoints Questionnaire

Some of the issues that come up as a result of the "Career and Education" section deal with the woman's work priorities. Many women see themselves as workers only until the time that they become mothers, which, by implication, will be a full-time career at that point. Women haven't had many choices in their careers, and even now earn 59 cents for every dollar earned by men. Despite all the new pushes for women's equality in the workplace, and the economic and psychological pressures to work (and earn fulfillment at it), staying at home with a child may be much more appealing than rising at six, pulling on pantyhose, dashing out the door, and turning yellow under florescent lights all day. Admitting that these feelings are not only natural but logical can be a real relief, and it often takes guts to divulge this truth.

Men can complete that section in two ways—putting themselves in their wives' places for some items, or completing such items as if *they* were the woman bearing the child. Many of the items in the "Career and Education" section are geared to women, because women are in the most tenuous positions professionally. They have to contend with physical changes of childbearing that men don't, and they're often scrambling twice as hard to maintain their rungs on the tipping career ladder.

This isn't to say that men have few career concerns. There are pressures to stay in a secure job due to financial obligations. And they may deeply care about their partners, feeling the significance of the woman's career as if it were their own. But it's crucial to note that women generally do have a greater career risk than men, and that women's reservations about parenthood and even about wanting to succeed are common and justified.

The section on "Personal Concerns" spans a variety of issues. Worry about the physical effects of pregnancy is becoming prevalent, given the recent emphasis on physical fitness and control. If you belong to a gym and have worked ferociously to earn your firm muscles and slender form, it's natural to be concerned that all your work is for naught. This is the issue of control: when you're pregnant, your physical development is out of your control—nature takes over. Whether you see this as a wondrous miracle or a distended disaster is highly personal.

The timing of a child is another issue that carries doubt. There's no potential parents' crystal ball you can peer into to know if now's the perfect time or if you should wait for your oil well to become a geiser. An important tool for you to see how you'll adapt to parenthood is to look at existing patterns in your life. When you've made other important decisions, have you wavered back and forth, full of buyer's remorse, or have you acted and never looked back? You can expect the same reaction to the parenthood decision. Have you treated your pets as children? If so, look at how they've fit into your life, and the division of labor and responsibility you've assigned. They're great barometers to your future reaction to having a child.

Emotions and value-charged issues of moral responsibility are easy to philosophize about. It's important not to negate the notions of "duty" and "right," but each child is conceived with a view to the circumstances occurring at that moment. The existential question is often raised: What is our purpose on earth? For some people, the answer is love, which can come from existing family, a close marital relationship, or rewarding connections with others—or from their own children. Again, this is a very personal issue.

The section "On Parenthood" focuses on common fears and joys of various stages of parenthood. It's paradoxical that the static term "parenthood" describes a status that is constantly changing. Parenthood is getting up during the night to hold an infant of 10 lbs who can only communicate in screams. Parenthood is helping a toddler to her wobbly feet for a trot across the playpen. Parenthood is sitting vigil at the bedside of a child with the flu, and proudly greeting other parents at an 11-year-old's piano recital. The problem with parenthood is that it's impossible to capsulize because it's completely unknown. The only thing you *can* know is your own present fear and anticipation about each stage of development.

Most couples mention two ages when deciding about having a child. Infancy is either cherished or disdained. Suddenly your entire life is directed toward the care of a helpless human—even if you hire help, your thoughts and concerns center around the needs of the newborn—and the object of all this attention can't even respond in kind. He'll gurgle or smile or fuss, but never provide an intellectual challenge. For women and men used to a fast-paced interchange with adults, this can be a frightening change.

The second age that scares prospective parents is adolescence. Most of them point out that mores have spun beyond the strict standards of their own youths: sex, with frequent teenage pregnancy; drugs of all hues; alcoholism; disdain for authority; lack of respect for parents or the family; status consciousness and demands for the latest designer jeans; fashionable hairstyles across the color wheel;

portable stereos and stylish models of cars. No longer is the child physically smaller than the parent. You can't easily spank a 17-year-old, so it's a time of worry that the parental relationship will disintegrate as the hormone-flushed adolescent becomes out of control.

Another concern is not the child, but yourself in old age. It's terrifying to think of yourself—an active, achieving person—as alone and needing help. It's a difficult burden for an adult child to bear if an aging parent depends on him or her for emotional and financial support. Admitting that you're afraid of old age, incapacitation, and death is also difficult. But it's crucial to separate those fears from the fantasy of being sustained by your child.

Statements "On Relationship with my Partner" begin with what you already know. You know exactly where you stand—the kind of lifestyle you lead, the importance of stability versus spontaneity, the amount you fight. You can only speculate about the impact of a child, and chances are, if you're satisfied now, you'll predict the child can only bring decline. These are natural concerns, but they're based on only half the information. The other half of which you are deprived until you actually have a child and it's too late is the personality and role of your offspring. A colicky baby can lead to fights over who's doing what wrong, or can unite the parents toward making him comfortable and solving problems together. A smiley, cooing angel can enhance shared pride. Again, look at patterns in your relationship to determine how you might react to these eventualities.

One recurring issue is that of bottom-line responsibility, the last item in the "Relationship with Partner" section. Women fear that, if all things are equal, they'll be the ones expected to leave the board room for a phone call from the school nurse. Men usually swear they'll be responsible, too, but underneath it all they feel their wives should handle the crises.

This is partially due to their lack of fatherhood practice. Most little girls play house and play with dolls; boys are told to "go out and play." Role modeling during the 1950s and 1960s featured Mom making brownies, just waiting for the kids to come home from school. Translated, that means Mom's responsible for the kids' well-being, no matter what. Even "raised consciousnesses" have a hard time shaking this background.

Men are usually more rankled than women by another section, "Economic Factors," because the same socialization that produced women's bottom-line childcare responsibility gave men a financial obligation. Financial concern is cited as the reason most postponing couples put off having a child. Yet those who are committed to child-bearing—usually the planners—may be in far poorer straits. It's a matter of attitude. The ones who sincerely and completely want children say "We'll manage," while those who aren't quite sure set up elaborate financial criteria for their lives.

The "Lifestyle" section deals with change. It's essential to speculate on being a single parent, even if the chances of becoming one are remote. Again, past patterns can provide a clue to dealing with the necessary restrictions a child would impose. However, the amount of restriction actually necessary is debatable. Some parents feel a duty to give the child a stable environment, while others see the offspring as an extension of themselves, able to fit into any established pattern.

Obviously, agreement or disagreement with the statements on the "Viewpoints Questionnaire" requires speculation about the future. That's why examining your present and past patterns of decision making, life-style, and relationships is constantly crucial.

When considering "Family Composition," most people think of stereotypes. They hear that having just one child will mean tantrums from a selfish, bored pipsqueak, so they accept this as truth, without fully understanding the situation.

A second factor influencing family composition is your own childhood. Only children who were themselves lonely vow they'll never inflict that on a child. But "onlies" who basked in parental attention and then went on to achieve may believe that theirs is the best life imaginable.

Of course, the modern fantasy is of a quaint single-family home and two cherubic children making monster Leggo castles in the front yard. Nowadays, Mom is deriving satisfaction from her responsible job rather than spending days at PTA meetings, but there's still that tenacious two-child ideal. Then there's the issue of timing—past stereotypes had families completed by the mother's thirtieth birthday so that the folks could be young with their brood. Think about how you feel about your own parents' age when you and your siblings were born. Were they too old, or perhaps too inexperienced, to do the job right? The major training for parenthood in our culture is through example; it stands to reason that the longer a potential mom or dad has to observe varying parenting styles, the more they'll know when their own time comes. On the other hand, by the time some adults are ready to have children, they're involved in a lifestyle they resent changing.

Concerns about "Health of the Child" also stem from experience. If you work with handicapped children, for example, then the spectre of a dreaded accident happening to you is magnified. If there are genetic problems in your family, you will want to consult a professional geneticist or your private physician.

Nearly everyone fantasizes about what their child would look like. As a supplementary activity, take a moment to envision your child. What age is the child? Is it a boy or girl? What does he or she look like? What is the child doing? Where are you looking from—across the room or down at an infant in your arms? Compare this vision of your child with your partner's. Keep in mind that this dream is an ideal—a picture of the child you *hope* will be reality—and that such mental snapshots don't have to be labled good or bad.

Views "On Important Relationships" are central to the child-bearing decision. The first questions cover investment in having a child and the balance of investment between you and your partner. Are you pressuring him or her to go along with your own desire? Could that be causing resistance that wouldn't otherwise be there? Do you have the uncomfortable feeling that you love your partner more than she or he loves you, because you'd be flexible enough just to see him or her happy? These are some of the issues that are raised when your relationship is at stake.

Pro- and antinatalist pressures are rampant among family and friends. How do your own values coincide with traditions and sentiments in your family? Are you rebelling against tradition, rediscovering it, or abiding by it gladly? Many couples who enjoy the support and security of their families' protection and values consciously choose to put these feelings above their own inclinations to have or not have a child.

The final section, "On Society," focuses directly on basing personal decisions on the greater public good. Population multiplication, limited resources, and other societal concerns are often cited as ingredients in the childbearing decision, but they're not often final determinants. The gnawing of emotions—away from the whole issue or in favor of it—ultimately inspires a move. The choice about having a child is more personal than philosophical, so doom-and-gloom predictions seldom deter even the most ardent pessimist who resolutely wants to be a parent.

The "Viewpoints Questionnaire" helps you compare your values with those expressed by other potential parents. The quotations were condensed from comments volleyed in a workshop setting. You have the advantage of time and privacy to mull over each statement, and you probably haven't considered most of them before, even if you have carefully contemplated the childbearing decision.

The next step is to clarify more specifically your expectations of parenthood. In the "Viewpoints Questionnaire," you considered thoughts of others; now you have the opportunity to express your personal beliefs and circumstances. The next form, called the "Expectations Questionnaire," generates *realistic* expectations for yourself and your partner. This is where a little sorcery would come in handy. The major purpose is to compare your views with your partner's and, if you choose, with the experiences of others you know and trust.

Instructions for the Expectations Questionnaire

Parenthood is divided into ten areas, listed at the left of the form. The first five are areas you're already familiar with, and you can use your observation of existing patterns to make your predictions. The second five areas require greater guesswork, and you'll have to rely on what others report and on your intuition to project what will happen.

For each of the areas, write your expectation for yourself and your partner down the center section of the page. You may run out of space, since each area is so complex. Add on as much paper as you need; the more elaborate your predictions, the more grist for discussion you'll have.

After you've noted your thoughts, look at the columns down the right of the page. If your expectation became reality, would you consider each aspect of your life to be positive, negative, or neutral? Don't check everything "neutral"; face your judgments so you can come closer to your underlying feelings.

Finally, check off whether each of the ten areas is Very Important, Somewhat Important, or Unimportant in the overall picture, compared with the other areas listed.

Expectations Questionnaire

Step 1: Read over the areas to the left.
Step 2: Write in your expectation.
Step 3: Check whether the prediction would be positive, neutral, or negative if it came true.
Step 4: Check the importance of each area to you in your choice.

"How will having a child affect my partner's and my . . .	"What will happen?" Expectation for myself	Expectation for my partner	Positive (good)	Neutral	Negative (bad)	Very Important	Important	Unimportant
1. Career and/or education?								
2. Financial situation, now and later?								
3. Relationship with each other?								
4. Relationship with family and friends?								

			Positive (good)	Neutral	Negative (bad)	Very Important	Important	Unimportant
5. Freedom, privacy and spontaneity?								

How will my partner and I deal with . . .	Expectation for myself	Expectation for my partner						
6. Pregnancy and birth?								
7. Supervising, training and being with the younger child (birth to 8 years)?								
8. Supervising, training, and being with the older child or teenager?								
9. The possible health, traits, and personality our child could have?								
10. Bringing up a child in today's world?								

After you've fantasized about your answers and written them down, compare them with those of your partner. Use the discussion guidelines in Chapter 6 so the interchange is fair and most productive. As you talk, listen carefully to the underlying values both you and your partner express, as well as those that are desired but more flexible.

Perhaps you'd like to plot out a few "alternative scenarios," pictures of the future that might occur. For example, you might want to repeat the form according to the possible directions your careers might take: "If I stay with Bedrock Chemical, I'd have security and little travel; if I return to graduate school and then start my own business, I may have to relocate and we'd depend more strongly on your income." Or repeat the upper half of the form to consider life with a child of various ages. Maybe your career would be on hold during the baby's infancy but soar afterwards. All these factors interact— affecting your and your partner's relationship, freedom, privacy, spontaneity, finances, etc. The goal is to achieve a consensus regarding how your life will most probably be affected by the addition of a new child.

Use your "Expectations Questionnaire" to discover any areas you have trouble fantasizing about. Maybe it's a cinch to chart the changes in your financial picture, given the cost of orthodontia, a new addition on the house, or the Wee Ones Childcare Center down the street. But when it comes to speculating on bringing up a child in today's world, well, your crystal ball becomes cloudy. It's easier to project in certain areas than others, but if you've missed important ones, collect information and fill in the blanks.

Checking whether each of your predictions would be positive, negative, or neutral if it came true meant placing values on your possible futures. Maybe you consider staying home for a year with your child as detrimental to your career (negative, regarding the area of "career or education") but enriching for you in general (positive, under the heading "supervising, training, and being with the younger child.") They cancel each other out right away, reinforced by your check indicating each area's predicted importance to your overall choice.

The "Expectations Questionnaire" was an exercise in: (1) considering specifically how your life with a child would differ from your present situation; (2) evaluating how good or bad these differences would be to you; and (3) putting all the areas of change into perspective with each other. The "importance" columns on the far right of the form help you negotiate with your mate about your plans. You'd probably compromise on managing the less important areas but may hold firm in carrying out (or changing) predictions that are crucial in your view.

The Continuua Questionnaire

So far, you've agreed or disagreed with other people's thoughts expressed in the "Viewpoints Questionnaire." Then you've generated your personal prediction of your future life with a child on the "Expectations Questionnaire." Now you'll be more carefully considering the broad predictions by zeroing in on potential events.

The "Continuua Questionnaire" lets you look at concerns by degree, rather than assuming events or thoughts are black or white. The form lets you visualize ranges of response—from good to bad, from some to a lot, from always to never. There are gradations of financial impact a child could have, variations in parenting styles, and shadings in the acceptability of your childcare options. This questionnaire provides ranges of outcomes you could expect and offers you a chance to realistically decide a likely position for yourself.

Now, independently from your partner, complete the "Continuua Questionnaire" by placing a check mark at the point on the horizontal line that most closely represents your values, expectations, and feelings. It's tempting to just put check marks right down the middle, but don't be equivocal—try to firmly plant yourself on one side or the other. That way you'll have more information for discussion with your partner and more for yourself to mull over and revise.

Continuua Questionnaire

Check your position on each continuum as if you had a child (or as guided by the statements on the ends of the continuua).

My partner's career will suffer.	My partner's career will flourish.
My career will suffer.	My career will flourish.
The child's primary caretaker will hate childcare.	The child's caretaker will adore childcare.
The primary caretaker will pause briefly from work.	The caretaker will make childcare his or her career.
Childcare options seem impossible.	Childcare arrangements will be easy.
The woman's physical state will suffer greatly.	The woman's physical state will improve.
Parenthood clashes with my view of myself.	Parenthood fits perfectly into my self-concept.
I'd be a poor parent.	I'd be a fabulous parent.
My partner would be a poor parent.	My partner would be a fabulous parent.
My relationship with my partner would suffer.	My relationship with my partner would improve greatly.
I'd feel tied down.	I'd feel liberated.
My parenting style would be very strict.	My parenting style would be very permissive.
My partner's parenting style would be very strict.	My partner's parenting style would be very permissive.
Our standard of living would nosedive.	Our standard of living would continue to improve.

My own income would cease.	My own income would continue to rise.
I couldn't cope with being a single parent.	If need be, I could easily take over single parenting.
We'd be outcasts among our present friends.	Our friends would appreciate us even more with a child.
Our parents leave us totally alone in the baby decision.	Our parents won't let up with their urging.
If we have a child, it's got to be immediately.	We can wait ten years or longer to have a child.
Our child would probably have health problems.	The risk of health problems for our child is extremely low.
I'm leaving the entire decision to my partner.	The childbearing decision is entirely mine.
The world our child would face would be a mess.	Our child's world promises to be far better than today's.

For me, each period of my child's development listed below will be . . .

	Fabulous	**Very Difficult**
1. Pregnancy		
2. Birth		
3. Ages 1–3		
4. Ages 4–9		
5. Ages 10–14		
6. Ages 15–18		
7. Adulthood		

The questionnaire was designed to make you ponder the judgments (i.e. values) you would assign to each item. Maybe for you, childcare is "impossible" when you have to drive half an hour to drop off the kids at your mother's. For someone else, "impossible" means having absolutely no one, except yourself, to rely upon—sitters and daycare are unaffordable, friends or relatives are out of town, and your paycheck must pay the rent. There are also differences in what defines a "permissive" versus a "strict" upbringing.

This questionnaire presented you with polar opposites that you had to define clearly and then evaluate in relation to yourself. You might want to repeat the questionnaire or return to any items that confused you. For example, if you took a look at the item on the woman's physical state and asked, "Is this *during* or *after* pregnancy?" then put a check on the continuum for your prediction at each point, during *and* after pregnancy. Distinguish between the two by a little note, or by using two colors, or by using a check versus an *X*. All the questionnaires are designed to be personalized this way; the more you put into them, the more you'll learn.

After you have completed the questionnaire, go back to the beginning and put a star to the left of the answers that left you dissatisfied or confused. Maybe you confessed that you'd feel tied down at home taking care of a baby, and you'd long for the contact of peers at the office or just the freedom to take a leisurely browse through the five-and-dime. Perhaps you'd put a star next to that item because you're not pleased with the prospect of facing all that frustration. The starred items then become situations you can plan to change. A little research might reveal three other people on your block with little ones at home who are itching for stimulating company and someone to trade baby-sitting with as much as you are.

Contemplate your responses and the possible means of changing events that aren't appealing; then share your findings with your partner. Maybe you'll discover that *both* of you would feel tied down—the man because of responsibility and lack of freedom, and the woman because of feeling cooped up with a burping baby. If both of you agree that this is stifling, you can plan together. Daddy might talk to other fathers and find out that the pressure fades quickly, that Junior really won't mind being left behind or tucked into a backpack; or he might want to *think* about those feelings of responsibility, contemplating rather than denying them. A counselor or understanding spouse can help explore the roots of negative emotions and can help decide how important they are in the overall picture of having a child.

Facts to Further the Decision

So far you've relied on your own inner resources to supply answers to childbearing-related questions. The values, expectations, and feelings you expressed on the "Viewpoints Questionnaire," the "Expectations Questionnaire," and the "Continuua Questionnaire" were very personal. Each of the forms probably raised several issues and left new questions to be answered. Now, before you complete a final tool, the "Benefits and Drawbacks Questionnaire" (which gives you a score in favor or against having a child), see if facts confirm or negate the beliefs and expectations you hold. Add all this material to the interviewing of friends, family, professionals, and strangers you've been doing, and you'll have a fairly large set of truths on which to base your choice. You're manufacturing a crystal ball.

What Will A Child Cost?

Assume that the cost escalates with age, as indicated in the chart "It's Only Money." It's likely that a typical middle-income family will end up shelling out most of the cash listed—and the figures are bound to be higher by the time your baby requires his or her wad of greenbacks. For comparison, Thomas J. Espenshade in 1979 tabulated estimates of what a child costs. The Population Reference Bureau in Washington D.C. published his findings: a moderate estimate for childbirth alone in 1979 was $3,272. Child support to 18 years totaled $62,525. Four years of college added another $20,000 *then*, for a grand direct cost of $85,797. This doesn't even touch the wife's "opportunity costs," the sum she would've earned had she stayed in the workforce rather than tending to Junior's upbringing.

Cost of a Child: It's Only Money

This list of expenses is loosely based on an accounting done in 1977 by **New West** magazine, with updates to 1982. In some cases, costs may vary widely by geographic region, availability, or price fluctuations. Any unreasonable figures deserve checking out yourself. Perhaps there are other expenses you'd add—or some you'd eliminate. Just remember that you'd want your child to have the best of everything you could afford.

Age 1: $5,450

Obstetrician	$500–2,000
Hospital (3 days @ $175)	525
Delivery	300–500
Nursery (3 days @ $100)	300
Supplies	50
Baby wardrobe	200
Feeding equipment	75
Diapers (disposable)	350
Pediatrician	200
Food	500
Extra room for baby (@ $100 per month)	1,200
Baby-sitters/nurse for two weeks	150–750
Toys and books	50

and probably . . .

Baby's savings account	100
Photos (professional and family)	100

Age 5: $6,125

Food (including fast-food restaurants)	800
Housing	1,200
Clothing	500
Medical care	200
Dentist (including cavities)	400
Nursery school	850
transportation	500

Toys, books, records	150
Babysitting	250

and probably . . .

Room redecoration (crib to bed, etc.)	300
Lessons	150
Special birthday (clown, etc.)	150
Vacation or live-in baby-sitter	500
Hair/barber	75
Child's pet(s)	100

Age 11: $10,730

Food	900
Housing	1,200
Clothing	650
Medical care (includes one broken bone)	500
Dentist	175
School-related expenses	100
Hobby supplies/toys	250
Allowance (@ $2.50 weekly)	130
Bus fare/cost of chauffeuring	500
Sports equipment, team registration	100
Entertainment/movies	75
Baby-sitting	500
Haircuts (first permanent)	150

and probably . . .

Private school	3,000
Lessons	300
Special outings (Disneyland, circus, etc.)	50
Special birthday	150
Vacations or live-in baby-sitter	500
Summer camp	1,300
Pets (including a dog)	200

Age 16: $17,800

Food (includes fast-foods, restaurants)	1,200
Housing	1,200
Clothing (includes fads)	500

Medical expenses (includes dermatologist and mononucleosis)	650
Dentist	150
Orthodontia	2,000
Books/records	200
Entertainment/movies	250
Dates	250
Transportation/use of the family car (with insurance)	800
Haircuts	200
Family vacation	350
Allowance	600

and probably . . .

Private school	3,000
Student trip abroad	1,500
Musical instrument lessons	400
Special events (rock concerts, etc.)	100
Teenager's private telephone	150
Room redecorated	500
Stereo, camera, other necessary gadgets	500
Incidentals (shampoo, acne cream, magazines, etc.)	100
Deb or other Big Party	1,000
Contact lenses	300
College entrance exam study course	350
Algebra/geometry tutor	350
Dog (continued)	200

Expenses to Consider

College tuition (public institution)	5,000 (over 4 years)
College living expenses (dorm, etc.)	30,000 (over 4 years)
Wedding	
Girl	7,500
Boy	2,000
Mother's lost work opportunities (@ $20,000 per year)	

The prospect of living without all this money can be frightening. But just to get a sense of perspective, check around with parents you know. Did they feel strapped because of their children, or do they blame any need to scrimp on other circumstances? Do they consider their children a worthwhile investment, or might the return have been greater on the commodities market? Parents of infants can give you a more exact quotation on the price of Pampers, while a 12-year-old's dad could fill you in on the price of soccer team registration and garb.

Complete your financial investigation by browsing through the infant's department of your nearest department store, then cruising over to the toy counter to price the latest computerized toys. Check with your family to see who's willing to loan you which crib, carefully stored clothing, or toddler pull toys. Consider ways you could save money, through trading your time, creating needed furniture, clothes, or playthings yourself, or sharing items. Below are a few other ways you might improve your financial picture.

Changing your attitude.   Resign yourself to living a leaner life style. Convince yourself it's good for society not to be wasteful. Consider it creative to use low-cost foods, recycled goods, and borrowed or hand-me-down furniture. Or, if you are only reallocating the money you have, cultivate the attitude that you are investing in a worthwhile human being; that you can learn as much from traveling locally as you can by jetting far away; that building a nice home environment is important to you and your child's development.

Think "part-time."   Supplement a tight budget with part-time, seasonal, or intermittent employment or projects (garage sales, weekend work, helping in a friend's garden, etc). Trade baby-sitting services with other parents. Trade other talents you have for friends' talents repairing things, shopping, etc.

Get help.   Government and other agencies often provide help clients who have children. You can take out a loan, borrow on insurance policies, get help from family. A financial manager or other professional can help you invest what you have or improve your budgeting or spending habits. Help with taxes can save large sums. Investing in real estate or other sources of return could mean a secure future.

Change your plans.   Change your style of living. Sharing quar-
will reduce costs. Moving back with family or nearer to relatives can
chop housing and childcare costs. Joining group insurance plans or
changing auto insurance companies can help. Sell your car and use
public transport, or get a second car so both partners can work.

Be comforted by the fact that most parents who successfully raise
their children and keep up the mortgage payments never looked at
the long-term costs of their endeavor. The prevalent attitude is "I'll
face that expense when the time comes." Somehow, there's always
enough soup to feed the hungry stomachs.

Genetic Concerns

A second area of concern where facts can help you decide about
children concerns inherited or age-related traits. Many prospective
parents who work with special children panic at the thought that such
a child could be theirs. They've seen the painstaking effort required
to move a severely retarded child through the day. They've dealt with
distraught moms and dads who can't figure out why Johnny is failing
reading. They've felt the heartache of new parents discovering that
their child needs a series of operations or will live a shortened life.
These possibilities are scary. Professionals who confront them every
day sometimes start to think these problems are common.

Teachers of the handicapped, medical personnel, and social
workers assisting the disabled receive a distorted view. Yes, the
seriousness of the problems of special children is very real: they
require much love and extra attention. But to be scared out of parenthood solely on the chance "it" could happen to you is uncon-
structive. *Most* children are healthy and normal. Chances are, unless
specific indicators are present, yours will be too. Dwelling on what
could happen (but isn't likely) is as inappropriate as ignoring all the
happier possibilities.

Take a look at potentials and consider all the advances within
the past several years that have improved handicapped childrens'
lives. A retarded child can bring immeasurable joy. Those with phys-

ical problems can still laugh over the cat chasing his tail; they can still love with the intensity of other children without physical challenges; they can rally families into mutual support.

Genetic counseling can pinpoint the likelihood that your child will suffer from defects transmitted by genes or chromosomes. The National Foundation–March of Dimes provides free information to the public on genetic counseling, available in all parts of the United States and most European countries. Contact your local university medical center or health clinic.

A March of Dimes pamphlet lists five questions which can help determine if you should go for genetic counseling:

Is the mother-to-be past the age of 35?

Has the mother had a history of frequent miscarriages?

Are the parents-to-be close relatives?

Has the family had a child with a birth defect?

Is there any member of the family with a possibly inherited disorder?

Is there a history or suspicion of a history of genetic disease in the family?

One of the major concerns of women over 30 is the risk of Down's syndrome (mongolism). Victims of Down's syndrome possess an extra chromosome that causes mental retardation and distinct physical characteristics (almond-shaped eyes, one feature, linked victims with the Asians from whom the syndrome got its early, popular name). As the mother's age increases, so does the risk of Down's syndrome and a handful of other diseases. At age 25, Down's syndrome occurs in one out of 1,205 births. At age 30, the incidence is one in 885. At age 35, odds climb to one in 365, and by age 40, they're one in 109.

The procedure called *amniocentesis* can detect Down's syndrome in the developing fetus so the parents have the option of abortion or at least can prepare for proper care. At 16 weeks' gestation, a sample of the fluid surrounding the fetus in the amniotic sac is removed and cultured. The results also reveal several other genetically linked problems (as well as the child's sex). The results come two to four weeks after the sample; abortion at 20 weeks can be especially stressful.

Amniocentesis gives new options to couples hoping to minimize risks. Nancy spoke with me about her experience with amniocentesis. She was 38 when she became pregnant with her first child. She'd ended a disastrous first marriage and finally felt secure and confident enough in her second relationship to fulfill a desire she felt growing over the past three or four years.

"I knew before I became pregnant that I'd have amniocentesis," she says, chestnut hair parted over her serious blue eyes. "I was terrified of having to abort a child I desperately wanted, and which, by the time the word would be received, would be moving inside me. But, on the other hand, I had no doubt that I would abort if the fetus had Down's syndrome. I simply could not be an effective parent to a child that required so much attention, and I'm filled with sadness when I see children like that. I want my child to have so much more—." She broke off suddenly, emotion flooding her, before regaining composure to explain what her amniocentesis was like.

"My husband, Bob, came with me to the hospital, part of the university complex. First, the doctors found the position of the fetus through ultrasound, a procedure where my stomach was scanned. It was painless, and on a screen, I could see the shapes of the baby's head, the sac, and even my internal organs. Then the doctors swabbed my stomach and inserted a needle to draw out the fluid. I'll confess that it hurt some, but Bob was squeezing my hand as a distraction, which helped."

In some cases, the needle must be inserted repeatedly before a sufficient amount of fluid can be successfully drawn. "The proccess wasn't the worst part of it," Nancy asserts. "The waiting was." It took four weeks for a culture to be grown from the sample of amniotic fluid. During that time, Nancy and Bob saw a genetic counselor twice, the same woman who arranged the procedure for them. "We'd already picked out names for the baby," Nancy continues, "and I was already anticipating the excitement of the child. Bob and I had to keep each other from becoming too attached—we kept calling it 'the fetus,' and wouldn't go out and buy a layette. It was especially hard because my parents were so happy for us. They kept dropping sentences like 'The baby shower will be on the fifteenth.' Both of them knew we were having amniocentesis and might abort, but I somehow don't think they understood the seriousness of it."

Had the doctors discussed the risks of amniocentesis before the procedure? Nancy nodded. "They said there was a chance of spontaneous abortion, increased vaginal bleeding, and even of puncturing the amniotic sac. But the percentages of complications from the procedure itself are relatively low. We made sure we investigated the record of the hospital before agreeing to have amniocentesis done there. We were shocked, actually, at the variation in statistics. Some hospitals perform the procedure almost routinely, while others still find it relatively new. We opted for the most experienced personnel we could find, and also checked to see which lab they used. Some are quicker than others, and occasionally one might make a mistake, which we couldn't bear." Nancy added that she'd read an article in the May 1979 *Consumer Reports* magazine that explained the procedure and also followed up on all subsequent recommendations for reading made by the counselor.

"Bob and I consider ourselves very planful, careful people," Nancy concluded. "We could never ignore a chance to know everything we could in advance." But one thing Nancy did not want to know in advance was the sex of her child. She delivered a healthy boy, and has taken a year's leave from her job as a social worker to take care for him.

Nancy is one of only about 20 percent of women over 35 who use amniocentesis, which costs from $200 to $700. But cost is probably not the most important reason why older mothers have not more fully taken advantage of the test. Many are unaware of it. Others are afraid—not only of the process, but that they could not abort a child they knew was defective. It takes deliberate effort to seek counseling and receive amniocentesis; it's a lot easier to ignore potential defects and simply allow the pregnancy to progress with normal observation by the obstetrician.

Pregnancy and Birth

Libraries and bookstores have shelves of books detailing the physical processes of pregnancy and birth. Don't put off a careful investigation of all the physical changes you can anticipate during pregnancy and afterwards, with the rationalization that you'll have plenty of time for that *after* conception. Though the pregnancy period is only nine months, a wink in the ongoing process of parenthood, it's the part you'll experience first, and events on the immediate horizon are most scary and easiest to postpone.

As you logically consider the facts, don't negate your feelings. Grab onto your emotional reaction to pregnancy and childbirth. When you see a pregnant woman on the street, what's your first reaction? When you talk with someone who's obviously in her ninth month, where do your eyes tend to wander first? Many mothers report that during this time it was their bellies and not their mouths that seemed to do the talking—and receive the most attention.

Consider also how pregnancy will affect your careers. Will you be taken seriously, or will co-workers assume that after the child is born, the baby *must* take first priority over work? How do you perceive co-workers who are pregnant?

Consider, too, the facts you lack. Do you really know what giving birth is like? What is the first sign of labor? What happens at the hospital? Do you understand the different types of natural birth, medication, or the purpose of an episiotomy? If not, make a note to follow through and find the answers.

When you get information from friends and relatives, realize that people tend to talk about foul-ups and discomforts. "Good Shepherd Hospital won't let your husband be there for a Caesarian," a friend will begin, thinking she's informing you. "When the monitor showed they'd have to operate, they just pushed me past my husband into the other room, leaving Mark puzzled, worried, and disappointed. I didn't know what was happening either, and they wouldn't even answer my questions." You can see how "information" has turned into a horror story.

Some people remember the pain as terrible, hospital personnel as incompetent, procedures as strange and expensive. Whether or not this is an accurate recollection is debatable; whether or not you benefit from these frightening accounts is more certain. You don't.

Friends whose deliveries were flawless, quick, pleasant, and rewarding will probably tell you about their experiences, too. And given the increasing sensitivity of hospitals and medical personnel to the needs of new families, it's likely that more and more women will have positive experiences to report. Somehow, though, expectant parents harp on the unfortunate aspects of what they hear. A single horror story can stick with you longer than a dozen recommendations. And attitude can really make the difference. If you approach birth-day as a terror to endure, it will be. If you see it as a wondrous adventure, your expectation will probably be fulfilled.

Here are several topics you might want to research at the library or bookstore, or through your physician:

Pregnancy
Infertility (discussed briefly in a subsequent chapter)
Possible complications of pregnancy and birth
Miscarriage
Prenatal fitness
Prenatal nutrition

Birth
Birthing chairs
Cesarean birth
Bradley, LaMaze, and other prepared childbirth methods
Rooming-in
Alternative birth centers
Midwives
Events in a normal delivery

Postpartum
Postpartum depression
Breastfeeding; the LaLeche League
Maternity/paternity leave from work
Parent-infant bonding

Career and Education Options

Some people are shocked to realize that for them, parenthood is an escape. Maybe you're stuck in an unfulfilling job; taking care of your child seems ever-so-much more attractive than the daily grind. Or perhaps you've spent years preparing for a fast-paced career and, once in it, realize that the dizzying pace is just a little *too* fast. Taking a leave to nurture your child seems like just the right respite. It's also common that women who have worked in fields they don't consider a "career" aren't sure of the direction they *do* want to pursue. Some careers would require returning to school for years; others have attractive elements with contrasting aspects of boredom or distate. So getting pregnant is a way out of a perplexing dilemma, a means to postpone a difficult career decision.

Earlier, we met Danielle and Arthur. As you recall, he wanted to avoid parenthood—and unconciously to continue his dependence on Danielle. In this case, having a child would have forced him to take career responsibility, because suddenly there would be a need for stability and a steady income. The real problem for Arthur wasn't becoming a parent but, rather, a lack of confidence in his career ability—he was an artist afraid of failure, afraid of criticism, afraid of not succeeding in the art world.

In Chapter 3 we also met Barry and Michele. In their case, Michele wanted her career to be motherhood, and she explored alternative directions to be sure that parenting was not a substitute for other choices. She took interest and aptitude tests to discover a field she'd enjoy, and investigated activities she could pursue as an alternative to having children. But Michele was a teacher and had always centered her life around children. She was willing to dedicate herself to the "profession" of motherhood with the same zeal she would become a school principal—motherhood was a chosen occupation and not just a replacement for an aimless future.

If you're feeling dissatisfied with your job and fantasize that cozy mornings cuddling your baby would be an appealing alternative, it's time to pause. Don't enter parenthood until you're comfortable with yourself and your chosen career. If you're happy with your life, anxious to rise each morning to go to work, pleased with the outcome of your labors, then you won't depend on your child for your happiness. It's terrible pressure for a child to know its his responsibility to make you happy. Even little kids can sense when they're the focus of your attention (it's true; they comprehend far more than they can express) and in time a child may feel smothered or suffer from guilt if he doesn't perform to your expectations.

Also, if you look at your child as a substitute for a career, then all your eggs are in one basket—you can't opt out and simply switch occupations. You can always quit a job you detest, change fields, or sail off to a South Seas island to avoid civilization altogether if your present career choice doesn't work out. But you can't send your baby back; parenthood is a responsibility that stays with you forever. "But I can just get childcare and go back to work," you're probably murmuring. And you're right, but just don't think it's simple. There's the rush to drop off little Amy on your way to work, worry about after-school activities and weekends spent entertaining rather than recuperating from a hectic week. Once you have a child, you can never entirely return to a career-focused, independent life again.

Maybe you're ripe for this permanent change. But if you have doubts, wait. Explore career options. Try out a new direction. See if your career fulfills you. You may discover that you're too busy to give a child much thought anymore, and then you'll know that a childfree life might be the one for you.

A child should be a bonus, an added pleasure to a life that is complete in itself. The best mothers have self-confidence; they know they'd be happy even if they didn't have a child, and would dedicate themselves to another worthwhile activity. The child is an extension, an added gift. Most men see children this way. They don't usually consider parenthood as a substitute for a career direction. They think of their career as one aspect of their lives and a child as another, just as many women separate their jobs from their marriages.

Here are a few suggestions to help you think creatively about career barriers to having a child. With some innovative thinking, most problems can be overcome.

Change your attitude.   Change your attitude about the future; convince yourself that it will be fun, noble, or valuable to do what is ahead. Try to convince your partner, your family, your boss, or anyone else you care about. Or just ignore them and find support for your view. Groups like the National Alliance for Optional Parenthood support nonparents; many religious groups, parents' organizations, and childcare set-ups can give support to parents.

Think "Part-time."   It needn't be all or nothing. Continue what you're doing or begin what you want to do on a part-time basis. Perhaps it's possible to take work home or split a position with your partner or someone else.

Get help.   Why should *you* do it all? Can your partner do it instead? Can you hire someone to help with the child while you go to school, study, or work? Or maybe there is a family member who could help on a part-time or shift basis. Or hire someone to help with your career (an assistant so the job doesn't take so much of your time) or your studying (subscribe to a lecture notes service; hire a typist to do your term paper).

Change your plans.   Take off in a new direction. Perhaps you have skills you can use in a new field, or branch out. Maybe there are jobs you can do from home. Or move your office into your home. Get a new job in a city or industry where there is childcare. Hold down two or more part-time jobs, or have your partner try that. Invest in something where the monetary return allows you not to work. Lower your standard of living so you can work in a lower-salaried but more convenient occupation.

Childcare

An adjunct to the career dilemma is adequate childcare if you *do* decide to have a baby. Investigate what's in your neighborhood. Each area has a variety of licensed facilities, nursery schools, individuals who can baby-sit, and cooperatives. A growing number of businesses and large corporations are beginning childcare centers at plants or offices. University campuses frequently offer such services or list referrals.

An option for the parent planning to stay home is to take charge of four or five other children as well as your own. Sometimes such arrangements must be licensed or approved by local officials. Sometimes the schedule can be made flexible so that a group of parents rotate their duties. The point is that there are more alternatives for both occasional and regular childcare if you ban together with others.

Below is a list of childcare alternatives that summarizes various options you can use separately or in combination.

Childcare Alternatives

1. *Daycare centers* are open year round, often subsidized by the government. They're like a nursery school, providing hot lunches and naps,

and fees are reasonable. The hitch is that parents must qualify based on income. Because of funding cuts and areas of high need, the number of centers and positions may be small, so waiting lists may be long.

2. *Family daycare* is licensed supervision for up to six 3–6-year-olds in the home of a private individual. Many times mothers will care for their own brood and take in others to make a total of six. There are often government subsidies, and fees may be charged on a sliding scale based on parents' income. Because the homes are licensed, they must meet certain standards that can assure you of some quality control.

3. *Private, profit-seeking daycare centers or nursery schools* offer programs and activities, but there are usually no governmental standards to meet, and ability of personnel is variable. Chains of centers are scattered across the country: "Living and Learning Centers" are on the east coast; "Kinder-Care" is in the south and midwest. In the west and midwest is also a childcare franchise, "Mary Moppet." Fees are higher than subsidized programs, but volume and competition usually keep prices within the budget of middle-class couples.

4. *Independent proprietary centers* are similar to family daycare in that they are run by mothers in their homes. But these are businesses without government sponsorship. The National Association for Child Development and Education, a Washington, D.C. group, will mail you a list of these if requested.

5. *Private nonprofit daycare* is often sponsored by organizations to benefit their members. Large corporations might begin an on-premises program for employees, and some colleges provide assistance for students and staff. Hospitals, factories, churches, and recreation centers might also offer this service. Fees are low, often on a sliding scale, since daycare is seen as an enhancement to the objectives of the firm, college, or community.

6. *Nursery schools* can be an informal daycare-type situation or an elite miniature academy. They share the purpose of adding instruction to baby-sitting. There are usually no standards for staff, but the better schools hire trained teachers, often increasing their cost. Prices for looser arrangements may be as low as $60 monthly; more selective institutions may run as much as $3,000 per year. Many of these schools have limited hours, though now many do accommodate parents by offering a six-hour day.

7. *Parent cooperatives* are informal groups of parents who join together for the care of their own offspring. Informal is not unorganized, however, and most have governing boards and hire screened staff. Some

require that parents contribute a minimum of their time; others waive this rule for the payment of an additional fee. The goal is generally to break even, so charitable events may be staged to keep fees low.

8. *After-school clubs and centers* are usually profit-seeking groups that provide organized activities for school-age children. Frequently, they offer door-to-door bus service, allowing the parent freedom from chauffeuring. Kids often enjoy them because they provide arts and crafts, field trips, sporting competitions, and sometimes academic tutoring. The cost is usually moderate, and parents' worry is minimized.

9. *Baby-sitters* have the advantage of bending to your schedule if they're in your home. You can often hire a housekeeper willing to double as a childcare supervisor for minimum wage (though higher salaries often help draw better-prepared applicants). Live-ins are usually the first choice of high-level professionals who quickly add, "Then there's the lack of privacy and expense of the additional room." There are many benefits, however, including a reliable source of care and the confidence that your child is safe at home.

   Some sitters prefer to work in their own homes, handling one or two clients on an as-needed basis. Rates usually start at $3.50 per hour for these services. Baby-sitting agencies will refer you to a trained, reliable employee for a higher fee, often running to $10 an hour, but you receive the backing of the firm.

10. *Mother/father combinations* are emerging as "the new compromise" of the decade. Bargains are being struck where Mom will leave her job for a couple of months, then Dad will take a year's leave and stay home with the baby. Or perhaps Dad is home a lot anyway or is in the office only part-time. A combination of his attention, Mom's, and a sitter's could carry the childcare load without placing total responsibility on one party. Some couples are ready to make a trade and let Dad be the nurturer while Mom sees to family economics.

11. *In-laws,* particularly Grandparents eager to dote on their granchildren, can become loving and reliable sources of childcare. In some cases, it's appropriate to reimburse the relative either in cash or through gestures or goods, so that there's no feeling of imposition. In-laws and parents are usually most cooperative if they're considered occasional baby-sitters. In some extended family settings, or where large families find Grandma with some of her own children still at home, your child's presence for part of the day might seem natural.

12. *Friendship networks,* where you trade baby-sitting hours, may be the most frequently used but least recognized source of childcare today. Check out not only the families on your street, but also in a four-block

radius. Then you can either work out a structured plan, so that each mother gets an afternoon or certain hours free, or develop an informal arrangement of "I'll watch yours, next week you can watch mine." The often-heard phrase "Go over to a friend's and play until I get home" is as much childcare service by the friend's mother as it is social interaction for the child.

Use this time to explore your opinions about each of the childcare options. Some women say "I'd never leave my child in a center all day—I'd want to be there to give him my attention. Otherwise why bother to have him?" They're answered with "The social benefits of being with other children outweigh the disadvantages. And with childcare I won't feel tied down so I can give *quality* time when we're together." How do these arguments strike you? Are you biased against leaving your child with a sitter? How about for a short time? Now is the time to visit several childcare centers and compare personnel, activities, facilities, and the apparent satisfaction of parents and children with each arrangement.

The Benefits and Drawbacks Questionnaire

You could continue collecting facts, interviewing parents, pondering your expense sheet for weeks, and come no closer to a final decision. In fact, there comes a point when you're confident that you've investigated quite enough, thank you, and now the rest must come from yourself.

The "Benefits and Drawbacks Questionnaire" synthesizes all the reading, thinking, and interviewing you've done. It is based on research by a group at the University of Washington, Seattle, in the mid-1970s. They asked parents about all the influences on their choice to have a child and reduced them into areas of concern. I've embellished and reshaped their findings into this questionnaire, which attempts to hit upon all possible aspects of the childbearing question.

I've grouped each of these into ten major areas. Each of the items is intentionally ambiguous so you can project your own values, expectations, and feelings to give meaning to the phrases. For example, one of the categories you'll judge is "Child's effect on career opportunities." That's a broad phrase, and you'll have to return to your expectations (as expressed on the "Expectations Questionnaire" and the "Continuua Questionnaire," as well as from the information you've been reading and collecting) to decide, first, the likely effect of a child on your career and, second, whether this would be a benefit or drawback to you. If there are any instances where you are not sure what a question means, think of all the possible ways the statement could be interpreted, jot them down, and then make a separate "benefit or drawback" judgment for each of them.

As you look at the questionnaire, you'll see there are five judgments you can make. The crucial option is to check that a statement is "Not important to me either way." The chance to say "I consider this irrelevant" separates this from other scored questionnaires. There are so many questionnaires flung at the public which are supposed to definitively tell you about your characteristics, such as whether you're an intellectual or afraid of snakes. Most have a set scoring scale, something like "between 85 and 90 points means you're moderately afraid of snakes." Feelings about having a child can't be scored like that. All questions and considerations are not equal for everyone; there is no one absolute ruler by which parenthood can be measured. That's why, by checking the middle column on the questionnaire, you can customize your score to include only the aspects that have meaning for you.

Now, complete the questionnaire separately from your partner. Scoring directions will follow.

Name: _____   Date: _____

Benefits and Drawbacks Questionnaire

Check how important a benefit or drawback each
statement would be if you had a child. Be sure to
use your **feelings** as well as your logic.

	An important benefit of having a child	A benefit of having a child	Not important to me either way	A drawback of having a child	An important drawback of having a child
I. Career and Education					
The child's effect on my education					
Having a child to stop or go back to school					
Child's effect on time to study					
Child's effect on career opportunities					
Child as a reason to stop work outside of the home					
Child as an extension of the role of homemaker					
Parenting allows me to pursue interests other than employment					
II. Personal Considerations					
Experience of being pregnant and giving birth					
The risks of childbirth					
Health of the mother					

	An important benefit of having a child	A benefit of having a child	Not important to me either way	A drawback of having a child	An important drawback of having a child
Physical appearance					
Having a child as part of growing up					
Maturing and being a whole person					
The opportunity to be a good parent					
The opportunity to reproduce myself					
Child's effect on my feeling young and flexible					
Fulfilling moral and ethical beliefs					

III. Parenthood

	An important benefit of having a child	A benefit of having a child	Not important to me either way	A drawback of having a child	An important drawback of having a child
Caring for the new baby					
Supervising, training and being with a 1-to-3-year-old					
Supervising, training and being with a 4-to-9-year-old					
Supervising, training and being with a 10-to-14-year-old					
Supervising, training and being with a 15-to-18-year-old					
Teaching a child specific skills, like sports, music, crafts					
Helping the child to achieve					
Sharing recreational activities with the child					
Child as a companion throughout his or her childhood					
Child as a companion to me in old age					
Holding and playing with a young child					

	An important benefit of having a child	A benefit of having a child	Not important to me either way	A drawback of having a child	An important drawback of having a child
IV. Relationship with My Partner					
Competing with the child for my partner's attention					
Competing with my partner for my child's attention					
Child's effect on our having a good time					
Child's effect on free time spent with my partner					
Child's effect on strengthening or weakening our relationship					
Child as a symbol or product of our love					
Child's effect on feeling trapped in the relationship					
Child's effect on the kind of birth control we can use					
Effect of trying to become pregnant on sexual satisfaction					
Effect of being pregnant on sexual satisfaction					
Agreement or conflict on how to bring up the child					
Cooperating in providing a good environment for raising a child					
My partner's ability to be a good parent					
V. Economic Factors					
Cost of maternity care and hospital bills					
Cost of equipment and clothes for the baby					
Providing food, shelter, clothes, etc. throughout the child's life					
Cost of educating a child; saving for future education					
Housekeeping and childcare costs					

	An important benefit of having a child	A benefit of having a child	Not important to me either way	A drawback of having a child	An important drawback of having a child
Child's contribution to me in old age					
Effect of the child on the overall money we can spend each month					
Child's effect on having a good house, furniture, etc.					
Child's effect on the amount of money we have for travel and recreation					
Child's effect on the type of housing we need					
Standard of living in the future					
Change in my partner's or my income					
Child's effect on benefits (taxes, government support)					

VI. Lifestyle

	An important benefit of having a child	A benefit of having a child	Not important to me either way	A drawback of having a child	An important drawback of having a child
My ability to be a single parent should my partner not be available					
Child's effect on our ability to move when we want					
Child's effect on the type of neighborhood or city we live in					
Effect of a child on traveling					
Ability to go out at the spur of the moment					
Sense of being a "family"					
Effect of the child on home clutter and noise level					
Child's effect on having "family experiences"					
Effects of a child on household tasks, responsibilities, and workload					
Effect of the child on the kinds of community involvement we have					

	An important benefit of having a child	A benefit of having a child	Not important to me either way	A drawback of having a child	An important drawback of having a child
Social pressure to have children from family and friends					
Ability to expand or maintain the variety of people we see					

VII. Family Composition
Child's effect on our ideal family size					
Having a boy					
Having a girl					
My age at the birth of the child					
My partner's age at the birth of the child					
Completing my family so my partner or I can go back to work or school					
Child's relationship to existing children (friends, relatives)					

VIII. Health of the Child
Intelligence of the child					
Traits passed on to the child					
Psychological adjustment of the child					
Risk of mental retardation or other birth defects					
Passing on a genetic disease in the family					
Maintaining the physical health of the child					

	An important benefit of having a child	A benefit of having a child	Not important to me either way	A drawback of having a child	An important drawback of having a child
IX. Important Relationships					
My partner's feelings about having a child					
My partner's health and happiness as a result of having a child					
Child's effect on relationships with our parents					
Child's effect on relationships with other relatives					
Continuing the family name or traditions					
Child's effect on relationships with friends					
Being like other people					
Keeping with the same circle of friends					
X. Society					
Fulfilling religious beliefs or teachings					
Concern for population					
Concern for the use of natural resources					
Concern with political systems affecting our lives					
Grand totals:					

In favor of having a child

Against having a child

Score in favor of having a child:
Add together scores in columns "An important benefit . . ." and "A benefit . . ."

Score against having a child:
Add together scores in columns "An important drawback . . ." and "A drawback . . ."

Scoring the Benefits and Drawbacks Questionnaire

To get your personalized score showing inclination for or against a child, follow the steps below to find point totals for each of four vertical columns. The "stronger" answers on the outside columns will earn more points than the less forceful choices. You will also be able to weight any particular considerations with additional points to really reflect your concerns.

1. First go down the column marked "An important benefit of having a child," on the right and count up *two points* for every check you placed in this column.

2. Then go down the column marked "A benefit of having a child." Give yourself *one point* for each check in this column.

3. *Do not* count up any points for the checks in the column "Not important to me either way." Since these areas aren't important, they won't be counted in your score.

4. Next, total the checks in the column "A drawback of having a child," giving yourself *one point* for each check.

5. Give yourself *two points* for all checks under "An important drawback of having a child."

6. Go through the considerations again, and add in *bonus points* for the important considerations that you know are really the important ones. The number of extra points will be determined by the importance of that statement relative to the others. This is "weighting" your score to be more accurate for you.

   For example, the mother of a 13-year-old was deciding whether or not to have a child with her new husband, who dearly wanted one. She was happy with her daughter and wasn't enthused about more mothering. But the crucial factor in the choice was her current husband. Depriving him of the child he wanted so much might ruin their relationship, she feared. That concern caused her to add 20 points to an item on relationships, allowing her new score to more accurately reflect her feelings.

7. To see how strongly you feel for or against having a child, add together the points from the two columns showing "A benefit . . . " and "Important benefit . . ." of having a child. (This is your score in favor of having one.) Then add together the points showing "A drawback . . . " and

"Important drawback of having a child." (This is your score against having one.) The higher your score either for or against, the stronger your reasons to have or not have a child.

Interpreting the Questionnaire

There are 91 statements on the "Decision-making Questionnaire." Without bonus points, the highest possible score is 182 either for or against having a child. Chances are your score will be split, and there will be many items that aren't important, and therefore won't affect your score at all.

First, take some time alone to understand your score. Here are some steps to help you think about your answers.

1. Note which items you did *not* score—that is, the things that weren't important in your decision either way. These are the areas in which you can be flexible; if your partner does care about them, you may be willing to bend or compromise for him or her.

2. Note the items you felt strongly about (the 2-pointers and bonus-pointers). These are least open to discussion on your part. Look them over again and this time judge which of your interpretations of each statement are most likely to come true. Also think about which you're least sure about. Circle the things you know won't change and are therefore quite probable (important values you hold or things you're sure will continue or exist in the future). These you just have to live with, and they make up the heart of your expectations and beliefs for or against having a child.

3. Next look again at the 2-point and bonus-point answers. This time see if they group under any particular headings. For example, are your important concerns centering around your relationship with your partner, financial problems, or the health of the child? If your answers seem spread out, try to find a common theme.

   It often helps to think back to your own childhood and the associations you have with different aspects of the parenting you received. Jot down notes to share with your partner about any memories or insecurities affecting your feelings.

4. Look at *how many* statements you felt strongly about, counting the number of 2-pointers and bonus-pointers. Remember, there is no absolute scale against which to compare your score. It's an idiosyncratic

reflection of your own special values, expectations, and feelings. Generally a score of 70 or more in either direction shows that this is a very important decision for you. A low score, especially one under 20 either way, shows that you checked many aspects of parenthood as not important. This may also reflect an analytical nature, with a tendency to ignore or rule out emotional influences.

If your score is below 20, go through the questionnaire again and try to force yourself to decide if the statements are benefits or drawbacks. See how many points you change your mind on the second time.

Using the Questionnaire with Your Partner

Use the "Partner Decision-making Sheet" included here to organize your discussion. First, transfer the column scores from your questionnaires—the scores showing inclination for and against having a child. Also transfer the combined scores that make up your inclination. Then follow these three steps.

Partner Decision-making Sheet

Use this sheet with the results of the "Decision-making Questionnaire" and the preceding section on "Using the Questionnaire with your Partner."

Write in the column point totals from the "Decision-making Questionnaire":

Worth

2 points	An important benefit of having a child		Add together to find inclination to have a child } ____ total
1 point	A benefit of having a child		
1 point	A drawback of having a child		Add together to find inclination against having a child } ____ total
2 points	An important drawback of having a child		

List the subheads or areas of the questionnaire where your strongly felt, 2+-point answers clustered:

_____

_____

List the 2+-point answers you circled because they are likely to occur or are values that will stay the same:

_____

_____

_____

On a separate sheet, list alternatives for the future so you and your partner will both be satisfied or be able to accept the situation.

Decision Alternatives

"After considering my values, expectations, and feelings, and those of my partner, the best course to take is . . ." (circle one only)

| Have a child soon | Postpone 2 years or less | Postpone 2-1/2 to 5 years | Postpone over 5 years | Remain childfree | Recognize strong differences in opinion* |

*If there are strong differences in opinion, how do you propose to deal with this in the near future?

_____

_____

1. Compare and discuss the *number of points* each of you collected. Because bonus points are added to indicate importance, the partner with the highest number of points probably feels strongest about the decision. Talk about this difference.

2. Compare and discuss *areas of importance*. On the "Partner Decision-making Sheet," list the headings under which your important two-and-bonus-point answers clustered (e.g., career and education, economic factors, or relationship with family). In discussing these, see if your concerns overlap or differ. If you and your partner have a similar set of concerns, you have a good basis for negotiation. If your concerns seem miles apart, your values and hopes for the future may be disparate. Some problems cannot be resolved, so it comes down to the hard choice about which is more crucial: pleasing your partner and preserving marital tranquility, or your bottom-line feelings about having a child.

3. Compare and discuss *specific concerns*. List the "Benefits and Drawbacks Questionnaire" items you circled, and compare them with your partner.

Then list alternatives to change your future, if possible. You may want to dig up more information, reread parts of this chapter, or head for a counselor to get ideas.

Also share the concerns and memories you recalled when you thought about your own childhood. If your partner can see where you got your ideas, she or he can more compassionately understand why you feel as you do.

Making Sense of It All

Now you've completed the rational portion of the process (except for questions posed for specific types of decisionmakers—planners, now-or-never deciders, conflict couples, singles, second-time-around parents). How do you put it all together? First, return to the "Viewpoints Questionnaire" and look over your responses. Would you change anything? Jot down areas in which your own values have changed, and refresh your memory about strongly held values.

Then return to the "Expectations Questionnaire" and the "Continuua Questionnaire," and evaluate how your predictions compare with those you hold today. Are there still areas left to negotiate? Are there still predictions you need more information to make? Are some of them distasteful or discomforting? Jot those down too. Revise any expectations that need changing based on new information.

Then return again to the "Benefits and Drawbacks Questionnaire," reconciling your selections and score with the first two questionnaires, as well as your final discussion with your partner. Jot down any changes, questions, or ideas related to it.

Lastly, look once again at the "Partner Decision-making Sheet" you just completed, armed with renewed knowledge of the other questionnaires. Ask yourself:

1. What values did I discover in myself and my partner that I was not aware of before I began this process?

2. Which expectations about my life are under my own control? Which do I shape around my partner? Am I satisfied with the amount of control I take over my life?

3. How much credence do I put in this rational decision-making process? Am I willing to invest my underlying, truthful feelings in it or is it something mechanical I'm doing for my partner or to satisfy guilt or apprehension?

4. What do I want out of life: a satisfying marriage, fulfilling work, dedication to my children, a contribution to society? Are any of these mutually exclusive?

You've just stepped back to assess your larger values and thoughts. Even if you're still not sure whether or not you want to have a child, you should feel proud for completing all the forms and doing all the soul-searching, values defining, and crystal ball-gazing. You must have addressed issues you'd never considered before, and you probably understand far better the reasons why you think the way you do. You've consulted your partner and probably enhanced your relationship just by taking the time to talk about a serious and basic issue, and you've gained an education from other people around you through your observation and interaction about parenthood. You should feel good about these accomplishments.

8

Special Considerations

Chapter 7 discussed problems and issues most people wonder about. You may have additional concerns. This chapter addresses more specialized questions facing particular groups of decision-makers.

Questions for the Three Types of Decision-makers

Remember the three types of couples who face the childbearing issue—now-or-never couples who debate having a child or remaining childfree; conflict couples, where one partner wants a child and the other doesn't; and planners who have a clear preference. Each of these groups has its own concerns, so included here are three special questionnaires designed to examine issues not addressed earlier. Use them in conjunction with the feelings, values, and expectations you've already expressed to identify your own personal choices.

Now-or-never couples can't procrastinate much longer. If you feel the years creeping by, even if your vim and child-like enthusiasm for life haven't ebbed, the "Deciding Now-or-Never" page pertains to you. Remember to combine your responses with those of the previous exercises. Answer each question or decide if you agree with each statement in the left-hand column; then look to the right to see what your response might mean.

There are four major areas of concern for now-or-never couples. The most feared aspect of making a firm decision is the finality of closing doors. No one likes to see the last streak of light narrowing behind the creaking portal. To step up to the door and latch the lock forever, through sterilization or having a child, denies options that might seem valuable under different circumstances. Although now-or-never couples like to be in control of other aspects of their lives, somehow it's easier to let time gently pass, until there's no reproductive option, than it is to act.

Name: _____

Deciding Now-or-Never

Questions	Implications
On Closing Doors Is the issue the need to act now, or whether or not I want a child?	If it's pressure that's getting you down, better to let the biological time clock expire than have a child just in case you'd regret remaining childfree.
Do I often regret decisions, or have "buyer's remorse"?	If so, **wait** until you're pretty sure before having a child; it's better to regret what you missed than resent your child.
Do I tend to act decisively in other areas of my life?	If so, your hesitancy is telling you that having a child now isn't the best course to take. If not, evaluate how often you've regretted **not** acting. If you've frequently regretted inaction, then you could be more ready than you realize to have a child.

Questions	Implications

On Parenthood and Aging
Does the task of training a child often change people into authority-types?

If you agree, you may expect yourself to become more authoritarian. Consider if the **fear** of changing into a settled person is scaring you unnecessarily away from a desired child.

How would I feel about my past and future if I were age 55 and had no children?

If you'd feel good, you're probably not postponing parenthood just to avoid feeling old — and you probably have many activities that are a rewarding substitute. If you'd feel bad, you may fear aging, need the support of family, and underneath it all, want a child.

Which statement is truer: "Children keep you young," or "Children wear you out"?

Both statements might be true for you at different times. The statement you selected is indicative of your response to parenthood.

On Being an Older Parent
Do you prefer new situations, new jobs, new people; or familiar restaurants, a steady, secure job, and long-time friends?

Parenting requires flexibility to bend with new situations; people comfortable with familiarity may be less willing to change their lives to accommodate a child. Remember that a child who is totally dependent on you must be first priority.

Are you as physically active as you were ten years ago?

Tending a child requires stamina. If your energy has been declining, evaluate whether you will feel up to the tasks needed for a 10-year-old after another decade has passed.

Are you comfortable in a group where you are noticeably older?

If not, consider that parenthood after, say, 35, will probably mean lots of activities with younger parents.

Do you find children more appealing or less appealing than you did ten years ago?

A growing appreciation for children may mean you're ripe for parenthood; a decline in their attraction suggests you'd be able to pass parenthood by.

On Biological Concerns
Is there a reason to suspect special genetic or other risks?

If so, genetic counseling before pregnancy is recommended.

Is the woman's body in good shape for a pregnancy?

If not, decide the steps necessary to get in shape, and the likelihood you'd be willing to take them in the future.

If amniocentesis revealed a defective child, would you abort?

A tough question: "no" may mean the selflessness to care under any conditions; "yes" may mean compassion **or** could reveal doubt about wanting to have a child.

A second "now-or-never" item is the association of parenthood with aging. Even when people in their thirties handle extravagant house payments, advanced college degrees, top-flight jobs, and 12-page resumes, it's hard for them to think of themselves as almost, gulp, *middle-aged*. They often associate freedom with youth and a family with being tied down. So they keep postponing, saying they're "not ready yet." Then menopause comes, and they wonder where the years and opportunities went.

A third area of concern to now-or-never couples is both the joys and problems of being an older parent. Some postponers think that the wisdom, experience, confidence, and competencies they've gained prepare them for the rigors of parenthood. Others worry that they're so set in their ways, they won't be willing or able to accommodate the many changes a child brings. (Many of these issues are discussed in the "Parenthood After 30" section of Chapter 10.)

Finally, now-or-never couples wonder about the biological risks of waiting to have a child. No one knows the date menopause will take away the childbearing option. When the hardship of caring for a defective child is at stake, few are anxious to gamble.

Conflict couples' concerns are spelled out on the question and implication sheet called "Resolving Conflict Between Partners." The first task is always to assess the severity of the conflict. You probably knew right away there was a disagreement, but felt you could swing things your way with a little coaxing and fact-wielding. When that wasn't successful, you turned to new means—and realized that the extent of the problem was deeper than you'd hoped.

It's natural to deny the problem for awhile: Who wants to suffer? Avoiding the subject or not taking the steps you may have reluctantly agreed upon is one way to put off a confrontation. Taking longer to face the problem is also a way to put off having a child, a step one of you is obviously not ready to take. The "Resolving Conflict Between Partners" form focuses on compromise. The idea is to detect any softening by one of the partners, to see if eventually she or he may be able to accept the other partner's stronger desire.

There are two other special concerns to mention: setting deadlines and splitting up. Deadlines are only as good as both partners' willingness to stick by them. If the deadline passes and there's no change in attitude, then separation may be the only alternative.

Name: _____

Resolving Conflict Between Partners

Questions	Implications
On Severity of the Conflict Is one partner rigidly opposed to having children on principle?	The likelihood of changing a partner's mind is higher if there are specific reasons for beliefs. Being opposed "on principle" leaves less room for negotiation.
In your arguments, does one partner usually give in?	If so, it's likely that the person will again be more willing to bend. But on such a crucial decision, some usually easy-going people suddenly stand firm. Decide how this decision is different from others you've faced; realize that if no one gives in, someone will automatically lose, because action is then postponed even longer.
Would you go to a therapist over this issue?	Then you know this is a serious problem. If you'd go to a marriage counselor, it may indicate that you place your marriage above the need for a child.
On Reaching Compromise **If you want a child:** Can you imagine a happy life without children?	If so, you might be able to compromise, finding rewards in substitutes for parenthood.
Do you value your relationship with your partner above all?	If so, you're more likely to bend your childbearing stance than risk a split.
Are your contacts with children (a) satisfying, or (b) frustrating, due to desire for your own?	If they're satisfying, a long term involvement with children may preserve your relationship and be fulfilling. If you're frustrated now, it's likely time will worsen your distress and increase your desire for a child.
If you don't want a child: Is your partner willing to take major responsibility for a child?	If so, you may be able to have the best of both worlds: a pleased partner and little parenthood hassle. Yes, you would have emotional responsibility, which you must consider.

Questions	Implications
If your partner became pregnant accidentally and had the child, would you resent her?	If so, bringing a child to the situation could exacerbate the problem to the point that the marriage splits anyway. If not, how easily could you accept and even enjoy parenthood? The stronger the chance, the more you're willing to bend.
On Setting Deadlines Does the proparenthood partner want a child right away?	If so, the conflict is more severe than if he or she can wait. Who knows, the confirmed nonparent could change his or her mind eventually.
Is a major career turning point expected within two years?	If the turning point would mean more income and security, then reaching that point could make the hesitant partner more willing to have a child. That date might be a good deadline for the decision.
Is the no-child partner waiting for an undefined event or situation before having a child?	If so, the real problem may be an underlying uncertainty about career direction, self-image, relationships, or something else, which should be resolved before having a child; it's best to recognize and work on that first.
On Splitting Up Would a split over this leave you both bitter and angry toward each other?	Then your values place self-satisfaction above the union. A child brought into the situation would worsen your marital problems.
Could the pro-child partner find a new mate easily?	If chances to find a new mate before menopause are low, assess if it's worth this risk for the **possibility** of a child.

Planners confirming an inclination don't want to leave any considerations out. After you've laid your infant to sleep in the cradle is not the time to say "oops." If you've come through all the reading, discussing, and writing still cheering your choice, the sheet of questions and implications titled "Confirming an Inclination" may provide additional insights.

Avoid self-fulfilling prophesies. Some people make a mental "script" for themselves when they're children that they internally vow to keep, no matter what. Your ambition to be a cowboy was probably abridged as you grew older, but perhaps your determination to be "just like mommy" was not so easily shaken. Even though your temperament isn't quite right for parenting, or you can't foresee a time when you can give yourself to a child, that underlying script awaits its reading. Unconsciously, there's no way you'll allow yourself the room to do anything differently.

Admittedly, it's difficult to alter your unconscious mind, but sometimes these scripts or biases are nearer the surface than you think. The questions on the "Confirming an Inclination" sheet can help you see the biases you may have carried into the decision-making process. Everybody has at least *some* doubt about the choice; without it, you couldn't see both the bad and good realities of parenthood.

Name: _____

Confirming an Inclination

Questions	Implications
On Remaining Flexible Did I approach this decision seeking to confirm what I knew?	If so, you may have ignored or shut out points for the view you don't hold. Better to be open to everything—then your choice will have been well-considered rather than rushed.
I know what I want, but I have to settle aspects of my life before acting on it.	If you agree, don't rush into anything. You may find that as your situation changes, your view of children shifts, too. It's best to evaluate your desires at each point in your life, unbiased by any out-of-date determinations.

Questions	Implications
On Choosing to Have Children I would like to learn a lot more about parenthood before plunging in.	If so, use caution. After you've done the questionnaires and research suggested in this book, and **still** feel unwilling to have a child, you have underlying doubts and should wait until you feel sure.
I want children but can't decide when.	You may be unconsciously trying to avoid parenthood if you're unwilling to project when kids will fit in your life. What is the likelihood events will **ever** be right? If never, you might be happiest without children.
I want children but can't decide how many.	A relatively small problem—don't decide now. Just say "We'll start with one," and evaluate your feelings about how many more to have later.
My partner needs to be as sure as I am before we'd go ahead.	This is a warning flag, possibly signaling unexplored conflict between you. Work that out first.
On Choosing to Remain Childfree My partner and I are sure enough we never want children that we're planning sterilization right away.	If you agree, there's no problem. If you disagree, there's still time to change your mind, so reuse this book in six months.
We most likely won't have any children, but we will continue to use reversible birth control.	If you are under 30, then it's quite possible that you'll change your mind as you approach 40. If you are 35-plus, it's most likely you'll keep postponing and eventually remain childfree.
I'm not concerned with others' reactions to our decision.	If you agree, you're less likely to be swayed when growing numbers of peers have children or when family and friends disapprove of your choice.
I feel confident I've considered my choice thoroughly.	If so, you're more likely to stick by it. If not, don't consent to sterilization or other permanent birth control until you're confident every aspect of the choice is explored.
If I had unlimited money for the rest of my life, I might reconsider and eventually have a child.	A crucial question, since money can buy freedom. If you answer "yes," don't use permanent birth control—you may come into an oil well or an increase in desire that will change things.

Differences Between
Men's and Women's Concerns

Some concerns are specific to men or women. These concerns may involve less-than-flattering thoughts about a mate or reveal embarrassing events as underlying reasons for wanting or not wanting a child.

Men's Concerns

Here's a summary of the most common of men's concerns.

1. *Maintaining the male image.* Sometimes it's difficult to break away from socialization and peers. Other times, men admit that the roles with which they've been brought up are well ingrained and aren't likely to change.

Typically, men feel a discrepancy between what they say they'll do to help with the child and what they actually envision as their everyday role. "I don't want to go fussing around with diaper pails and little sleepers after a long workday. Women have been trained to do that stuff since they were kids. It's so much easier for them," is a frequent comment.

The traditional male image tends to simply dismiss childbearing as a woman's domain. This type of man might prefer drinking a beer in front of the television to joining his wife in the nursery. The way these men look at it, "the little woman" can have a child to play with; they'll find out about fatherhood when the child can talk.

A third aspect of the traditional male image relates to work. Intellectually, the husband may want to become involved in early childcare but fear his employer would doubt his dedication if he put a child ahead of work.

2. *Carrying on the family name.* Most men have been raised to bear the banner of their names proudly. They've been told that their achievements are a credit to the family; that their failures will ruin the family reputation. The sense of family identity, according to the men I've talked to, is planted more firmly in sons than daughters, because until recently, it was only men who were assured of keeping their names throughout their lives.

"It's not the word itself that's so important," one of these men revealed. "It's that I'm part of a family link, part of an ancestry that goes back centuries in history. It's a means to guarantee continuity; immortality, in a way. The idea of a string of people all sharing a common bond for centuries is very important to me. I want to carry on our religion and our values, too."

In the past, this link with humanity via family identity was one of the major benefits of children to fathers. They didn't have much direct play or cuddle contact, often acting as official punisher of their offspring ("Just wait til your father comes home!"). They therefore derived much satisfaction from the social rewards of simply siring a large brood. This attitude is hard to change.

3. *Leaving a piece of yourself.* This idea is related to the one above. But here the annals of history aren't the concern; it's the direct education and values a father teaches his child.

You might love hockey and want your son to have athletic skills. Or you might want to pass along a coin collection you received from your grandfather. Or maybe you'd like your child to share your love of history. If so, you probably look forward to seeing a reflection of your own parenting efforts in the personalities of your children.

4. *Fulfilling father–son fantasies.* How many men do you know who look forward to the activities they'll share with their daughters? The fantasy instilled since childhood is of a father pitching a ball to his athletic son; a dad placing his smiling cowboy on the pony ride; a pop winking at his 15-year-old as he reaches in his wallet on his son's first date.

There aren't many fantasies about an infant spitting-up. Father–son fantasies begin the day Junior gets his first haircut. Dressed in a blue romper, the child is perched, smiling, on a board across the barber's chair. Twenty minutes later, whispy locks cluttering his oversized smock, Junior emerges a little man, with pomade slicking down his crewcut. During childhood, there are the usual Cub Scout camp-out fantasies and numerous athletics-related dreams.

A cluster of imaginings seems to involve the teenager. There's Dad teaching his son to drive; giving lessons on how to use cream and razor for the first shave; toasting his teenager's first beer; and the all-time favorite—carpenters adding wooden letters to the family business sign to read "Smith . . . and Son." These are the images that make parenthood attractive for men. They're the intangibles that stir feelings of pride and love.

Women's Concerns

Women have an easier time confiding their fears and complaints, (stereotypes of the coffee klatsch and multi-hour phone conversations are grounded somewhat in fact.) Women have usually practiced sharing their feelings and providing support for one another. Their concerns include:

1. *Being responsible for the child.* Deep down, most women know that they'll be the one who comes running when Toddler falls down. They admit it when they feel protective instincts. Women often guess they'll *want* to be there for the child.

This attitude would have been lauded just a couple decades ago. Now it becomes toublesome. Women say they want their marriages to be unions of equals; that skill rather than gender is the criterion for accomplishing a job. In more traditional days, it was assumed the woman would have total responsibility for childrearing; now the same fact seems to violate egalitarian principles.

2. *Changing physically.* Fears about the effects of pregnancy, birth, and lactation are expressed often. More than ever, women care for their bodies, tuning them regularly and feeding them only the best. Some women see pregnancy as a opportunity to experience a new physical reality, and plan to bring their enthusiasm to a prenatal exercise regimen. Still there's the element of the unknown.

3. *Conflicts between traditional and new roles.* Role conflict has been a major thorn in the side of the blooming feminist movement. Reared to believe that raising children is life's ultimate fulfillment, women are suddenly told that a career can bring them the same kinds of rewards. Feminists argue that work has always satisfied men's needs for achievement; why can't women enjoy the same advantages?

It can be a difficult choice. After waiting years to start a family and also becoming engrossed in their own careers, women fear they won't ever have time for kids. Sometimes they wish they never had so many opportunities. Without them, most would've just gone ahead and had children and not been faced with a painful one-or-the-other decision.

If you have a child and give up your career, you may regret that, too. My friend was the head buyer for a department store when she took maternity leave. She's been home for two years and loves it, but feels guilty about not returning to work. She keeps saying, "By now I would've been head buyer for the whole chain." She doesn't think she'll be able to go back now and make the climb as rapidly. If you have your own business, where do you think it will be without you in two years?

The decision to combine parenthood with work is as difficult as choosing between one or the other. The desire to "do it all" usually leaves women unhappy simply because of the limits of human energy. For women whose careers are synonymous with their identities, the change to parenthood is one of the most costly transitions they can attempt.

Step-parents

About 15 percent of the couples who attend my decision-making workshops include a partner with children from a previous marriage. These couples are wondering whether to begin a family of their "own." Often, the parent is reluctant to begin diapering, teething, and burping a baby again, while the new mate would like to have a child. Sometimes the second mate has parented a partner's children several years, and only because these children are now living elsewhere does the childbearing question arise.

Recall Wayne and Susan. Their marriage suited them both just fine, but Wayne had experienced parenthood and Susan felt deprived of that privilege. They had certain concerns not shared by couples facing the new parent challenge together for the first time.

What are the special concerns of step parents? They deal with existing households and relationships, and include:

1. *The relationship of a new child to existing children.* Different considerations arise depending on the type of living situation. In households where children are present, how would adding a child from the two of you affect the children you have? Would they be

jealous? Is there a chance that the step-parent would treat her or his natural child differently? What role would existing children play in the upbringing of their new sibling?

When no children are present in the home, there are other considerations. How will having the new obligations of a baby affect the time you give your existing children? When they come to visit, how would having your own child affect accommodations and activities you enjoy? How would your older children react to the introduction of a younger sibling that commands more of Dad's or Mom's attention than they do? What steps can you take to ensure that existing children understand that their relationship with you is secure?

2. *The degree to which the new parenting experience will be colored by memories.* The partner who's "been through it" before probably has some preconceptions about raising a child. A woman who had her first brood a decade ago may assume that she'll have to carry the same load now as she did then. But such assumptions may be inaccurate because of changes in attitudes, new childcare options, and most importantly, a different person with whom to share it all. A man whose wife did most of the mothering tasks may expect the same—passing by opportunities to get involved and receive more enjoyment this time. The parents should ask these questions:

- How is your present relationship different from the one you had for your first parenting go-round?
- In what areas can you reasonably expect your experience to be the same or different?
- How willing are you to forget some aspects of your previous experience and try out new parenting skills?

For the first-time parent:

- How able are you to recognize and ignore your partner's inappropriate predictions?
- How confident are you of your intuition as opposed to your partner's experience?
- In what ways can you make sure that you child's upbringing is an equal result of both parents?
- How can you evaluate when you or your partner is right about a course to take?

3. *Environmental concerns.* "It just doesn't seem right that I have another child," Donald announced. "I had four in my previous marriage. At the time, the population problem wasn't much discussed. When my wife got pregnant each time, we didn't even debate what to do. But now I see that there is a limit to the earth's resources. I've already reproduced two of myself *and* my former wife." Donald's concern is understandable. Yet his new wife, Alice, hasn't had a chance to reproduce at all.

When it comes down to deciding, however, the environment is less an issue than personal desire and ability to cope. Worry about the intangible "environment" or "overpopulation" seems remote when you return to your comfortable home in the suburbs. So the real questions to ask are:

- How will having an additional child affect the use of resources?
- How important is this concern in my decision?
- How does my concern for the environment balance against my partner's desire to have a child?
- In what ways can we modify our life-style so that we are preserving the resources still available?

4. *Financial concerns.* A first child involves significant financial outlays—a lot more than the $85,797 which was the Population Bureau's 1979 moderate estimate for direct-out-of-pocket costs. Adding those costs to present child support payments will squeeze your budget further. The main questions regarding finances include:

- Would my partner and I feel psychologically burdened by the responsibility of paying for our child plus children from a former marriage?
- How far into the future will child support from the first marriage continue?
- Is our income likely to go up to accommodate new expenses?
- If we postpone having a child, will the financial situation ease?

For Single People

It used to be hush-hush when a single woman became pregnant. The embarrassment was hidden by long visits to relatives, "vacations," or "illnesses" spent at maternity homes, but this seems distant from modern mores. It's finally become an option for single people to deliberately have a child, rather than as the result of careless love-making. More and more women who don't foresee marriage in the near future are becoming pregnant on purpose, choosing not to have an abortion, or looking for a man to contribute his sperm but not his life to a child.

Here are some issues singles, especially women, need to consider before attempting parenthood.

1. *Finding a father.*   Evaluate if it's morally acceptable to you to become pregnant and not tell the father.

- What kind of advance arrangements with a potential father can be made to avoid problems in the future?
- Is artificial insemination a viable alternative for you, or is it important to have greater control over the characteristics of your child?

2. *The importance of providing a role model of each sex.*   Some women wonder if a man's influence is required as an appropriate role model (especially for a son).

- What kind of role model is a tired, working mother, even if she shares satisfying time with her child?
- How good a model is a working dad?
- How can you bring a variety of role models into your child's life?

3. *Stigmas of single-parent families.*   In earlier days, children living with only one parent were considered rejects from a "broken home." This is no longer true, but some people feel a one-parented child gets cheated. After all, there are still few publicly supported means of assisting single mothers or fathers—good childcare is still a luxury; finding suitable housing is a squeeze in today's market; costs of necessities are rising faster than one income can accommodate. Consider that residues of traditional views of single-parent families may return to haunt you or your child.

4. *The penalties of "illegitimacy."*   There's no such thing as an illegitimate child; each person is equally valid, independent of

ancestry, status of parents, handicaps, or extraordinary abilities. But some people and institutions don't see if that way. They pry with words, printed applications, and policies. Maybe you're in a supportive atmosphere right now, but judge if your child can continue to be protected from these social guardians, and if not, the effect it would have.

Homosexuals

Many homosexuals have stepped out of the closet and joined mainstream of society, more openly adopting many of the customs heterosexuals have taken for granted. In gay marriages the same sincerity, ritual, and declaration authorized by government for heterosexuals prevails. What's the logical life progression for both the gay and straight world? Love, marraige, baby carriage. Traditionally, gays have omitted the third step, but increasingly they want to have it all.

Some considerations for gays anticipating parenthood are:

1. *Gay women: choosing a father for the child.* Is having sex with a man acceptable for this purpose? What are the pros and cons of artificial insemination? What role would any biological father play in the life of your child?

2. *Gay men: How likely is adoption?* Would you have to remain "in the closet" if you adopted a child? Would you be happy with an older or handicapped child? Can you arrange for private adoption?

3. *The family orientation of the child.* Would the child be confused by the presence of two "mothers" or "fathers"? Would your model of a family be healthy for a child? Would the child get a distorted view of the prevalence of homosexuals and homosexual relationships? How would you explain your situation to the child? What do you see as the special benefits of growing up in a gay household?

4. *Stigmas of gay families.* How would the opinions and comments of others affect your child? Would the child be placed in a defensive position, and could this cause damage? How would having/adopting a child affect your gay identity? Would you curb activities related to your sexual preference or change your habits in any way? How would you respond to the reactions of others?

9

Emotions Determine the Choice

The Want Factor

When you polled parents about their experiences, you asked them why they had children. Probably most of them shrugged their shoulders and replied, "Because we wanted to." Some may have said, "It just happened," when the woman became pregnant unexpectedly. This suggests most people don't accurately verbalize reasons for parenthood. They can, when pressed, often come up with eloquent explanations. But at the time, there are usually few logical determinants of the decision.

Instead, people have children for a myriad of undissected reasons. And even these vaguely recognized notions are brushed aside by "want." The components of "want" are often unconscious. That's why all the list-making in the world can still leave you with a curiously unsatisfied feeling. Also, when having children is approached logically, somehow the outcome always appears negative. You can quantify the number of dollars a baby will cost, and it's always detrimental to your budget. You can predict that the amount of peace you'll have will diminish, and no one's going to call that a plus. Risks

167

of health problems for mother and child are always present, and potential problems always speak kindly for the status quo.

The arguments in favor of a child don't come from facts and lists. They're emotions that stem from sensual experiences. You see a child grasping for a teddy bear out of reach, and feel the urge to push the toy closer. You hold the petal-like fingers of a baby and marvel that such a perfect being has been produced. You teach a child the alphabet and glow in a shared secret. So it's really only fair to look at the emotional side of having a child. You've considered it rationally and now deserve a balance.

Freedom from Values

Focusing on emotions may be foreign to you. You're used to attaching values to every notion; that's how sharp business people work. But in the coming exercises, you're invited to forego values and consider your feelings as being equally legitimate. There's no "right" about depression or "wrong" about ecstacy.

Some organizations may claim they know "good" and "bad" reasons for having a child. Saving a flagging marriage, for example, is a "no-no." Trying for a boy is similarly frowned upon. Wanting to see a miniature you is dubbed selfish. Longing for a human being to love you and be your own is also unacceptable. But who's to say there aren't tinges of all these reasons amidst the most honorable feelings of "want"? Who's to say it's bad to be selfish? After all, people who choose *not* to have kids are selfish, too—or so the mainstream opinion would say. Values dictating what's bad and good, acceptable or unacceptable, don't really have much power in determining the final childbearing choice.

An Exercise: Fantasizing to Arouse Feelings

Before you concentrate on feelings about the future, here's an exercise to help you observe your feelings about the past. You'll be thinking about your emotional reaction to some specific questions, so in order not to lose them (and so that you can have a record of your feelings today for comparison with feelings at another time), get out pencil and paper. Make yourself comfortable and try to free the daily tensions from your mind (perhaps try a few stretches) so they don't interfere. This will be an entirely private experience, so let yourself go emotionally, name the feeling that comes to mind, and jot it down. The more you allow yourself to feel, the more you'll gain. Consider:

1. *Your own childhood.*   Remember when you were in elementary school. Who were your friends? What was your daily routine? What happened during your young years that you will never forget? What do you wish you could erase? Which memories will you always treasure?

As you think of each of these topics, return to your childhood. Grab hold of the feelings and relive them. Capture them by putting a name on each of them. Let yourself cry or smile. Give yourself the luxury of time to notice what you feel.

2. *Your parents.*   How do you remember your mother (or your mother substitute)? Did she change over the years? What triggered the most rollicking laughter you ever shared with her? What brought out tears of sadness? Feel things from her point of view, if you can. What made her proud of you? What did you do that made her worry? What do you think were the parts of parenthood she found easiest and hardest? How does this make you feel about being a parent?

Now think about your father (or your father substitute). How did your relationship with him differ from the one you shared with your mother? What's the most vivid memory you have of yourself as a child with your father? What feelings does it bring out in you? How do you think your father viewed his role as a parent? How did he feel about each of his children? How does this make you feel?

3. *Your current life.*   What do you like to do most? Think about the good feelings you get when you're in the midst of it. Really feel them. What is there in your life now that you dread? Feel the fear, the panic, the laziness, the pain that it instills.

What is most important to you now? Where do you want to go? How does this future make you feel? Scared? Enthused? Regretful? Think about the warm things in your life, and imagine them continued into the future.

4. *Your relationship with your partner.*   When was the last time he or she made you cry? Remember and experience that sadness. When was the last time she or he made you feel a surge of love, appreciation for the caring she or he provides? Relive those nice, toasty feelings. Savor them. How did you feel when you first met? How has your relationship changed, emotionally? What do you feel when you're apart for a day or a week?

You've been thinking about present and past feelings. Now keep that mood to fill out the next questionnaire.

Sentence Completion

As quickly and smoothly as possible, fill in the ends to these sentences. Many are alike, but just keep the answers coming, trying to think of new feelings and views that are aroused.

1. A mother is _____ .
2. A mother is _____ .
3. A mother is _____ .
4. A mother is _____ .
5. A mother is _____ .
6. I am _____ .
7. I am _____ .
8. I am _____ .
9. I am _____ .
10. I am _____ .
11. A father is _____ .
12. A father is _____ .
13. A father is _____ .
14. A father is _____ .
15. A father is _____ .
16. My partner is _____ .
17. My partner is _____ .
18. My partner is _____ .
19. My partner is _____ .
20. My partner is _____ .

Now look over what you've written. First, what are the feelings that come when you read the sentences you've formed? Are you sad, happy, melancholy, perplexed? Now decide how far from your notion of a mother and father you and your partner are. Do you hold a mother and father on a pedestal, and do you see yourself peering upward from below? Or is a mother or father an evil character, there to discipline you unpredictably? Do you see yourself far removed from that ugly picture? Or do you fit perfectly with your notion of a parent? Does your spouse fit harmoniously with your vision of what a parent should be?

Think about these differences and the feelings they arouse in you. Keep writing down your thoughts. If the mechanics of writing get in the way for you, try speaking into a tape recorder. Capture your feelings; don't let them slip away. Your emotions may change day to day or minute to minute. You are trying to discover the triggers of different types of emotions as well as the feelings themselves.

Using Experiences to Generate Feelings

So far, you've been examining pros and cons of parenthood in rapid succession. The next activities require a bit more thought over a few days' time. You'll be imagining that the woman (that's you or your partner) is pregnant for a period of three days. You need to have this time span so you can observe how your feelings change as you "live with" a given decision. After you fantasize about the pregnancy, the upcoming child, and the changes they will bring, imagine the other side of the coin, permanent nonparenthood. You'll "live with" the fact that neither of you can physically have children ever. The decision is out of your hands, and having it made for you should help generate some emotions to make your desires clear.

For the next few days you will record your feelings on forms provided here. They are meant to organize your reactions to imagined pregnancy and nonparenthood.

Each morning, look at the page marked for that day of the process. It sets the mood and gives you an "assignment." It also will tell you an area of your life to focus on, as you experience all your reactions to every aspect of the role you play.

During the day, "live with" the role for that day. Really get into your role, imagining all the ramifications of impending parenthood or nonparenthood. Keep these materials or a pad handy to jot down any flashes of insight, questions, or doubts.

In the evening, after you've had time to reflect on all the events of the day, return to these materials and complete the "Daily Record Sheet." Use the notes you've made, any discussions you've had with your partner, and your emotional as well as intellectual reactions to parenthood and a childfree life.

Using the Daily Record Sheets

Look ahead to the "Daily Record Sheet" marked "First Daily Record Sheet: Imagining Pregnancy." You'll see it has a place for your name and the date. Under that are the directions for that day.

Each day you will imagine the coming child's impact on all of your life. To help you narrow your thoughts, a focus area has been designated.

When you return to the record sheet in the evening, the first task will be to write in all the feelings you can recall. The sheet might say "Excited at coffee break when thinking about the baby's name. Depressed at exercise class when I thought of my expanding belly. Proud—when I told my piano teacher and she beamed with me. Glowing—eating my healthy sandwich, realizing that *I* was making a whole human being."

There will be three components to what you've recorded. First and most important are the feelings, each with a name as specific as possible. Next comes the time of day or activity you were doing when the feeling came to mind. Third is the thought or sight that triggered the feeling.

After you've recorded your feelings and their triggering times and thoughts, write on the record sheet the more rational questions that these bring up in you. For example:

• Will my body be permanently distorted after the baby's born?
• Will I have time to sit and read the newspaper, dawdling after dinner?
• Will the child tie me down?

Name: _____   Date: _____

First Daily Record Sheet: Imagining Pregnancy

Today's directions: You have decided to have a child and have found out that you or your partner is pregnant. Today, think about how the child will affect your **important relationships** (partner, family, friends). Observe your emotional reactions.

In the evening: Write how you felt today when you thought about the child's effect on your important relationships.

Jot down your main concerns:

How often during the day did you think about the coming child? (circle one)

| Every hour or more | Every couple hours | Three or four times today | Once or twice today | Not at all |

When you thought about how the child will affect your important relationships, how often did you feel:

	Mostly	Quite a bit	A little	Not at all
Sad or depressed				
Happy or enthusiastic				
Worried				
Frustrated				
Glad or pleased				
Other feelings: _____				

Based on how you felt today, mark how you feel now about having or not having a child right away. (circle one)

| Definitely want one | Want one | Confused/Conflicted | | | Don't want one | Definitely don't want one |
| | | Same as before | Less than | More than before | | |

Concerns are usually fears that arise because you can't accurately predict the future. If you write them down carefully, you may realize that some are unfounded; that others aren't worth worrying about; that some are serious and should be discussed and prepared for.

After you write down all your concerns, go to the next section of the record sheet, which asks how often you thought about the coming child. Circle whether you thought about the child or your inability to have one every hour or more, every couple hours, three or four times, once or twice, or not at all.

This is a helpful question, because it gives you a chance to see how much you're involved in the childbearing decision. If you circled "every hour or more," the choice is quite significant, and you're willing to work to make the best decision. A casual thought once or twice often reflects less involvement, perhaps instead showing a desire to "play by the rules" by going through with the role-playing game only minimally.

The amount of time you spent imagining the coming child or nonparenthood can also tell you how difficult the actual decision will be. It's so much easier to become engrossed with work, a dinner date, or an evening of study than grapple with all those messy, frightening emotions. Distracting activities let you successfully avoid the task of analyzing your feelings about parenthood.

The next section of the "Daily Record Sheet" asks you to check off how often you felt each of six listed emotions. This contrasts with the first question on the sheet that lets you generate your own list of feelings. This question *gives you* the feelings and asks you to remember the situations when you felt them.

During the day did you feel sad and depressed most of the time, or was that emotion just a fleeting moment? Did frustration arise every five minutes, or was it nonexistent? There is a space for you to write in other feelings so you can later see which feelings occurred most.

After you've reflected on your day by answering these questions, step out of your imagined pregnancy or sterility. The last item on the page requires you to assess the day's feelings and their effects on your decision. If you were depressed all day, admit that you definitely don't want a baby; if you glowed with parental pride, state that your desire for a child is definite. Choosing the more extreme answers will be useful when you graph out your responses after your "pregnant" and "nonparent" days are over.

To give you more precision in measuring any uncertainty, there are three subchoices. Confusion or conflict can be less than, more than, or the same as before.

The record sheet looks the same for all four of the days to come. It's just a tool to help you structure or organize your emotional responses. The important thing is your awareness of yourself. And it's important to note not just the reaction, but also its source.

Choosing Daily Topics

I have suggested topics to focus on while you imagine pregnancy and nonparenthood. They're open to change, though, if there are areas of greater importance to you. Or you might want to rearrange them to fit activities you have planned on the days you're role-playing.

The first day of pregnancy is directed toward its impact on important relationships, particularly partner, family, and friends. Because you or your partner's condition is new to you, you'll probably be making a few announcements, and the reactions will be worth thinking about. Also, if you begin the week of role-playing on a Saturday or Sunday, it's likely you'll spend some time with others.

For example, if you begin on Sunday you may spend the day with your family, enjoying a fancy sit-down meal followed by board games and talk. You might want to make an "announcement" and use the occasion to get feedback from others.

The second day of pregnancy is directed toward feelings surrounding career and education. If on Sunday you received the reaction of family and friends, on Monday you can look at the impact of the coming child on your job and co-workers. "I thought of how my morning routine would be altered," Rebecca, the undecided hospital administrator, remembered. "I realized I'd probably have to get up an hour earlier *every day* to get the baby ready and drop him off at the childcare center. I sat at my desk wondering if I'd worry about my child being mixed in with those other kids' germs, unsure that he'd have the quality of mothering I would give him. All this made me anxious and depressed."

Because most people are involved with their work or schooling on a weekday, that's the best time to really focus on the impact of pregnancy on that area of your life.

The third day of imagined parenthood has been dedicated to feelings about yourself. Often, by the third day participants get used to the pregnant state. They have looked at the reactions of other people and have decided how these make them feel. Now that there is less novelty, they can see how parenthood affects their own self-images.

If the three topics for concentration during your imagined days of pregnancy aren't the ones foremost on your mind, feel free to substitute others, focus on different topics during the day, or even extend the periods of "pregnancy" and "nonparenthood" if you need more time. Here are a few alternative topics to consider. They're basically variations on the subheads from the "Benefits and Drawbacks Questionnaire" you completed.

- Being a parent to a child of the age you fear most
- Financial concerns
- Living a certain life style
- Becoming a family: changing the family group
- Being a single parent
- The kind of child you could have
- The type of world in which your child would grow up

Begin imagining your pregnancy tomorrow, using the "First Daily Record Sheet: Imagining Pregnancy." Remember to use the forms like a journal or diary and to privately record your reactions to the experience.

Imagining Pregnancy

Pretending to be pregnant should translate the possibility from sheer fantasy into reality. This means revising your actions as if you or your partner were actually pregnant. For example, lots of people just can't start the day without a cup of coffee. But given recent research that caffeine could harm a developing fetus, you have to evaluate if you—a pregnant woman—would drink it. If you're the male partner, would you still brew that pot of coffee for yourself in front of your wife? How closely would the man watch over what his pregnant wife consumes?

Smoking has a direct and negative effect on a growing fetus. If you smoke regularly, will you quit? Will you rationalize that this is only role-playing and continue smoking? Or will you treat this like a real pregnancy and see how difficult it will be to alter your life?

Asked how she felt when she imagined being pregnant, one woman replied, "I was a lot gentler with myself. I didn't go jogging like I usually do because I was afraid I'd shake up the baby. I directed the rearranging of our furniture instead of helping out." Yet the medical consensus is that continuation of an established jogging program is usually fine unless it becomes uncomfortable. And sliding sofas shouldn't disturb the well-protected child either. In other words, pregnant women might alter their physical activities in some ways, but not in all of them.

Preparing for baby doesn't just mean buying booties and cutting down on coffee. It also includes arranging for the newcomer in your home. Where would the bassinette go? Would you repaint the den in pastels? Would you move from your adult-oriented apartment complex? As you think of how the infant will affect your life, pay careful attention to the feelings inspired. Focus on emotions. For example, if you love your garden apartment overlooking the tennis court, would you be willing to move because of a child?

During your "pregnancy," pick out names you would give a boy and a girl. Would the child retain the mother's last name or earn a hyphenated title? Would a boy be a traditional John, Samuel, Junior, or III? Would a girl be Jennifer or Linda? Or would the name you give your child be more unusual?

Once the child has an identity, think about all stages of his or her life. What should you do now to prepare for a toddler? Start working on an elaborate jigsaw puzzle of the United States to enhance early education? Investigate the best neighborhoods with convenient child care? Cultivate a good relationship with your mother-in-law? You may want to bone up on old, new, or returning math. Anticipating

Name: _____ Date: _____

Second Daily Record Sheet: Imagining Pregnancy

Today's directions: You have decided to have a child and have found out that you or your partner is pregnant. Today, think about how the child will affect your **career or education.** Observe your emotional reaction.

In the evening: Write how you felt today when you thought about the child's effect on your career or education:

Jot down your main concerns:

How often during the day did you think about the coming child? (circle one)

Every hour or more	Every couple hours	Three or four times today	Once or twice today	Not at all

When you thought about how the child will affect your career or education, how much did you feel:

	Mostly	Quite a bit	A little	Not at all
Sad or depressed				
Happy or enthusiastic				
Worried				
Frustrated				
Glad or pleased				
Other feelings: _____				

Based on how you felt today, mark how you feel now about having or not having a child right away. (circle one)

Definitely want one	Want one	⌐——Confused/Conflicted——⌐			Don't want one	Definitely don't want one
		Same as before	Less than before	More than before		

being the parent of a teenager could mean setting aside money for a college education or investigating social groups for your child to join. Now that you're a parent, there's lots to do.

Revealing the "pregnancy" to friends or family encourages earnest talk from them about the value of children. Hearing about their decision process might help you as well.

Role-playing can become habit. One woman was so convinced she was pregnant that she worked her life around it. "Our friends asked us to go backpacking with them this summer—that's eight months away. I didn't even think about it, telling them I couldn't because I already had something scheduled for those weeks. Then I realized that I'd set aside July for having a baby."

Miraculous things can happen when you're tuned to the pregnancy wavelength. This actually happened to Wayne and Susan, who overcame Wayne's hesitance to have a child with his second wife. "I was really thinking about this child, and how we'll make a cradle and take LaMaze classes and sew little terrycloth sleepers," said Susan, in the midst of her decisionmaking. "Then out of the blue my mother telephoned me long distance from across the country. She said she had a dream that I was pregnant, and that it was so real she just had to call me to see if it was true." It seemed as if Susan's desire for a child was telegraphed home.

Being pregnant can bring you into the "club" of parents. Because you now have something in common, suddenly you listen more carefully when associates talk about diaper rash remedies. They include you in their remarks, willing to be helpful to a new friend. One couple got together with the woman's sister after years of estrangement. The sister had three children, and the woman wanted to know how her sister handled that with her career.

Some people report that they view the world differently as future parents. They make financial decisions more conservatively, spend more time around home, and remove harmful objects from a baby's reach. Being a parent gives them a whole new image of themselves. Remember that you're not only experiencing the activities and rewards of pregnancy but also the emotions. That's the whole point of the exercise—to grab ahold of the "want factor" that's aroused in you.

Name: _____   Date: _____

Third Daily Record Sheet: Imagining Pregnancy

Today's directions: You have decided to have a child and have found out that you or your partner is pregnant. Today, think about how the child will affect your **feelings about yourself** (your body, your roles). Observe your emotional reaction.

In the evening: Write how you felt today when you thought about the child's effect on your feelings about yourself.

Jot down your main concerns:

How often during the day did you think about the coming child? (circle one)

| Every hour or more | Every couple hours | Three or four times today | Once or twice today | Not at all |

When you thought about how the child will affect your feelings about yourself, how much did you feel:

	Mostly	Quite a bit	A little	Not at all
Sad or depressed				
Happy or enthusiastic				
Worried				
Frustrated				
Glad or pleased				
Other feelings: _____				

Based on how you felt today, mark how you feel now about having or not having a child right away. (circle one)

| Definitely want one | Want one | ———Confused/Conflicted——— | | | Don't want one | Definitely don't want one |
| | | Same as before | Less than before | More than before | | |

Two women I know had the same reaction to their imagined pregnancies, but there was a big difference in the reasons behind the tears and the triggers.

"I cried because I was so upset that I was going to have a child. I just couldn't face the possibility—it would really ruin my life," was the first friend's explanation. "I was so sad and depressed. The child growing inside me would mean the end of everything I've worked for—my wonderful relationship with my husband, my freedom, my independence. I never knew I felt so strongly about not wanting a child."

The second woman shed tears for an entirely different reason. "I cried because I was touched with the reality of pregnancy. I've been on the Pill for so long, I was petrified that I could never have any children. I was so overwhelmed with the possibility that I could do it, and filled with awe at the miracle of life inside me, that I was left speechless, emotional, and raw. I cried tears of gratitude and relief." The differences between these two responses show why it's important to name the feelings that pass through your mind.

Emotional Changes During Imagined Pregnancy

Now you've spent three days contemplating, role-playing, and reading about the coming of your own child. What does it all mean? Think back over the three days, rereading what you wrote on the record sheets. What about each day's experience was special? How did your activities each day affect your inclination to have a child? Did your desire increase as pregnancy continued (perhaps as you got more used to the idea) or did it decrease (maybe the novelty wore off and you discovered an emotional toll)?

If desire increased over the three days, you could be adapting to the idea of having a child and overcoming initial blocks of inertia that urge you to maintain the status quo. Sometimes it takes "getting used to" before you can switch a self-concept from carefree individual to protective, responsible parent.

If desire decreased over the three days, you may be looking for the personal attention and social status a child can bring, but not the actual duties or contact of parenthood. The novelty may have worn off as business or recreation consumed your interest. But beware: you can't just "forget' about your child, and you should explore alternative means to get on-going attention. Don't have a child until you can be enthusiastic for at least three days about the prospect.

If desire for a child fluctuated, look at the triggers of each emotion. The feelings you had with borrowed children and family count the most, because then you had an opportunity to experience both negative and positive angles. If antiparenthood feelings came when you were balancing the checkbook or considering room additions, remember that it's easier to feel negative about the realities of cash flow. If you were "pregnant" and did not seek out other mothers or spend time thinking about changes in your life, you're probably too consumed with your own daily activities to be involved with a child.

If desire for or against a child was never strong and you found it difficult to observe your feelings, there are three possibilities. You might find the issue of parenthood so painful that you're subconsciously blocking it. You might refuse to examine anything on an emotional level, choosing to work from a strictly rational perspective. (If that's the case, you can probably only see the negative side of parenthood, since recognizing the positive requires paying attention to emotions.) Good parents are emotionally giving, so practice observing your emotions before having a child. Lastly, there's the possibility that you simply are indifferent. If so, *don't* have a child. You *must* have commitment—if not to children, then to supporting your partner in his or her desire for a child.

Be sure to discuss your daily record sheets with your partner as often as possible. Discuss the events that triggered your feelings, as well as your concerns and fears about the future, and alternatives for changing them. Note the changing strength of your feelings over each of the days. Perhaps Monday was trying, a contest between your restraint and your tears. Perhaps Tuesday was depressed, but in better control, evolving into a Wednesday of resolution. How often did you think about the coming child, or were you "too busy" or unwilling to dwell on the topic? The priority you place on the decision reflects its importance to you. Compare this with your partner to clarify which of you is most invested in the choice.

Imagining Nonparenthood

After three days of impending parenthood, spend one day imagining the opposite—that neither you nor your partner can ever physically have children. This sudden switch allows you to observe the change in your outlook.

Imagine that neither of you can ever conceive a child. Use the last "Daily Record Sheet." When these materials were first used, participants tried pretending they'd purposefully decided to remain childfree. But it was hard for people to live with a decision they'd never made, and harder for them to consider it resolved when everyone around them knew it was a central issue in their lives. By taking the matter out of both partners' hands and blaming it on biology, the most extreme (and therefore clear) reactions are elicited. There can be less wriggling to slip out of the decision.

Perhaps you'd consider nonparenthood differently if only one partner and not the other were unable to have children. Take some time to fantasize about this difference and your emotional response to it. Use the one day to think about all the emotional ramifications of being a permanent nonparent, and record your feelings just as you did before on the "Fourth Daily Record Sheet: Imagining Nonparenthood."

It's tempting to "forget" about imagining permanent nonparenthood. After all, being a nonparent requires a minimum of change in your life, but the "knowledge" that childbearing is not possible brings many chances to react to the fact. There are many triggers to react to. Here are some triggers you might encounter:

- A mother pushing a stroller in the park
- A father carrying a baby in a backpack out shopping
- A family juggling diaper bags, toddlers, and packages climbing onto the bus
- Children squealing over the tide at the beach
- Pregnant women you see on the street
- Couples your age whispering together in a romantic restaurant
- Your friends' children playing with blocks in the livingroom
- Your mother talking about other people's children
- A children's birthday party at a neighborhood pizza parlor
- An elementary school with kindergarteners screaming on the playground

Name: _____ Date: _____

Fourth Daily Record Sheet: Imagining Nonparenthood

Today's directions: You have just found out that you and your partner cannot physically have a child, ever. Think about your life now and your future. Observe your emotional reaction.

In the evening: Write how you felt today when you thought about your permanent non-parenthood:

Jot down your main concerns:

How often during the day did you think about the effect of nonparenthood?

Every hour or more	Every couple hours	Three or four times	Once or twice	Not at all

When you thought about how nonparenthood will affect your life and future, how much did you feel:

	Mostly	Quite a bit	A little	Not at all
Sad or depressed				
Happy or enthusiastic				
Worried				
Frustrated				
Glad or pleased				
Other feelings: _____				

Based on how you felt today, mark how you feel now about having or not having a child right away. (circle one)

Definitely want one	Want one	Confused/Conflicted			Don't want one	Definitely don't want one
		Same as before	Less than	More than before		

These are external triggers. They are things you see around you. Now here are some external events that pull *internal* triggers:

- Doing anything you love to do alone
- Seeing your body in a slim-fitting outfit, a leotard, or in the nude
- Sleeping late on a Sunday morning
- Not feeling like making dinner
- Arranging a spur-of-the-moment game of tennis
- Reading the newspaper
- Seeing your partner sleeping in bed next to you
- Dusting your collection of glass miniatures
- Tasting an expensive, delicious food

These internal cues don't deal directly with children, a child, or a family, but they are reminders of what you have now that might change. You have to feel from inside if these changes produce joy or depression.

Try announcing to others you trust that you can never have a child. There are a few typical reactions you'll encounter. They may want to know everything—what is wrong with whom, how they can help you overcome an expected depression, how they can put you in contact with substitute children to fill that gap in your lives. This is the attitude that expects *of course you want children* and that not being able to have them would be a big psychological blow.

In some cases, the news can throw a concerned listener into a panic or disbelief. He may immediately start looking up fertility doctors for you or refuse to believe that you can't deliver the grandchildren he wants so much.

A third reaction from others is embarrassment, especially among men. "Friends seemed to assume that if I couldn't have kids I was less of a man," said one client. In turn, you may feel pain, embarrassment, or fear.

What else can happen when couples begin imaging nonparenthood? Here are some classic reactions you might experience.

1. *Relief.* If pretending parenthood brings uneasiness, pressure to provide financially for your family, or desire to turn back to care-

free times, you're likely to feel soothing, quick relief. Suddenly all the hassles or responsibilities you dreaded have been lifted off your shoulders. This is a classic response of "now-or-never" couples leaning toward "never" and "planners" who see children in their more distant future.

2. *Sadness.* This can arise from two causes. One is that your imagined pregnancy has come to term—no longer can you revel in a fantasy that obviously pleases you. The second cause is the prospect of sterility. There are all sorts of negative feelings aroused by this one—you're not a complete woman or man, you can't carry on the family name, you won't have parenthood as an aspect of your life. Some people call up fertility doctors to inquire about new procedures; others read articles about implanting test-tube babies. It becomes a challenge to defy the pronouncement that you're sterile. This reaction also shows a desire to have a child—and the stronger your feelings of loss, the more of that magical "want" for a baby you show.

3. *Anger.* Nobody likes to have the decision snatched out of their control. It's as though an obnoxious intruder barged into your life. This is an especially common reaction if you're used to controlling your environment. It shows that *you* want to decide, but anger in itself doesn't signal whether you want a child or not.

Once you've completed your day imagining nonparenthood, compare your feelings on that day with your emotions during the three days role-playing pregnancy. Is there a sharp difference in your inclination when you went from one to the other? Look at differences in your answers to the last question on each "Daily Record Sheet," the item asking you to step back and use each day's experience to determine your yearning for a child.

A change from wanting children during "pregnancy" to not wanting them during "nonparenthood" shows flexibility. You'd probably support and become enthused with either possibility. A change in the other direction, from *not* wanting children during "pregnancy" to desiring them during "nonparenthood," may also indicate that you're not ready for a child. It suggests you're not happy with the situation you have. This reaction might also mean you need to straighten out conflicts in your life now, perhaps your job or an important relationship, before committing yourself to parenthood.

After you've interpreted the differences in your "pregnancy" and "nonparenthood" fantasies for yourself, share your experiences with your partner. Did you both feel the same things? Did nonparenthood produce opposite reactions in each of you? Do you notice your views getting closer together, or splitting divergently? Did one of you more than the other show a dramatic change when nonparenthood began— that is, was there a big contrast with the three days of pregnancy for only one of you? Use your partner as a mirror and a resource; there's no one else with as much investment in your potential child.

Summing It All Up

You're now ready to evaluate all the exercises, thinking, reading, form-checking, and scribbling you've been doing. Go back to the first forms, questionnaires, and notes. Reread them. Then rescan the sheets from your experiential exercises. Think about how your concerns, pros and cons, reasons, values, and feelings changed. Look for themes and similarities. Look for your gut reaction to it all.

Mainly think about your present inclination to have a child. What you feel now is the total of what you've experienced. It's the result of the questionnaires and the reading, the interviewing of parents, the discussions with your partner. What else can you do to clarify where you stand? Perhaps there's more. But you have to decide when the best time is to face your true desires. Try doing it now.

This is a two-person process. It's not something to glibly circle. Two people will be affected by the outcome, so both of you should fully participate in the decision-making process. Set aside a time to make a choice, and give it at least as much respect as you would an important business engagement. After all, this may be the most important business of your life.

Final Decision-making Sheet

This form lets you summarize your experiences with all the questionnaires and exercises you've completed. Unfortunately, there's no magic formula for adding it all up. The answer still has to come from you, though now you're well equipped to recognize it.

Look at the "Partner Decision-making Sheet" you completed earlier. Transfer your tentative decision with your partner's at the bottom of that page to the "Final Decision-making Sheet." Look them over carefully and discuss how representative those conclusions are of your current feelings. Below that, each of you should circle your present choice from the ones listed there. Talk about it. Rehash your reasoning, your fears, your expectations. But force yourselves to mark something that's most comfortable for you both now. Write in the concerns, questions, and pros and cons that are "leftover"—still pertinent to you. Don't feel this choice is inflexible—you can change. But do realize that if you abdicate a choice now, eventually the decision will be made for you by the passage of time.

Final Decision-making Sheet

From "Benefits and Drawbacks Questionnaire":	Partner A	Partner B
Score in favor of having a child		
Score against having a child		

Inclination from first "Partner Decision-making Sheet": (one circle for each partner)

Have a child within 1 year	Postpone 2 years or less	Postpone 2-1/2–5 years	Postpone over 5 years	Remain childfree	Recognize strong differences in opinion

---

Now at the end of the experiential activities: (each partner circle one)

"After considering my values, expectations and feelings, and those of my partner, the best course to take is . . ."

Start trying to have a child within 1 year	Postpone 2 years or less	Postpone 2-1/2–4 years	Postpone over 5 years	Remain childfree	Recognize strong differences in opinion	Decide not to decide

	Partner A	Partner B
Major pros of parenthood		
Major cons of parenthood		
Concerns/questions		

10

Living with Your Decision

Receiving Feedback from Others

Once you've taken shaky pen to paper and selected an alternative—
whether it's to throw away your diaphragm or put off all thought of
children for another five years—the story doesn't end. You didn't
decide in a vacuum (recall all the interested friends and relatives)
and now you needn't carry your decision by yourself either. Feedback regarding your choice can be a mirror that reflects if your
decision fits you comfortably or is bound to be regretted.

There are many sources of feedback:

1. Start with your *friends*. Remember Jo and Marty, who at late
ages confronted their decision not to have children? When they told
their friends, the reaction was typical. "There was hostility in the air
at first," said Jo, "like I'd betrayed them. But as they looked over the
materials, they saw how serious a choice it is for me. They surprised
me with their understanding."

"And there was one more funny thing," Jo added. "They said that they were afraid that now that I don't want kids I wouldn't want to be their friend. They promised to try to be more cognizant of my interests and needs so that I wouldn't find them dull and leave them. I felt so good, I could've floated through the roof. These are women I went through school with. It reassured me that good, solid friendships are precious things to keep. I told them so. I think we all benefited from my decision."

Friends can also tell you how well your choice fits with their perception of your goals and personality. Because friends weave in and out of your life, sometimes they can give a more unbiased perspective than relatives can.

2. Another source of feedback is *family*. In some cases, it might not be wise to divulge your choice, but you probably can get valuable feedback if you make your announcement gently. There will be more on dealing with family in this chapter.

After flying home to discuss the problem, Kathy, considering adoption, viewed her mother from a new perspective, with admiration for the effort and devotion she used to raise her three children. "My mother never knew there was a choice," Kathy reflected. "And she was glad that I could have all the opportunities to have a career and then decide about motherhood that she never did." Siblings can report on their own experiences as parents. Aunts and uncles can relate their feelings toward you as a child close to them.

3. A third source of feedback is *professional counselors*. Clergy, social workers, psychologists, psychiatrists, marriage and family counselors are all trained to listen to your concerns and make constructive suggestions. In some cases, clients find that the childbearing dilemma is perhaps the only mentionable part of a deeper problem. Professionals can usually separate a short-term quandary from longer-term questions and needs. On the other hand, therapists each have an orientation that they bring into the counseling process. Before you choose a professional, assess whether you have a short-term case of the willies or something more complex. Then seek out recommendations from people you trust—a family doctor, people with similar problems, a professional association, or a community center—before making inquiries directly to counselors.

But also be aware that most professionals aren't yet sensitive to the issue of deciding about children. Inquire about their attitudes first. Some gynecologists tend to pat distressed women on the arm and murmur, "You'll have children in due time; all women want children." Clergy have been known to preach rather than listen to alternative views. Even some psychologists who understand new attitudes do not have enough experience with this problem to provide a wide variety of options.

4. A final source of feedback is *supportive acquaintances*. Women's centers often have discussion groups where the conflicts of career versus motherhood are understood and suggestions given. Men, too, are increasingly forming their own discussion groups, finding that traditional stereotypes give way to caring, warm relationships. Co-workers can be in just the right position to give feedback—not overly involved in your personal life, so they can be objective, yet knowing you well enough that discussing your choice would be comfortable.

There are times when mere acquaintances can give useful feedback as well. One couple shared a railroad train compartment with an older couple from England. It was almost because they all knew that they'd never see each other again that discussing the dilemma of childbearing was unthreatening.

Acting on Your Choice

"Ohmygosh," you may be thinking as you look over the "Final Decision-making Sheet". "This certainly *does* seem final. I've just committed to paper my whole future!" Perhaps you have—but only if you checked a determination to *act* immediately on your choice. Otherwise, don't feel that you're stuck with it like careless fingers bound with Crazy Glue. You see, there are really three possibilities once you've made the fateful decision.

Planners who want to confirm an inclination to have or not have children may actually *act* on their choices. "We were so elated about our decision that we spent the night having our own private orgy," Brenda blushed to me in confidence. "We couldn't wait to start the baby we knew was so right for us."

But still, until Brenda is actually pregnant, or Don has his vasectomy, or Kathy and Lou receive their adopted heartthrob into their home, their choices are all reversible. For everyone, regardless of how confident or unsure, some regret, some uncertainty, and further ambivalence is inevitable. Doubt will sneak in sometime, even after your children have grown or your accomplishment-laden life is behind you.

While planners or the newly decided may act on their choices, other couples *stall* a truly final end to the question. Some people who say they've "decided once and for all" to postpone children a specific one, two, or five years make vows and send out telegrams to proclaim that their choice is "the real thing." In their minds, they completely accept the reality of their decision. It's a permanent decision—that's it, period—the end—until one, two, or five years mosey around.

"We've decided we definitely want to start trying for a child in a year," might be your choice. "In the next year I'll even go into training for it. There are some things I need to settle in my life, and then we'll definitely go ahead with it."

But what about your desire to wait a year? It could suggest you have things you want to do other than have a child. It gives you time to change your mind.

Being rigid about your decision can have advantages. You can squelch a tendency to hedge by repeating your resolution. You can abandon distress by reminding yourself of the detailed procedure you went through to arrive at your choice. You can sleep more soundly knowing the decision isn't still up in the air. This is the way to go for some people: make up your mind or forever boil in turmoil.

Ahh, but there is an out. Some people *"decide not to decide"* about having a child. They go through all the questionnaires and discussions, read till their red eyes need toothpicks to prop them open, and flip all the pros and cons through their minds like a short order cook does pancakes. They end up with a stuporous grin, a cowlick from all the head-scratching, and a question: "Huh?"

Deciding not to decide is an honorable choice. It admits that you have a poor-quality crystal ball; that maybe you aren't in such a rush after all; that things are expected to change dramatically in the future;

that you actually *prefer* drifting along with your current situation. Yes, it's alright not to make a decision. Say it over and over: "It's OK . . . It's OK. . . ."

So you see there *are* three possible outcomes to the decision-making process: (1) choosing and acting, (2) choosing and postponing, and (3) not choosing.

11

The Decision to Have a Child

Once you've decided to have a baby, you can expect the changes to begin. First, you must accept your decision as final and begin to act on it. One way to solidify the choice in your own mind, as well as gain support of others, is to simply talk about it.

Making the Announcement:
Typical Reactions

You'll have to face some immediate consequences of your decision, among which are the positive and negative responses of others.

1. *Happy receptions.* Because your parents, peers, enemies, television heroes, and magazine serial protagonists all have kids, this is a pretty well-accepted decision. You probably will get a lot of positive responses—"I'm so happy for you!" "Congratulations!" and "Mazeltov!"—especially when the actual pregnancy is announced. You'll hear a lot of stories about "when I had my first." The smiling faces around you can't help but encourage you.

197

2. *Denial.* But be prepared for some surprises. "We told my mother that we had started trying for a child," Donna reported, "and we expected she would squeal with joy. Instead she shot back, 'Already?' I couldn't believe it! I thought she'd been waiting for a grandchild with poised knitting needles." It turned out that Donna's mother had been struck by her own aging and saw being a grandmother as a wrinkled white-haired senior—a far cry from the tennis expert and ad agency executive she actually was.

3. *Children as hindrances.* The birth of your child doesn't just affect you. The event has meaning for everyone around you, too. In a changing social climate, the meaning might take on a negative cast. Dick explained that many of their friends were professionals without children. Most of them didn't intend to have any, either. But he and his wife *did* want to be parents. "It became the reverse of most people's pressure," he chuckled. "Instead of feeling left out without children, we were afraid we'd be left out *with* them. We talked this over long and hard," he continued, looking at his wife Brenda, "and we almost made a dart board out of their pictures. Getting angry at our friends for inhibiting us was our way of liberating ourselves from their influence."

"We finally realized that if they don't want to include us when we have kids, it's their loss, not ours. We'll have a whole new world filled with parents and kids as well as freedom. *We're* getting the bonus in our lives; *they're* the ones who will feel left out!"

4. *Employers' concerns.* "What are you going to do *after* the baby's born?" your boss might ask. If you say you're going to take some time off, he or she will probably frown.

You might hear, "We didn't train you to go off and leave us to have babies. We made a big investment in you because you're well-educated, bright, competent, and professional. I suppose we were wrong on that last count. We were considering you for a promotion. You know it's our policy to elevate people from within the company. It's such a shame you've chosen to stay home."

You may feel hurt, angry, disappointed, or frustrated—but that's the reality of the career world. For both men and women, success means that career comes first, family second. Being a "professional" means someone else looks after the kids. Be prepared for this.

Antinatalism can affect men as well as women. "At first I told everyone that I would take off a year to stay home with our baby," Matthew confided. "Then I began noticing that the reactions didn't shine with the enthusiasm I'd expected. Many of the women were excited for me and said that my wife was 'lucky.' But the men really seemed uncomfortable with the idea. Like I was suddenly effeminate or crazy." As you recall, Matthew is a junior high school assistant principal.

"My colleagues wanted to know how I could stand to give up a year's income. They wanted to know how I could abide staying home with the dirty diapers of a crying child. They couldn't understand that there are benefits attached to fatherhood."

5. *The "new social moralists".* Prospective parents should watch out for another aspect of antinatalism: the "liberated" people who condemn tradition—critics who feel having children is self-indulgent rather than generous. Even in progressive environments, mothering can be looked down upon. It may be "in" to talk about childcare and self-pregnancy testing and natural foods preparation, but when you say you're pregnant, some people seem to reverse their words.

"They asked me how I could tie myself down," Michele remembered. "They thought that motherhood was alright for those who had already chosen it, but with so many new options, why pick that one? They suggested that I would be more fulfilled in a fancy job, and that I would prefer a high salary to the common 'woman's role.' "

So, prospective parents, brace yourselves for both positive and negative reactions to your new status. But you'll probably get more strokes than snarls. A study by Public Health professor Judith Blake at UCLA showed that one of the major benefits of children is the social acceptance and status they bring. People no longer have them for economic reasons, like they did in agricultural days, but kids still garner rewards because of the approval they gain from others. Some of this positive reaction will be sexist. "Hey, George, we knew you had it in you!" many men hear from cronies. They nudge you with their elbows and wink, as if being fertile is an accomplishment.

After the announcement, there will probably be moments of both excitement and doubt. It is natural to feel regret, and to ask, "What did I get myself into?" Magazine articles detailing the psychological cycles of pregnancy catch women's eyes monthly. After all, practically every woman does become pregnant.

"I thought I'd made a huge mistake," a 46-year-old mother of two told me. "I had my first at 31, which was considered over the hill at the time. I was moving up in my private practice as a psychologist and needed every moment to promote myself. I doubted any client would want to come to a ballooned mother-to-be. How could I be competent when my looks suggested my mind was on baby bottles and strollers?"

But looking back on the experience, she wouldn't have changed a thing. "My children are the pride of my life. I think I'm a better therapist because I have a broader view of the human condition. I see both sides of the mountain now—that of daughter and mother. I can understand the gaps a lot better."

The theme that parents repeat over and over is that they have adapted to their roles. They love their kids. They have no idea what life would've been like without them—nor do they care to speculate. So even though your doubts may reappear, keep this in mind.

Blake, an art director for a major newspaper, told about his caring for his 6-year-old daughter. "I wouldn't have gotten married if I could do that over again," he confides, "but I'm so glad I had Trina. She reminds me that my life isn't in vain, that I matter to someone."

Blake, divorced two years, still hurts from the experience. "Trina is a fascination to me. She grows and changes with such a perfect personality. She makes infinite sense. When everything else in my life is crazy, I can spend just two hours with her and I'm renewed."

Blake had many regrets in his life. He said that when Trina was on the way, he panicked and wished her birth wasn't reality. "I felt left out of the pregnancy and the birth. I didn't participate in the feeding and the diaper-changing. I guess these were early symptoms that my wife and I weren't close, but I didn't realize it then. It was only after we'd split apart and I was alone with my daughter that I appreciated her for the unique person she is."

Supermom—Faster than a Speeding Bullet

Try to avoid roles that trap you rather than liberate you. One is the "Supermom." You've heard about her. She does everything right.

She's up at 6:00 A.M. without the aid of an alarm clock (natural body rhythm whispers in her ear instead) to jog five miles and effortlessly do calisthenics. A half-hour of housework tidies the house for the day. She takes a shower and her hair falls neatly into place just by running a comb through the glistening strands. She dresses in a stylish skirt-suit of nubby tweed and wraps a silk scarf around her neck for accent (the proper balance of business and femininity). By this time her children and husband are awake. As they cheerfully ready themselves for the day, she prepares a natural breakfast for all and lays it out on a table replete with hand-sewn placemats and fresh daisies from the ever-blooming garden. Nutritious lunches are swiftly prepared and laid out as all sit down to pleasant conversation.

She kisses her supportive husband goodbye and drives one of her two charges to the smiling staff at the nearby reasonably priced daycare center. The other child is deposited at the school steps, where Teacher can't wait to receive this most precocious and well-mannered student. She then maneuvers her Porsche to its space at her law firm, facing a day of significant decisions affecting clients' lives and court victories hailed by her colleagues. Without a wisp of hair out of place or an eyelash in need of mascara, she meets the governor for afternoon cocktails, finishing just in time to pick up her grateful children and glide home. As the beef Wellington's pastry browns to a golden crust, Supermom dusts the entire house and vacuums the plush carpets. Her husband drifts in to passionately embrace her and exclaim what a jewel he's married, as the children add loving hugs at their knees. The exquisite meal by candlelight is followed by a quick clean-up and time to look over the children's perfect school papers while listening to them joyfully practicing their Beethoven on the piano. The youngsters gladly trip off to bath and bed, after which Mom and Dad enjoy political debate and replays of first-run films from their videotape recorder. At midnight they retire to their waterbed for mutually satisfying lovemaking throughout the remainder of the darkness.

An accurate portrayal of life for the working mother? Hardly! The problem is that Supermom has become a role model for lots of career women who want to "have it all." There's nothing wrong with trying, but you can be disappointed and frustrated to realize that it's tough to even grab *part* of it.

Supermom is a mythical creature—a statue on the pedestal next to the traditional housewife. Now that you've decided to have a child, don't let anyone con you into thinking you can pose on that same marble stand.

And Introducing Superdad

And what about Father? There's a new stereotype emerging for him, too—one that would leave Jim Anderson of *Father Knows Best* agog. Superdad awakens at 6:00 A.M. and puts on the baby's formula to slowly heat. Meanwhile, he makes breakfast for his wife, showers and shaves, and kisses the corporate president goodbye for the day. Baby is just arising in time for a lovingly dispensed bottle and cuddle-fest, as Daddy croons his most gentle nursery rhymes. Time for a change, accomplished swiftly and easily while company business is completed by telephone. Then it's off to infant exercise and swim class, where Baby paddles three pool lengths of the Australian crawl.

Dried off and smelling sweet, Baby coos in Daddy's backpack as he does the marketing, returns home, and bakes all-wheat granola bran loaves. More cuddling and formula; then a jaunt to the health club where the Dads there take turns watching their progeny as racquetball games are won. Then it's home again to breeze through some housework, check back with the answering service to confirm that the stock deal went through, and begin the luscious meal that's such an expression of his creativity. At 5:30, he's poised, clever tequila cocktails in the shaker, as his appreciative wife returns from wheeling and dealing six figures into the family income. They share chateaubriand and fascinations of each other's day; then spend a rewarding evening teaching their infant prereading skills to improve her intelligence. They retire, as every other couple, to mutually satisfying lovemaking through the night.

Perhaps this portrait of Superdad seems slightly ridiculous. Perhaps you think the myth of Supermom has received a lot more press, and that Superdad is fairly far off in the future. The truth is that this particular Superdad is modeled after a very real person who has taken a year from his successful business to cuddle, cook, nurture, and scrub. Paternity leave may soon be considered as valid a reason for time off as maternity leave. Maybe Superdad seems silly to you now, but more and more men will be forsaking the macho image for a domestic one. Superdad was presented so you'll think about your own role stereotypes and your own potential role as a parent.

The "Crisis" of Parenthood

A child brings changes to a marriage. It's gospel. Ask any parent you know. Ask academic researchers. Parenthood has been labeled a "crisis" by some of them, and studies of life satisfaction show dips when the tiny addition is made. Brace yourself for it. But it's my suspicion that the people who feel an unsettling jolt when Junior arrives aren't planners. They probably haven't fantasized about all the ramifications of little footsteps and bigger bills. They most likely weren't really prepared for everything that accompanies parenthood. They are probably just ordinary people—most of whom become parents and resign themselves to coping with problems as they arise. You've anticipated potential pitfalls, so unpleasant surprises will be minimized.

Preparing for Pregnancy

There are some things to do, of course, to get ready for pregnancy and your child. Even before you conceive, it's wise to line up a good obstetrician. Often the hospital in which you deliver will be determined by the obstetrician's privileges, so check into hospitals, too. Also consider options other than hospital birth—some doctors favor home delivery; others think it's risky. Many will go with alternatives if you and your partner meet specific criteria; notably no foreseeable problems with the birth. Cost might be a factor in your choice. Whatever you choose, do it early. An initial prepregnancy examination might reveal conditions or potential problems that can be taken care of before they appear.

Before pregnancy, you might also want to consider genetic counseling, especially if you suspect that you might carry such a disease or tendency. In addition, a woman about to become pregnant should get a complete physical to see if she needs any special preparation for motherhood. Sometimes weight loss, preparation through diet, special exercise to limber muscles, or even a simple change in attitude can prime you for a carefree pregnancy.

Then there's conception itself. "Tonight's the night!" can bring excited quivers of delight or shivers of uncertainty. At least this part of the process is guaranteed to be enjoyable. Or is it? Trying for a child may bring some very *unsensuous* effects on your sex life. That familiar caress may suddenly feel strange, as the purpose changes from recreation to procreation. The pressure to produce can mysteriously stall ovulation, limit sperm delivery, induce impotence, and change lovemaking to a mechanical ritual. The key word, say the therapists, is "relax." Repeating it 50 times before getting into bed may or may not help. A backrub, a soak together amid frothy bubbles in the tub, or an unpressured dinner in front of the fire may be more effective.

Infertility

Let's say you're trying—over and over. Months go by. Nothing happens. You begin to worry. You've now begun a vicious cycle. Your anxiety about being unable to conceive can affect your fertility. And your infertility fuels your worry about the problem. It goes around and around. But the truth is that getting pregnant doesn't happen instantly when you discontinue the Pill or throw away the condoms.

The Pill itself can cause delayed conception, especially if you've been taking it for awhile. The change in hormones can mean no ovulation for several months. Or it can mean that imperfect or too many ova are released. Medical opinion suggests that it's best to use other contraception for about three months after discontinuing the Pill as a precaution against fertilizing a defective egg.

But after at least a year of trying without success, most couples gulp and utter the word: "infertility." Andrologists are doctors who specialize in fertility problems for men; obstetricians and gynecologists are their counterparts for women. There are many tests for finding the source of the problem, and there's a growing number of procedures for correcting them. There's a lot of hope.

Los Angeles fertility specialist Albert Kapstrom, M.D. says most fertility testing can be completed in five to six weeks. Normal procedures include the following. First, an initial exam and an X-ray (to find closed tubes, weakened cervix, benign tumors, or other problems) is prescribed. A test to see if the tubes are open (called Rubin's test) might be recommended. Carbon dioxide can be blown into the uterus, and the tube's resistance to the gas is measured.

Tests on sperm count and female antibodies or allergies to the sperm can also be done. An "after-intercourse test" checks the mucus to see its acidity and the ability of sperm to survive in it. Ovulation can be monitored by examining a basal body temperature chart or through an "endometrial biopsy" or "mini-scrape" of the uterus lining performed by the doctor. Sometimes a hormone profile is indicated if there are questions about thyroid or other hormone levels. Surgery using a small telescope (called an "endoscope") might be recommended to correct pelvic adhesions, tubal blockage, or other abnormalities.

As you can see, continued testing can often pinpoint problems and bring solutions to infertility. More and more is being done to ensure that those who desire children can have them.

Having Children After Age 30

There's a lot of talk about parenthood after age 30, as if it's a new phenomenon, or 30 is over the hill. Women who have their second, third, or subsequent child after the magical age aren't considered so unusual. But if a couple delay their first, well, that's a headline. After all, the myth says, there are three horrible reasons why waiting till 30 means gloom and doom for all concerned: (1) At age 30, pessimists predict, you're too settled in your selfish ways to make room in your lives for a child. (2) At 30, they warn, you're very likely to produce a defective child. (3) After 30, they contend, you're just too dragged out to keep up with the endless patter of little feet.

'Tain't necessarily so. At age 30, lots of modern couples are just getting together, proudly looking back on graduate school, traineeships, and finally starting accelerating careers. If jetting around the country to close a sales deal is "settled"; if moving up from apartment to condo to house is "tied down"; if testing marital waters with a series of loving relationships is "in a rut"; the usual definitions have gone berserk. Getting started in the business of life simply requires longer than it used to. With life expectancies up and forced retirement down, there's more overall time to get going before the long cruise. And peoples' standards of what it takes to be satisfied are becoming more stringent. This may turn out to be for the best. Feeling secure and confident before making serious lifetime commitments can only improve the quality of the marriages and children that result.

As for the accusation that delaying childbearing to 30 or beyond means high risks of unhealthy offspring, again the reply is "wrong." Though doctors may call a woman having her first an "elderly primipara" or "advanced primigravida," there's no reason to take the nomenclature as a pronouncement of danger. While it's true that incidences of Down's syndrome increase with maternal age, chances of having such a child at age 30 are relatively low: one in 885. And with amniocentisis, the process by which a small amount of amniotic fluid is removed and examined for chromosomal abnormalities, the option to discontinue pregnancy is available. Birth defects such as cleft lip, club foot, heart defects, blindness, and mental or emotional illness occur in 1–3 percent of all births. The rate does escalate with maternal age, but most problems appear when the mother is over 40. By age 40–45, the percentages of defects double, to as high as 6 percent, but in most cases, by that time the childbearing decision has been made.

The charge that post-30 couples will be so drained of spunk that they drag behind their swift-footed progeny is immediately dispelled by older parents themselves. Says energetic 65-year-old Joan, looking back on the three children she bore after age 35: "My kids were only a plus. They kept me young. In fact, my youngest, age 23, is still at home. We love having her around. All her activities give me a chance to be in touch with the younger generation." Was raising a houseful of children while in her forties difficult? "Heavens no!" she laughs. "I just went along with it. I got into the carpools and made the cookies for the roommother's bake sale and chauffeured the kids to choir practice. Remember, this was what mothers did in the fifties and sixties, and I enjoyed every moment of it. Life was never dull, and it still isn't!"

How was "elderly" fatherhood for Joan's husband? "He thinks our kids are the greatest. He went to Indian Guides every week with our son. He built a playhouse in the back yard for all three of them to play in. He went crazy on Christmas Eves putting together all those assemble-it-yourself bicycles and electric trains."

Joan continued in her musical, optimistic tone: "If we had it to do over again, we'd do it just the same." Then her advice to couples considering later parenthood: "Do have them. Children will keep you young, just like they did for me."

The message Joan carries is that people over 30 don't have a foot in the grave. In fact, with more career options open to women, they may have one foot planted in the nursery and the other in the court-room—behind the bench. A Los Angeles judge decided on her first child, now age 6, after she passed 30.

"My daughter has been a total joy," the proud mother reports, "and a very special area of my life. I make a point to drive her to school, to have some quiet moments to talk early in the day. Then, after work, I spend at least two hours with her. She eats her dinner, I read to her or we paint, and I bathe her and tuck her in bed. She is my first priority. Then I have dinner with my husband and end up working until 12 or 1 every night."

In just about every peer group at least one member's parents added a child to their lives past age 30. Few of the offspring say that "old age" slowed their folks down or inhibited parenting ability. In fact, U.S. Census figures from June 1978 reveal that just over 7 per-cent of all women who bear children have their first past age 30. This figure covered women between 30 and 59, at the time the survey was taken.

Why *should* you have a child after 30? Because for the first time in your life, *you want one*. Because you've finally resolved those career dilemmas, the struggle to make a down payment on a house, and the need to decide who you are. Because you've found that your relationship with your partner is a solid one, something you can count on. Because you've discovered that without a child, you'll be missing a whole new area of life.

Yes, I'd Like Children — But How Many?

After you've twisted and squirmed about having *any* children, the question of "how many?" seems anticlimactic. "We'll start with one," is the usual reply. Yes, twins and triplets notwithstanding, everyone starts with one. But few stop there. Often it's because myths determine family size in deceitful ways.

Take the myths about only children. "Only children are spoiled." "Only children get lonely." "Only children become conceited and self-centered." Of course, this isn't the story you hear from the adults that became of "only" children. Toni Falbo, sociologist at the University of Texas at Austin, is one of them, and has studied onlies' characteristics. She compared 1,720 college students of assorted birth orders on several types of interpersonal and achievement orientation. The results are a mixture of surprises and "I told you so" confirmations.

In the latter category is the finding on self-centeredness. "Only" children were significantly higher on this item than first, middle, or last siblings—middle children being the least self-centered. Onlies were also significantly higher on internality—a dimension showing that they feel they are the main causes of their own destinies. Conversely, lastborn children were least likely to say they mold their own fates.

Falbo found no significant differences between the birth orders on self-esteem (onlies fell between middle and lastborns); externality (onlies were lowest on this measure of control by outside forces, followed by middle children); and loneliness (minimal differences between birth orders).

Two aspects of achievement orientation were measured: competitiveness and educational aspirations. Most competitive, by a significant margin, were firstborns, followed by middle, only, and lastborn siblings. There were no significant differences in educational aspirations, the birth order of desire for high-level degrees being firstborns, onlies, middle, and lastborn children.

What does all this mean? That the experience of being an only child *is* different from having siblings. But each position in birth order has its own benefits and drawbacks. If you have three, for example, the lastborn appears to have a greater chance of low self-esteem than

others. But the same lastborn is less competitive than his peers—
which may be an advantage leading to fewer ulcers and increased
peace of mind. The point is that parents shouldn't decide on the
number of children they have simply because a certain family size
is "right." Each family size is only "right" in the parents' minds—
not necessarily right for the well-being of the child.

It's generally accepted that "only" children's outlook and
achievement is similar to that of firstborns. The reasoning goes that
both have the exclusive attention of their parents—and that greater
contact with adults means better learning. A child imitating an adult's
speech will sound more articulate than if she copies only an older
brother or sister. A child with the guidance of a parent will catch
onto rules, manners, and developmental tasks faster than if he spends
most of his time playing with other children. A child who receives
her parents' direct attention will feel more special than one whose
time in the limelight is limited.

Think back to your own childhood. It's wagerable that whether
you were a first, middle, last, or only, you look fondly on your own
position and your own family in size. Even if you fought viciously
with all your brothers and sisters, you've probably mellowed to the
point where much of it is laughable. And if you were in the handful
of people who had a truly regretful childhood, it's doubtful that rearranging the birth order of your brothers and sisters would have done
much to change that. Personality means more than ordinal standing.

An only child may have to be inventive to play independently
and to fight off boredom. An only child will probably feel *special*—
not *different* from other children—because he has a unique role in
the family, and all of his parents' attention is focused on him. If this
sounds like a sales pitch for the only child, perhaps it is. It's also an
attempt to squash the idea that if you have *any*, you have to have
two.

Just what is so appealing about having two children? One thing
is the opportunity to have a child of each sex. This assumes, of
course, that there are large differences between children of different
genders. Are little girls sweeter and more docile than boys? Is it your
secret passion to dress up a real, live doll in frills and petticoats? Most
mothers can assure you that girls throw the same temper tantrums as
boys! Unless you're intent on instilling sexist values and customs,

there's little reason to treat a little boy any differently from a little girl. So the need for having "one of each—a boy for you and girl for me" is diminished.

Other reasons for two children are "So they can play with each other"; "So they learn give-and take"; "Because we want to be sure to have a boy to carry on the family name"; and "Because we love children and want to have more of them around." The first three reasons can be debated. The last can't. You need to have that last reason on your own list to justify having more than one.

But even loving children doesn't justify having an unplanned number of them. Each child needs to be individually evaluated for the role he or she will play in the family, for the amount of direct parental time he or she will receive, for his or her impact on everything and everyone. Each child should be wanted as a unique individual, a personality—not just as the first or third or fifth.

"My parents had so many kids, they ran out of names," one workshop participant shared. "We had a happy family, but I was the sixth of eight children. I saw my mother as a distant authority figure. I was usually disciplined or tickled or ignored more by my older brother than anyone else. He took over my parents' job, in a way, and took charge of me. Looking back, it's rather cruel for a child to feel that she's raised by a brother rather than a parent." This is only one view, of course, but there are other reasons for limiting family size as well.

Foremost among them is concern for conservation and the realization that the resources of our earth are finite. In this sense, two or three can't grow up as cheaply as one. A second child uses twice the disposable Pampers, twice the nonbiodegradable plastic doo-dads, twice the number of baby food jars as one. And that's just in infancy. Think of all the toilet flushes, wash cycles, and shower rinses that a person creates throughout a lifetime.

These are some of the reasons that overpopulated countries like China and India are offering incentives and threats to get people to limit their family size. The one-child family is the new Chinese ideal, and those who go along with this suggestion are rewarded by the government with higher job productivity, government subsidies, and an overall better quality of life.

Many Americans disdain the applicability of this to their own lives. "I've got enough money to support them, so why *shouldn't* I have them?" they challenge. "No child of mine will go without, so why deprive them of existence? My having one or two more won't affect the starving multitudes in India." That's what I call a narrow-minded view. We all do live on the same earth.

In answering the "how many?" question, it is wise to consider the retort "We'll start with one." If you are sensitive to the needs, desires, and changes of your first, you may be completely satisfied, able to use up all your parenting "want" on a single huggable person. If that's not enough, and you've loved your experience so much you'd like more of it, consider the next child. And use this book again.

12

Decision Without Guilt: The Option to Remain Childfree

So you've hemmed, hawed, and debated. And it comes down to the fact that you can't foresee ever wanting to have a child of your own. You decide, once and for all, that you will continue as a non-parent—and you decide to act upon it. What are the choices?

One, of course, is to continue using the birth-control method that's worked for you. Because couples who ultimately decide to remain childfree don't want to take chances, they usually have been careful in the past to contracept. Christine and Don were one such couple. Once their decision was made, they talked with me at my office about their next steps.

"We always had a hunch that children wouldn't fit into our lives," Christine explained. "So we were insistent on using the most reliable contraceptive available. That's why I've been on the Pill for nine years. I joke about it, but really, I'm afraid they'll suddenly find some horrible long-term consequence. I tell friends, 'I'll wake up one day and my arm will fall off,' and the nervous chuckles that follow confirm that, indeed, all agree there is a risk of something dire happening. That's one major reason why making the commitment to nonparenthood is important: so we can take more definite steps to ensure that there's never an 'accident.' "

"That's why I volunteered to have a vasectomy," Don interjected. "I'll admit that I'm scared of the knife, but the thought of Chris taking those hormones another 15 years is scary. I care enough about her that my temporary discomfort is unimportant." He exchanged glances with his wife.

"But the thing I hate is closing doors," she admitted. "I hate to make an irreversible commitment on anything, even if it seems right now like the logical thing to do."

"Why don't you consider a sperm bank?" I asked. They grew intent and asked for more information, surprised that their door to future options could be left ajar.

Sperm banks have received attention because of a recent attempt to collect semen of Nobel Peace Prize winners for insemination in intelligent recipients. The goal was to increase the chances that a childless woman requiring artificial insemination would produce a brilliant child. Debate has bumped around the idea that it's morally wrong to create a "super race" and that it's none of humanity's business what kind of child is created, so sperm banks have gained a rather unsavory popular reputation.

Sperm banks actually began as a sensitive solution to a touchingly sad problem. Men with testicular cancer, about to undergo radiation or other therapy which was likely to render them sterile, were given the chance to preserve samples of active sperm. The option was of particular value to men in their teens or twenties, afraid that all possibility to have children might be lost. They were allowed to fill vials with semen, which was frozen in liquid nitrogen to the point where all molecular movement stopped. The sperm could be stored in "cryogenic" tanks, insurance that despite sterility, fatherhood through artificial insemination could occur.

In the late 1960s, vasectomy increased in popularity, and storage of sperm "just in case" became reality for such patients. The register of sperm banks is now larger, as the price for deposit and storage becomes less prohibitive. Sperm banks are also used as a reservoir for anonymous donor sperm, used to artificially inseminate women whose partners are unable to impregnate them. In some cases, several donations of a husband's sperm may be frozen and collected, with the hope that by concentrating the dose, it would be possible to overcome a low sperm count.

Christine and Don selected a sperm bank affiliated with a group of fertility doctors at a local hospital. The initial deposit fee was $150, and Don was allowed to leave as many vials as he wished, though the doctors suggested that a minimum of 12 be stored. "I was embarrassed, to say the least," Don recalls. "They had me go into a bathroom they called the 'masterbatorium.' Ha Ha. It had an aquarium with colorful salt water fish. I could watch the sea anemone's tentacles sway in the bubbling water. I also had before me a stack of erotic magazines meant to titilate my fancy. But I felt so inhibited I stayed in there almost an hour before finally producing."

"I waited in the waiting room, though I was invited to assist the process," Christine added. "I probably felt as weird as Don did, and tried to concentrate on an old copy of *Town and Country*. I kept wondering why it was taking so long. I thought men were supposed to be able to do it any time, any place." The pair giggled.

"I returned to make each of the deposits. They suggest you don't have sex for a couple of days before each visit to guarantee that there's a high concentration of sperm in the ejaculate," Don explained.

"We saw the cryogenic tub where they were going to store our sperm," Christine said. "It's a silver cylinder, about four-and-a-half feet high. I kept wondering what would happen if the power went off. Would we lose our potential child?" She grinned. "But they showed us the back-up power unit. They said that healthy babies have been made from sperm stored as long as ten years. And with animals, the length of successful storage time has been 20 years longer."

"But there's no reason why it shouldn't last forever," Don qualified. "The molecules are actually in a state of suspended animation. Nothing's happening at all, so really, there's no way they can deteriorate."

Is that all there is to it? "No, we can't just forget about our 12 vials, and assume our heritage is assured. Every year they'll send us a bill for $50, our annual storage fee. So every year they *force* us to reevaluate whether we pay the $50 or let our claim to posterity just thaw out. We have to annually weigh the likelihood of whether or not we'll ever want a child."

"My guess is that in five years or so, we won't have to feel so insecure about our decision. We'll probably save the cash and stick by our commitment," Christine predicted. "But on the other hand. . . . " We shared a hearty laugh.

After the sperm was stored, Don faced his vasectomy. "I had gone for presterilization counseling," he recalls, "where they told me the chances for reversal and satisfied themselves that my choice was well-thought-out. They asked Chris to sign a witness form, although they didn't require a wife's signature or anything for me to have the operation." He showed me a booklet on vasectomy they gave him, with diagrams on where the inch-long incision is made in the scrotum, and pinpointing the vas deferens leading from each of the testicles to the seminal vesicles and the urethra. The booklet was written in such elementary language that it was of little use to Don and Christine.

"I had questions about autoimmunity," Don confessed. "I'd read that a man can produce antibodies to the sperm entering his system after the vasectomy, and that this can bring unpleasant reactions— a sickness I just didn't know enough about. I was told that there is an autoimmune reaction in about a third of the cases, but usually there are no serious consequences. The main problem occurs when the man has a vasovasostomy—an operation to rejoin the severed vas."

Don was talking about a new type of surgery to reconnect the vas deferens in order to restore fertility. More couples than I would've expected have come to the workshops wondering if they should go through with "vasectomy reversal" given the cost (usually around $6,000) and the discomfort of surgery. Cappy Miles Rothman, M.D. claims that with new microsurgery techniques, 90 percent of his operations are successful, with sperm again flowing through the tubes. Despite this, his patients only achieve a 60-percent pregnancy rate. He attributes this difference to autoimmunity.

Dr. Rothman showed me videotapes of healthy sperm and some that had been "knocked out" by the man's immunity system. The healthy sperm wriggled their polliwog-like tails vigorously, swimming in a one-directional pattern. But sperm from a reconnected vas looked confused. Some wriggled intermittantly; others swam around in circles. The problem arises when the tired sperm can't penetrate the woman's cervical mucus to get to the waiting egg. So even after a costly and perhaps painful vasovasostomy operation, some men are permanently sterile.

That didn't matter much to Don. "Even if Chris should die—heaven forbid—and I found another woman—also an awful thought—I probably wouldn't want to have kids. It's a commitment I've made now about the life I want to lead." Then he added sheepishly, "especially with the insurance of the sperm bank."

Christine and Don's concerns raised four issues. One was the advisability of using birth control pills as a permanent means of birth control ("Too risky," decided this couple). A second was the option of a sperm bank for preservation of sperm "just in case" some unforeseen quirk brought on regret about acting on the nonparenthood choice. The third topic was vasectomy—the male sterilization operation chosen by a large number of couples because of its relative ease, low cost, and wide availability, as compared with forms of female sterilization. Lastly, the option of vasovasostomy or "vasectomy reversal" arose as a means to undo an out-of-date commitment. The point is that deciding to remain childfree involves a *series* of decisions, rather than just one. And no decision is without its drawbacks.

Here is a note on sterilization for women. The fallopian tubes are cut or cauterized so that eggs cannot pass through to the uterus for implantation. Instead, they are harmlessly absorbed by the body. The *culpotomy* is a vaginal tubal ligation, technically simpler than sterilizations requiring abdominal incisions, but with a higher complication rate. Abdominal approaches are used in the *minilaparotomy* and the *laparoscopy*. Both are usually done in a hospital setting, though local anesthetic may be used. Usually no hospital stay is necessary, and patients can resume most normal activity within 48 hours.

After her laparoscopy, I talked with Laura, unmarried but certain she never wanted children. "They kept trying to change my mind," she recalled, "to test me. They asked what would I do if I married a man who desperately wanted children. My answer, of course, is that any man who wanted me would have to accept this aspect of my character. My decision not to have children is as much 'me' as my dislike for avocados or my green eyes. There's no compromise on some things.

"The people at the clinic kept insisting I was too young to know my future for the next 10 or 15 years," Laura went on. "I replied that I may not know the future, but I had come to know myself—and I knew that I just did not care for children. Finally they were satisfied that I wouldn't throw a lawsuit in their faces in a couple years." Laura then described her experience.

"Before I went in, they did several tests—blood, urine, X rays. For the surgery, I was out. The doctors made two tiny incisions—one in my belly button and the other lower. One was used to inject carbon dioxide to 'blow up' my insides so the surgeon could see more clearly. It was also used for the laparascope, the tiny microscope used to view the area. The second incision was used to insert a tool that coagulated my tubes." Laura seemed detached describing the details, as if none of it happened to her. Then her posture shifted.

"Afterwards I was groggy, but I was driven home and went to sleep. I felt all distended—like someone had put a balloon under my skin, but that gradually went away in a few days. The incisions were only slightly sore. I took aspirin 'just in case' but I probably didn't need to." She grinned as she pulled down her corduroy pants to show her tiny red scarline.

"The only difference in my life is that now I feel liberated. No more worries about accidents or doing things to my body which may be unhealthy."

Would she recommend sterilization to other women who don't want children? "Definitely," Laura replied without hesitation. "But they'd better be 100-percent sure, because there's really no reversal rate." The rate for complications from laparoscopy is low, statistics show, with the number decreasing with the experience of the surgeon. For further information, see Hatcher, et al., *Contraceptive Technology 1980–81* (New York: Irvington Publishers, 1980).

Harriet and Max also chose sterilization, but they couldn't decide which one of them should undergo the operation. "I'm extremely squeamish," Max admitted to me. "The thought of going to the dentist for just a check-up—much less any dental work—sends me into a panic for weeks in advance. I have to really work up to it, every day repeating 'It won't hurt, it won't hurt.' The idea that someone would take a scalpel to my balls is petrifying."

"But on the other hand, vasectomy is alot easier than tubal ligation," Harriet balanced. "There are many more risks with a general anesthetic than with the local Max would receive." The couple debated the psychological versus the physical risks, alternating cringes with logic. Finally a decision was made.

"All right, I'll just get myself psyched up for it, that's all," Max resolved. "Beneath my lily-livered cowardice, I know that I don't want Harriet in any kind of danger. I'll just learn to live with the coming event."

"And we can store sperm in case things change," Harriet added. "I know they won't, but this way both of us are covered." Max had his vasectomy and banked his sperm.

"It really didn't hurt," he told me two weeks after the procedure. "The only pain lasted about two seconds when the anesthetic needle went in. I'd braced myself for agony, and in a way, I was kind of disappointed it was such a snap. I couldn't get all the sympathy for my bravery that way." He chuckled. "The doctor told me of a vasectomy club where the men wear pins made of removed sections of vas encased in resin. I told him he didn't have to preserve mine— I have plenty of lapel ornaments already."

Let's say you've chosen nonparenthood and have scheduled the vasectomy. It's your own private decision, but other people in your life may not see it that way. They know that you don't have any children and they may have been bugging you to conform to their views. Here are a few ways to handle others' reactions.

"We lied," one woman confessed. "We told them that I'm sterile." She giggled with delight at the deception. "No one has ever raised the issue again. At the time, they blushed and muttered, 'I'm sorry,' and didn't even have the guts to pry into the details!" She referred to her parents-in-law, whose hope for grandchildren had colored their every word.

Another woman said she'd lied, too. "Only we told my sister and her husband that Bill was impotent! When I left, I couldn't stop laughing! They have such pity for us—as if I must be the most frustrated woman on earth!"

Then there's Christine and Don's way: "We told the truth. We said that we'd decided not to have children because we didn't have time for them. Sure, we get a lot of questions, but I'd rather answer them honestly than play some charade."

Combating the Accusations

You've said it: you're not going to have children. You're going to remain a nonparent and won't change your mind. What reaction will you most likely hear? A negative one. Here are some strategies for answering some of the accusations people disappointed by your decision will probably hurl.

1. *"You're selfish!"* If you truly believe you *are* selfish, say so. Admitting this ought to quiet your critics. Parents and nonparents are both equally selfish and unselfish. Nonparents are unselfish when they know they would not make good parents and don't want a child to suffer. They're caring when they fear that they'd provide their own children with a repeat of the unpleasant upbringing they endured. They're responsible when they recognize that children involve drawbacks and realize that these would become hurdles in their lives. It takes a far more conscious act to contradict the pronatalist expectation than to accept it. Those who are deliberately childfree should be applauded for their courage and conviction.

Parents may actually be the selfish ones. While they often sound altruistic, selfish motives tend to influence their choice. UCLA Public Health Professor Judith Blake's research shows that children are valued for the social kudos they confer on parents. Friends and relatives "ooh and ahh" the ability of Mom and Dad to produce such a perfect specimen.

In a *Population Reference Bureau Bulletin* (April 1977), Thomas Esplanshade reports on a cross-cultural study of the advantages of having children. The selfish returns to parents of "happiness, love, and companionship" rank at the top of the advantages across all races in the Pacific nations surveyed. Then 21 percent of middle-class Hawaiian Caucasians cited "personal development of the parent" as a prime benefit of children. There's no doubt that people have children to get something out of it. Cuddling and dimple-pinching would not be appealing or worthwhile if the subject were an inert doll. The investment is made in return for love, a sense of accomplishment, a role in life, a mark on the world. Parents have kids for themselves.

So when you're termed "selfish," give back "It takes one to know one," and watch the ire fly.

2. *"You must not like kids."* It almost sounds un-American not to like children. Must a normal human being enjoy partially-baked personalities as much as fully-cooked ones? Your first retort should be "Not 24 hours a day," or "Maybe I like adults better." Your justification can include serious reasons or a quote á la W. C. Fields: "Anyone who hates children and dogs can't be all bad."

But the truth is that many people who choose to remain childfree *do* like children. They put their extra time and energy into the alternative activities listed in this chapter. They may have had a bear of a time deciding between whether or not to have some of their own. Indicting you for not liking children can be a cruel misjudgment of reality.

A more reasonable approach might be just to explain your views: "We have such respect for parenthood and for the importance of the responsibility, that we wouldn't want to take it on unless we were sure we could give it our all.

3. *"You're defying nature."* If God had wanted us to have unlimited numbers of kids, why did He give us contraceptives? A Roman Catholic might reply that artificial devices to prevent conception are unnatural and that we shouldn't play with them. But human beings, children of the Almighty, made them and whether or not you approve, we have them. And it means we can choose whether or not a child is the inevitable result of sexual relations.

Our lives are filled with unnatural things. We grind wood pulp and put it into ice cream. We fly like birds on hang gliders and mechanical gasoline-eating monsters. We cut open injured people, changing otherwise certain death to prolonged life. Who's to say any of these things are more unnatural than deciding not to have children?

Besides, we're human beings who act on intellect, not mysterious drives. "The mothering instinct" was a straw early psychologists grabbed to explain why women had children. The concept was never proven to be anything other than a theory. Freud linked it to penis envy. Then early feminist and social scientist Leta Hollingworth suggested in 1916 that the mothering instinct is a trait normally distributed in the population, like grumpiness, intelligence, height, or manual dexterity. Some people have a lot of it; others have none. Most people fall somewhere in the middle of the continuum. Just tell critics that it's not natural for *you* to be a parent—or else the instinct would win out.

4. *"You'll end the family name."* This is the male chauvinist's lament. There are a lot of assumptions to be blasted with this one because in America and most European countries only males traditionally passed on the family name. (This hasn't been the case in Hispanic or many other cultures.) "I always laugh at that one," said a nonparent named John Smith. "No one would miss another Smith. There are towns filled with them." The same is true for Millers, Joneses, Johnsons, and Jacksons. There are proud lines settled within each name, yes, but one less of each would not mean the title's death.

There's also the implicit assumption that only the male child retains the family name—but not so anymore. People take new names; they combine them, they hyphenate them. Even if you did have children, there's no guarantee that an identifiable shred of "the family name" would survive. Maybe you read about the fellow who took a string of numbers for his name or the artist, Judy Chicago, who felt an affinity for the city.

Nowadays, daughters also carry on the family name. Women are keeping their names in increasing numbers as they rise in shining business careers. Said Irene, "When we first got married in 1974, I hyphenated my original last name with my husband's. But that was too long, and he never took *my* family name, so I just dropped his. I feel much more comfortable, because my original name is my identity." And her old-fashioned parents are happy about their new-found immortality; they had three daughters and no sons.

The issue goes beyond the grouping of letters for most people, though. The thing they want carried on is the family look, the family characteristics, the family business or reputation. And the main goal is having all these things identified with them. They want credit for what their heirs accomplish. In a sense, that's understandable.

It's also archaic. People are no longer identified by what their grandparents did. Nowadays they're tagged only by what *they* achieve. There's nothing wrong with feeling proud of your family tree—and nothing wrong with preferring the branches intact—but somehow critics want to put that value on *you*.

A Resource for the Childfree

A group was created just to support people who decide parenthood is not for them. Some members of this group got together one afternoon to discuss their reasons for the choice and how they cope with it.

"People inevitably ask why we don't have them," Frank admitted. "That always bothers me. Nobody automatically asks them why they *did* have kids. And I point that out. Usually that shuts them up, but we do tell them our feelings."

"We do it for another reason, too," Frank's wife, Nora said, pulling her brown bangs away from her eyes. "We do it because we have an opportunity to plug the notion of options, to enlighten people that stereotypes aren't right for everyone. Often our listeners end up revealing that they shouldn't have had the children they did, that they shouldn't have become parents at the time of their lives when they did. They all begin their confessions with 'I love my children, but . . . '."

" . . . But since I had them, you ought to also," Frank ended. "We are proud of our lives. We don't need children to enrich what we have. And we're proud to be role-models for others who may just be discovering the childfree option."

The discussion was going on in the Los Angeles office of the National Alliance for Optional Parenthood, a nonprofit group founded in 1972 to promote active childbearing decision making and private support for those choosing to remain childfree. The organization is now headquartered in Washington, D.C., where its members aim to influence law, policy, and media. They believe there shouldn't be any bias—either for or against children—in official pronouncements or personal attitudes.

Originally, NAOP was a support group for people who chose to remain childless. In 1972, pronatalist propaganda was rampant and often unrecognized. Childfree couples needed a respite from the barage of questions and accusations. Gradually, however, social stigmas eased, and NAOP could focus on changing traditional expectations.

If you decide not to become a parent, you may find this group to be a helpful resource and may want to educate others under the auspices of this established organization. In Los Angeles, NAOP maintains a library of clippings relating to parenthood, pregnancy and birth, contraception, and population. Speakers volunteer to talk about teenage parenthood, making the choice, and the childfree life style. And the materials in this book were used and discussed behind the door bearing the NAOP logo.

"We get a lot of students doing reports on nonparenthood," reports L.A. NAOP president Dave Dismore. "More and more people seem to be affiliating with the option—and many of them are parents."

The point is that growing numbers of people are choosing not to have children. In fact, 18.4 percent of married women aged 25–34 years old are childfree, according to U.S. census figures for June 1978. This is up from just 12.05 percent in 1970 and 9.45 percent in 1965. You're not alone, and thousands of parents and other childfree couples are more willing than ever to support your right to choose nonparenthood.

One of the main objections to foregoing children is the potential for regret once it's too late to have a child of your own. "Will I wish I hadn't passed up one of life's most precious experiences?" "I hate to just let the clock tick me past menopause, when I'll have no recourse."

But most people fail to realize that there's always possible regret for charging ahead and having a child. What if you become a parent, only to discover you're not suited to the task?

Realize that there will be times of doubt, that you'll wonder what life would've been like had you been a parent. Realize that this is natural. Realize that avoiding regret is a rotten reason to have a child.

Alternatives to Childbearing

So what can you do about it? You can get the pleasure of children in many ways other than by having them yourself. You can weave alternatives into and out of your life as you choose, without taking responsibility for a child for the rest of your days.

1. *Leading a children's group.*   A weekly commitment may be all it takes to satisfy your urge to be with children. Boy or Girl Scout troops, Bluebirds and Campfire girls, Sunday Schools, and recreational classes need leaders and teachers. You can benefit from this type of contact with children because you can begin on-going relationships without too much involvement. What you will do, though, is spend time on your own preparing games, crafts, fieldtrips, and fundraisers. You'll keep track of 25 nature study badges and 15 order sheets for cookies, candy bars, or raffle tickets. It's many hours of hustling for the reward of a few hours per week of smiles, chases around the refreshment table, and achievements braiding lanyards. It can be a lot of fun to successfully coordinate a camp-out and teach kids the traditional songs to sing around the fire. You'll meet not only children but also their parents, and you'll also come into contact with the bureaucracy that administers the group you supervise.

2. *Once-in-a-while treats.*   I know of a busy fashion designer in Los Angeles who cares about kids—and she especially cares about the ones living in the ghetto and barrio, the ones whose folks can't drive them to scout meetings or afford the uniforms that would help them fit in with other kids. So this lady called the Department of Public Social Services and offered to help.

She didn't want to just write out a check and consider her duty done. She wanted to feel inside that she had given of herself to these kids. She wanted personal, direct contact. So she chartered a bus and hauled a couple dozen housing project residents to Disneyland for a day. The kids had a great time and so did she. She held their hands and bought them sticky cotton candy. She talked to them about her life and theirs. She wanted to take them all back with her to Beverly Hills.

The phone numbers of agencies serving children litter telephone books. Most charities are more than pleased if you'd volunteer, even one afternoon a month, to help in a special project. Of course they'd prefer a more regular donation of time, but they understand your desire to help and can provide lists of children who long for the attention.

3. *Foster parenthood.*   A longer-term (but not lifetime) commit-ment to a child can be found in foster parenthood. Children are placed in homes for care when their own families are unable to pro-vide an appropriate environment or if they are awaiting permanent placement. There's a big risk that you may become overly attached to your temporary child and will find parting quite painful. But there are many compensations of having a child full-time under your care. It's as close to actual parenthood as possible.

In most cases, county agencies reimburse the expenses of the child in your home. They require in return that an adult be present whenever the child might require it—usually precluding both part-ners' full-time employment. Being a foster parent also means that you need space in your home to accommodate an infant or a teenager and that you can handle the emotional problems of children facing traumas in their lives. For example, some daughters are taken from homes where their fathers have sexually abused them; toddlers may be placed when a single mother finds she just can't cope with par-enthood. While this may provide the foster parent with a psycholog-ical challenge, there is also a special reward knowing you were there when a child was most vulnerable.

4. *Becoming a Big Brother or Sister.*   Adults who want regular, intense contact with a child without 24-hour responsibilities may find it through this nonprofit group. Preteenagers are the major group of children available for the enrichment of a special adult's attention. Most come from loving families who are simply unable to devote much time to recreational and social needs. They may have limited funds for nonessential expenses, and the treats you provide can make the difference between a dull and exciting learning experience for a child.

Barbara, a single mother, became a Big Sister when her own son was finishing high school. "Here's Elsa's picture," she says proudly, unfolding her leather wallet. Glowing with fat, healthy cheeks, the Hispanic youngster in the school photo seemed to have all life could offer. "She has four brothers and sisters and is in the eighth grade," Barbara continued. "Her parents are very nice—I had them all over for dinner."

What do Barbara and Elsa do together? "I spend every Sunday with her," Barbara explained. "Sometimes we go to the museum;

other times to concerts or to a movie. Sometimes I just have her over and we talk or play a board game. The main thing is that we communicate. I ask her about her homework and her girlfriends. I make sure that she gets a nice gift on her birthday and Christmas. Sometimes I take her out shopping and buy her a small item of clothing, but nothing extravagent. I don't want her to seem favored over her brothers and sisters, and I don't want to embarass her family. I also don't want her to expect anything more than my affection and interest." From the long look Barbara gave the photo, her fondness was apparent.

5. *Working with children.*   Everyone's heard of an old maid teacher who grew old instructing her roomful of surrogate children because she didn't have any of her own. This fabled creature was subject to a bevy of stereotypes: that mothering is an instinct; that teaching is a woman's job because females are naturally equipped to work with children. But the essence of the image may be accurate. Working with children by day can satisfy a good deal of desire for nurturing.

One teacher I knew fell in love with each of her charges. She enjoyed preparing activities she knew the kids would love. She occasionally took one of her 7-year-olds on an outing to the circus, a baseball game, or the beach. Every day she saw the children progress and grow. Watching the simplicity of their logic and the innocence in their discoveries made her job one she treasured.

Scads of careers center around contact with children: daycare worker, nurse, speech therapist, pediatrician. It's unfortunate that many of the jobs caring for and teaching children are low-paying and of modest status. That condition remains from more sexist times when "women's work" was undervalued. After all, mothers dedicate their full-time-plus to the task without monetary remuneration and government benefits.

Some jobs dealing with the general public include substantial amounts of contact with children. Salespeople accept cash from hands of all sizes. Anyone working in the home—from census takers to washing machine repairers to domestic assistants—will have at least brief moments with the young set. People who work in settings like amusement parks, roller rinks, libraries, and parks will probably cater to small customers.

6. *Pets*. "Our dog is like our child," you may have heard couples like Rebecca and John confess. "He sleeps on our bed and knows when we're leaving, coming home, or when it's time for dinner." Pets can bring many of the benefits of a child with few of the drawbacks. They're warm and responsive and will give love unconditionally. They don't require baby-sitters or expensive layettes or feedings in the middle of the night.

They also don't progress past childhood. An aging dog can still be your "baby." You'll never see a pet learn to read or perform in the school play, but you'll definitely know warmth and loyalty (at least from dogs) and recognition. Cats may be more independent, but they too respond with affection. Each pet has a personality for you to know, accommodate, and admire. With a pet, you won't be alone.

Pets do require attention. You can't forget to feed them or neglect their emotional needs (otherwise you'll find a chewed sofa). The amount you give, though, is very small compared with the rewards you can receive.

7. *Friends' and relatives' children.*   There's nothing warmer than being the "Uncle Mike" who always comes with a surprise for his nephew. If you live near people with children, you can make regular visits a ritual in your life. In single-parent families, you can be a second adult to whom the child relates. Your ideas can provide balancing opinions on issues enlarging the range of experience of all concerned. A child can't have too much loving attention. Indulge a desire to teach and nurture by babysitting frequently (giving parents much appreciated free time) and being available at birthdays, holidays, and vacations as part of the family.

"We're always taking care of my niece," one woman commented, "and it's been exciting seeing her grow from a senseless blob into an intelligent conversationalist. We feel so secure in our relationship with her—it's as though she were ours, just in a more limited way. And our attachment to Betsy has strengthened my relationship with my sister enormously."

Then there are stepchildren. Recall Susan's case. "We have a very different situation, but like you, one in which the child I've become involved with isn't my own. Wayne had children by a former marriage. They don't live with us, but I've come to know them well from occasional weekends and vacations. They've been super about accepting me, and I've been able to have many of the benefits of their love without their constant presence in my life. It's a very steady warmth—a bond that is felt underneath what I do, every day."

If you've chosen to remain childfree, you need not remove children from your life. The seven alternatives to parenthood above each offer means to enjoy contact with youth free from lifelong pressures and financial burdens. When you're a parent, you can't escape responsibility. There are times when the child must come before all else. As a volunteer, substitute, or temporary influence, though, you have the option to call it quits when your involvement becomes more than you'd like it to be.

Deciding Not to Decide

We've talked about the decision to have kids and to remain permanently childfree. We've discussed how to get a vasectomy, see your role as a parent, fight nasty accusations, and handle antinatalism. But what do you do in the meantime if you just can't make up your mind? Some people continue to reevaluate everything logically until their brains shrivel and indigestion growls at every meal. These people often have trouble making any huge life decision.

Relax. Keep postponing. Usually the major cause of anxiety is fear of missing something important. But look at your life in the meantime! *This* is life! Your current life is a good gauge to predict how your life will be later. Is anything huge missing?

When the answer is "Yes, and what's missing is a child," then move. If it's biologically too late, then include more of the childbearing alternatives mentioned here in your life. You never have to be totally without children. No, the child you see regularly won't be your own, and yes, having one *is* "different" than being with someone else's child, but you've led your life in a way parents you know couldn't. You've spent active years the way you wanted; you've lived in freedom and tranquility the way that was right for you. No sense regretting. Keep moving onward to the things that satisfy most.

In the meantime, until that lightening bolt of clarity zaps you between the eyes, reevaluate the situation periodically. Take out these materials once every six months and go through them again. Make a list of how circumstances in your life have changed since you last used the questionnaires. Note if your views have changed too.

"Six months ago I was working at a low-paying job," a client told me. "I had such disdain for materialists who earned a lot of money for work I considered less worthwhile than mine. Then I was offered a job as director of public relations for a large firm. I happen to love it, and I'm making double the salary I was before. Suddenly a color TV and dishwasher don't look so disgusting anymore."

This woman learned a law of consumerism: "need" rises to meet the amount of money available to spend. Her values had changed with her circumstances, and the palatability of using some of her wealth for a child improved.

One reason couples choose *not* to decide is because they find their lives and relationships in a state of not-yet-satisfying flux. People about to receive a doctorate in history may fear a lack of available jobs. Those floating in a secretarial career may know underneath there's something better and want to try a more fulfilling path. Couples with teetering marriages prefer to regain balance and stability before adding the enormous responsibility of a child. These are excellent reasons not to decide right now about having a child. It's much better to settle external problems before undertaking new demands.

So what *do* you do about these things? Set a deadline for tackling all those "I'd rather not face it" issues. Then just charge ahead. For example, Joanne didn't know what she wanted to do with her life. She was bored in an administrative assistant job and knew she had talents that were unused. "But it was so much easier just to go along day-to-day. The search for an intangible reward just seemed too frightening, like something I should approach 'some day' rather than on my well-deserved weekends of fun. Each day rushing off to work, getting out correspondence, setting up meetings, running around to the grocery store, cleaners, and choir practice left me in a heap. Most nights I just stared at the tube, reluctant to move." A tale all too familiar. She thought having a child would end her feeling trapped in the office and allow more time to think about a long-term career. Her husband was satisfied with their life-style but said he would support her choice to have a child. Joanne's blond-framed face lit up.

"Then one day I ran into a girlfriend from college. She had written a book and was in a department store signing copies. I couldn't believe it. We came from the same beginnings, and she was successful and famous. I was just a servant to an uncaring organization. I got angry at myself. Every page of her novel I read made me feel worse and worse. I became determined to straighten out my life before it was too late."

So Joanne went to the counseling office of the college she had attended. She was given a battery of interest, personality, and achievement tests to help the counselor steer her toward possibilities she might explore. She called her author friend and set up a lunch date to talk about the kinds of experiences that led to such a successful career. She thought about all the activities she liked to do, especially those for which she had received compliments.

"I loved staging parties for friends, birthdays, or other celebrations," Joanne reported. "I loved making the invitations original and memorable, planning out the menu with special touches, setting up the place settings and timing it all so it went smoothly. Because of this, I considered running a restaurant, but decided that was too expensive and risky. Then I came upon the idea of a specialized party catering service."

Joanne discussed this and other options with the counselor. Her tests revealed a knack for dealing with people and superior organizational skills. "I guess that's why I was so valuable as an administrative assistant, Joanne shrugs. "I could always pull off the biggest meetings with the minimum of fuss." To learn all aspects of the catering business, Joanne signed on as an assistant with a large catering firm. She plans to strike out on her own in about two years. Her dilemma about having a child is resolved. "It was more that I wanted to be independent and happy in what I was doing than the desire to have a child. The permanence and newness of parenthood was what attracted me, not the actual duties of motherhood."

So congratulate yourself for postponing the choice to feel more sure about the future. Don't brood about your inability to decide. Feel comforted that everyone is ambivalent to some extent on this question. Just remain confident that when you really want a child, you'll feel it.

When Conflict Can't Be Resolved

In some cases all the list-making, reading, pleading, questionnaire-checking and emotions-evaluating can't solve your problem: you and your partner want different things. When she wants a child and he doesn't, there's no compromise. You can't confer parenthood on only one partner in a couple. Being childfree and a full-time parent is an impossibility. In this conflict situation, you're faced with hard choices. As you recall, Barry and Michele confronted them.

"It comes down to having a child with Barry or leaving to find someone else who wants one, Michele defined. "We've hashed this out now so that both of us are clear on each others' values and flexibility on this issue. Basically, there isn't any room to move. I want a child now, and Barry doesn't want any. I've gotten past the crying point. I know what I have to do."

"Yes, it's been affecting our relationship more and more," Barry conceded. "This is very difficult for me, because we've had such a loving relationship. There's really nothing else wrong with our marriage. But we're steeling ourselves for the future. I want Michele to be happy, and I hope she will see there's happiness in her future with me."

"I'm afraid I would resent Barry more and more for depriving me of the child I want," Michele admitted. "We just want to make this transition as smooth as possible." Her voice cracked, and the calm facade broke as tears gathered in her eyes.

The next step is to break up.

That's it—the extreme—the worst that can happen when the decision about having a child is unresolvable. If you think you might be headed in that direction, here are some suggestions and considerations.

First, get counseling. Local mental health centers provide services on a sliding-fee scale. Religious organizations, such as Jewish Family Services and others, also have reasonable rates. Private psychologists, psychiatrists, marriage, child, and family counselors are other resources. Shop around to find someone who is sensitive to this issue. Talking out your concerns with a professional can help you clarify your positions, and you can receive feedback from someone trained to explain all the options.

Secondly, do some weighing of the following considerations:

- What is your investment in your relationship? How does your bond with your partner weigh against your desire to have a child? The longer you have been together, the more difficult it may seem to start over with someone else. Are you dependent on your partner? Could you make it on your own for the rest of your life if you were unable to find a new partner who agreed with your views on childbearing?

- How important is your desire to have or not have children? Is it more or less important than having a secure relationship, being happy in work, being economically comfortable, or continuing what you have now? Rate your position about childbearing in comparison with the other concerns in your life. If it's in the middle or lower down on your list, perhaps with time you will change your mind. How feasible is a future change?

- At your age, what is the likelihood of finding someone new? The partner who wants the child must assess time constraints. Men have fewer pressures to hurry up and find a new mate, since their reproductive capacity continues indefinitely (though sperm production does decrease with age). Women need to look at their current relationships with men to assess how easy it would be to begin new friendships. How picky about traits would you be? "I know it would be hard for me to find someone new," one woman confessed, "because I'd want someone just like Morrie," the husband whom she left. Look at your opportunities for meeting new partners. Talk to single friends to judge whether you would feel at ease dating. Consider the reality of the process of replacing a loving relationship with another just as warm.

- How will your life change if you split? Can you handle dividing your, possessions or moving into a new apartment or house? What if you saw your partner after the split? Would you be jealous of his or her new relationships? (Conversely, how would your partner take to these changes?) How would your relationships with in-laws and mutual friends change? How do all these changes balance against your desire to have or not have a child?

If you do have a loving relationship with your partner, it's clearly worth some effort to maintain it. Fantasize about living without children (if you want them) and imagine all the things you could accomplish with the time you'd have free. Imagine all the places you can visit, the standard of living you can enjoy, the attention you'll have from your partner. If you're against childbearing, motivate yourself to see the intriguing side of children—their developing, changing personalities. Think of how the caring qualities of a hug take on a whole new meaning when they eminate from a grateful, tiny child.

Look at this problem against the overall quality of your marriage. Who usually bends when there's a stand-off? Who usually makes the decisions? Who okays expensive purchases? Does one person always expect the other to acquiesce? Maybe the dominant one doesn't realize the other partner's determination on this issue may not be as amenable to change as usual.

To improve the situation, practice tolerance. I'm convinced that the main ingredient of all troublefree marriages is tolerance by at least one partner.

Start by controlling a reaction to a minor inconvenience—leaving dirty socks on the floor or the toothpaste cap off. You don't have to ignore the problem—just try a new approach for dealing with it. If you usually get irritated, instead replace the cap, put it away, and count to ten. Two hours or more later, mention your discovery: "Did you know you left the toothpaste out and open?" If you put off the childbearing decision and practice tolerance until it becomes automatic, maybe both of you will eventually be able to compromise on a baby issue.

Recall Michele and Barry, who fought because she wanted a child and he didn't. In their seven-year marriage, Michele had always given in to Barry's desires, gladly making him happy. But when he changed his mind about having the child they'd agreed upon, Michele was forced to become assertive. She moved in with a girlfriend, scaring Barry into taking her seriously. He's now becoming favorable to fathering a child.

Also remember Arthur and Danielle, who eventually set a deadline to achieve the career success necessary for Arthur to feel confident about parenthood. If that time comes and success is still out of reach, both his career and reluctance about the child will be reevaluated.

In both cases, the marriages will be changed. Michele feels she'll never trust Barry again; Arthur feels resentment against Danielle. Unless you're not worried about damaging your relationship, keep communication open and don't say "never."

13

Creating a "Children: To Have or Have Not" Workshop

The materials and discussion in this book can be used alone. Most readers will probably use them on their own to ponder all the ramifications of parenthood, but others may want the support and feedback of a group of would-be parents.

It's simple to divide the activities presented here into a neat package suitable for a workshop led by someone making the childbearing choice or, better yet, a trained mental health professional. The advantages in staging this kind of gathering are:

- *There's an established timeframe* for couples or individuals to systematically progress through all aspects of the decision. Many of the couples who come to the workshops I lead report that they enrolled because they had trouble making a definitive choice and wanted to "make the decision once and for all." Setting aside two weeks to intensely focus on this single issue helps indecisive people face their ambivalence within an allotted time period.

- *Objective observers,* the other participants in the workshop, can provide insight on their views of your own situation. If a mental health professional (social worker, marriage and family therapist, psychologist, or psychiatrist) is present, he or she can offer the perspective of someone practiced in sorting out motivations, desires, and dreams.

- *The relief of knowing you're not alone* in your situation or in your values and thoughts is an immediate, enormous benefit. Suddenly ideas that might have felt like confessions become the norm.

- *A variety of circumstances and perspectives* among participants lets you compare your own situation with others. Most workshop groups are a mixture of now-or-never couples, planners, and people in conflict. Differences and similarities among concerns help you decide how important the ingredients in your personal choice are.

- *You have an opportunity to give information to others,* a challenge of creative problem solving. Maybe you'll hear someone report a reaction or notion that doesn't ring true. You can question them, point out possible solutions, suggest a "what if," and offer the benefit of your own experience. With this comes the satisfying reward of knowing you're helping someone else find an appropriate answer for their own dilemma.

- *The parenthood experience may be represented* by someone who is deciding on a second or subsequent child, or has ended a first marriage with children and is facing the choice with a new spouse. Though one person's experiences may be lopsided or colored by an interfering emotion, there's still at least one valuable vote for "the good stuff" of smiles, coos, and cozies which nonparents cannot recall.

Setting Up a Workshop

Before I discuss a suggested workshop format, let me review several mechanics of putting together a workshop. The process should begin at least two months before dates you select, unless you feel you've got enough participants among friends or clients you already know. Here are the necessary steps to arrange a workshop:

1. *Arrange for workshop leadership or sponsorship.* The three-meeting workshop can be an informal gathering of co-workers or friends, or an officially sponsored function. A corporation with many employees facing the childbearing decision has a stake in the outcome—it's looking for worryfree, productive workers. If it holds a growing number of achieving women among its upper ranks, it stands to lose, temporarily or permanently, some top employees. Professional associations (Women in Business, Kiwannis, Chambers of Commerce) could sponsor a decision-making workshop, since having

a family is a major career-shaper. Organizations that serve the community (Planned Parenthood, Jewish Family Services, local mental health clinics) might offer the workshop as a service to members.

2. *Arrange a room.* If an organization or group does sponsor the workshop, they will probably have facilities that can be booked in advance. If a cluster of friends or nonaffiliated professionals ban together, check out the community rooms of local banks or savings and loans, the recreation rooms of condominiums or apartment complexes, conference rooms of large office buildings where a participant works, or local churches and synagogues. Requirements for the space are:

a. It must be available for a two-hour period on three consecutive weeks (e.g., for three Thursday nights or three Saturday mornings in a row).

b. It must comfortably seat 6–20 people in a circle facing each other. That means no ganged chairs. It's also desirable to have seating so everyone is on the same level—it's disconcerting to be the only one plopped three feet below the range of conversation on a floor pillow when everyone else is in a chair.

c. Participants should be able to write and refer to the materials easily, so there should be adequate lighting and plenty of room to move elbows.

d. Rest room facilities should be available.

e. The space should be free from distraction and located for privacy. In the workshop, participants often share intimate details of their lives and often find themselves crying. To protect the confidence of these personal experiences and assure that everyone can hear adequately, line up a room with a closing door and windows that muffle outside noise.

3. *Set limits on enrollment.* Often, limits will be set by the space available, especially if the workshop is held in a private livingroom. But if there's unlimited space, restrict the group to no more than 10 couples (or 20 individuals) if there's one leader, and no more than 15 couples (30 individuals) if there are two co-leaders. These are upper limits; a much more comfortable group is three to eight couples.

4. *Choose dates and times.* As mentioned above, you'll need to set aside three weekly two-hour time slots. Since a large proportion of people struggling with the childbearing choice are employed,

weeknights or Saturday mornings prove most convenient. An evening time slot that draws the most response is 7:00 or 7:30 to 9:00 or 9:30 P.M. There's even better response on Saturday, from 10:00 or 10:30 A.M. to noon or 12:30 P.M. That leaves the rest of the day to take care of errands or an outing. Often couples like to follow the workshop with informal discussions over lunch or an evening snack at a restaurant.

5. *Make sure the materials are available.* Check your local bookstore to be sure there are enough copies of this book so each couple (or each person, if you're offering the workshop to individuals) can begin the workshop with the necessary materials. Booksellers usually require at least two weeks to order and receive books they've sold out.

6. *Send out announcements or invitations* to the media or target groups. The workshop can be offered to single individuals, married individuals, or couples, with both spouses attending and required. Announcements should include the purpose: "To help couples sort out their values, expectations, and feelings about having a child"; "To ease conflict and distress over the childbearing decision"; "To help those facing "now or never" time pressure, conflict, or disagreement, or looking at ramifications of an inclination to have a child or remain permanently childfree."

Also include the format ("Three weekly meetings, two hours each"), the content ("Discussion and at-home exercises that look at the rational and emotional sides of the decision"), and the dates, times, location, leadership, cost, and registration procedure.

The price usually escalates with the qualifications of the leaders and the prestige of the location or sponsoring group. I've found that a sliding scale is helpful, but if the workshop is priced too low, its worth is somehow devalued in the minds of participants. They're thinking, "If it's only $5, then it couldn't be that great." But if they have to invest a more substantial sum—$35–$100 or more—they have a financial commitment to the process, are less likely to drop out when decision making becomes tough, and arrive with respect for the undertaking. Of course, a group of friends or co-workers shouldn't charge (except to cover any expenses that arise), especially if all the members are personally benefitting from the experience, completing the decision-making process with the group.

A press release, a one-page description of the workshop with all pertinent data written in sentence form, can be mailed to local editors three weeks in advance of the workshop. If possible, phone the newspaper to find the name of the appropriate editor and address the envelope to him or her directly. Then, if no notice has appeared a week before the workshop, call to remind the editor. Radio and television stations often have free public service announcements, so send them copies and follow up with phone calls. A sample press release is shown below.

News from L/CC
learning/communication center   Micrandon Elvenstar, M.A.
9701 Wilshire Boulevard, Suite 836   Contact: Diane C. Elvenstar, Ph.D.
Beverly Hills, California 90212   Directors

"CHILDREN: TO HAVE OR HAVE NOT" WORKSHOPS OFFERED IN APRIL

"Children: To Have or Have Not" is the question couples will answer at an April workshop sponsored jointly by Learning/Communication Center, Beverly Hills, and the nonprofit National Alliance for Optional Parenthood, Los Angeles. Three weekly meetings, to be held Saturday mornings April 4, 11, and 18 at Learning/Communication Center, 9701 Wilshire Blvd., Beverly Hills, will punctuate home activities designed to help couples examine their values, expectations, and feelings surrounding the childbearing dilemma.

The problem is a crucial one to a growing number of couples aged 25 to 40. New opportunities for women in the workplace (and a need for their income)—as well as new attitudes about personal gratification and the family—make parenthood a question of not only when, but if. Couples deciding about adding another child (often in a second marriage) face additional conflicts. The workshop is also designed for those who are inclined toward parenthood or permanent nonparenthood, and seek to plan purposefully regarding the ramifications and timing of that choice.

The workshop aims to resolve conflict and reduce distress. Week One's at-home activities focus on the rational side of the decision, using information and a series of personalized questionnaires. Week Two examines the emotional side of the issue, with couples reacting to three days each of imagined parenthood and permanent nonparenthood.

7. *Keep track of enrollment.* Since the number of participants is limited, you need to have a central enrollment receiving location or secretary. If a fee is involved, make sure the money is kept securely (perhaps in a bank account) at least until the workshop begins and you know there won't be refunds. As the workshop draws closer, confirm your reservations for the room and check stocks of the materials at your local bookstores.

As people enroll, inform them that this book is the required text, and let them know where it's available. Then suggest they read and complete exercises in Chapters 1–6. The workshop begins with the questionnaires and exercises in Chapter 7, and it will be helpful if everyone has a similar orientation through reading the book beforehand.

8. *Prepare to lead the workshop.* The workshop leader(s) should reread the book and fully understand the exercises. The person in charge might want to fantasize about questions that could arise as well as topics your particular group would find most rewarding. Perhaps there's a poison peril in your area—one issue might be the safety of raising a child locally. Perhaps the hospital facilities in your community are especially innovative, with special birthing rooms, midwives, up-to-the-minute fetal monitoring equipment. You might want to have that information handy. Consider any other local issues: attitudes towards fitness and women's bodies (in the sun zone, in certain circles of friends and co-workers), traditions to have large families (agricultural regions, certain religious groups), beliefs about women's role (in religious or ethnic groups).

9. *Lead the workshop.* The day before, plan for any refreshments (best are coffee with a nonfattening snack like fruit or vegetables and dip to be served at break). Check the room to be sure heating and cooling equipment are functioning. Test the chairs for comfort— throw pillows for hard folding chairs or benches will help.

The day of the first meeting, arrive a half-hour early to set up and welcome anyone searching for the location. By now, participants will have purchased this book and glanced through the agenda for the workshop. Welcome everyone, introduce yourself, and follow the agenda, using alert leadership skills to facilitate conversation, ask questions, encourage shy members, or play "devil's advocate." Don't be afraid of a lull in discussion, however. Sometimes a more reticent member is waiting for such a moment to add his or her thoughts. Keep track of time, and gently break off talk with "It's time to move along" when you simply can't accommodate more interaction in your time frame. But be flexible—the agenda is meant for convenience. The most important result of a group meeting is that participants are satisfied with their self-expression and amount of interaction.

A Workshop Agenda

At the First Meeting

Activity	Notes to leader
1. Reiterate purpose of the workshop.	State how you became involved with the topic, how the workshop came to be given.
2. Round-the-circle introductions: state name, what brought you to the workshop, type of decision being made.	Reiterate the three types of decision makers; let participants classify themselves.
3. Complete and/or discuss "A Before Questionnaire" (Chapter 6, page 92). Discuss surprises, thoughts that arose, differences with partner.	Remind that this will be ignored until the final session. It's purpose is to test conflict, distress, interaction style, inclination.
4. Break; refreshments (10 minutes).	
5. Complete "Expectations Questionnnaire" (Chapter 7, page 114).	Because of its length, the "Viewpoints Questionnaire" becomes an at-home activity. Describe the questionnaire (as in text) and allow 15 minutes for completion. Then encourage partners (if the group is couples) to trade papers and discuss for another five minutes.
6. Discuss issues raised by the "Expectations Questionnaire."	Approach the questions systematically or let conversation be free-form. If participants seem to share the same view, play "devil's advocate" and present other alternatives to consider.

Activity	Notes to leader
7. Provide an overview of each day's activities to be completed between meetings at home.	Go over the "In the First Week" agenda to follow; call for questions about procedure.
8. Final comments, adjournment.	Try to stick to the time frame, even if on-going discussion persists (10–15 minutes overtime is usually acceptable to participants).

In the First Week: Home Agenda

Each day, participants will complete one activity, leading to a tentative decision in time for discussion at the next meeting. Group members should read the accompanying text as they complete forms; then stop for that day and follow the agenda listed here.

Day 2 (the day following the first workshop meeting): Complete "Viewpoints Questionnaire" independently from partner; discuss your responses and read accompanying text.

Day 3: Complete "Continuua Questionnaire"; discuss with partner and read accompanying text.

Day 4: Read the material in Chapter 7 on cost of a child, pregnancy and birth, career, genetic concerns, etc. Write down your reaction to some fact or idea you encounter; then discuss what you've written with your partner. This will force you to be more attentive to what you're reading and will be the source of discussion for that evening.

Day 5: Complete the "Benefits and Drawbacks Questionnaire" in Chapter 7 to evaluate and then score your inclination in favor or against having a child. Follow the guidelines for interpreting your responses and score; then share your questionnaire with your partner, as suggested in Chapter 7.

Day 6: Go back over your earlier questionnaires, revising any responses you want to change in light of reading, discussion, or new insight. Then, with your partner, complete the "Partner Decision-making Sheet". (If you're a single person, simply express your own preference). Think about issues, questions, or facts you'd like to bring up in group discussion at the second meeting tomorrow.

Day 7: Attend second workshop meeting.

At the Second Meeting

Activity	Notes to leader
1. Overview of meeting's agenda; welcome.	Mention the tasks of the meeting as listed on this page.
2. Round-the-circle descriptions of each person's experience with the materials during the previous week. State name, reaction to questionnaires, score in favor and against a child, areas of surprise and concern.	Encourage participants to ask each other questions, add comments, or share relevant information, but don't get sidetracked and allow each person in sequence an opportunity to complete his or her report. Remind participants that they are providing self and peer-group help; that in essence, they are therapists for each other.
3. Summarize differences between rational and emotional observations as transition into the emotional perspective.	Refer to the exercise in Chapter 5 where readers practiced catching feelings by reacting to pictures. If there's time, you might show additional photographs and ask participants to jot down the feeling that's aroused.
4. Break (10 minutes).	
5. Fill in the "Sentence Completion" exercise on page 179 of Chapter 9.	This is a free-association exercise, so encourage participants not to censor their feelings. Allow ten minutes, and suggest that those with extra time begin going through the list again, adding more endings to the same sentences.
6. Share "Sentence Completion" with partner and quietly discuss.	Allow five minutes for partners to share responses.
7. General discussion in the larger group or, if there are two leaders, a group of eight or more couples may be broken into smaller, single-sex groups or simply more manageable clusters.	Facilitate discussion, encouraging participants to relate experiences of their childhoods or their adult parenting roles.

Activity	Notes to leader
8. Describe the activities for the coming week to be completed at home.	Urge participants to get as much hands-on experience with children as possible—and in a literal sense as well. Now would be the perfect time to "borrow a child," to push him on the swings at the park, feed and bathe an infant, play football with a teenager. Since the purpose is to observe emotions, emphasize that "the good stuff"—positive emotions—come from interaction with children, not just fantasizing about a potential child.
9. Final comments, adjournment.	Remind participants to role-play pregnancy and permanent nonparenthood as wholeheartedly as possible to gain the most from the process. Warn them that "forgetting" to role-play may be a way to simply avoid an unpleasant topic or distressing memories.

The Second Week: Home Agenda

Day 2 (the day following the second meeting): In privacy, with pen and paper (or tape recorder) complete "Fantasizing to Arouse Feelings" exercise near the beginning of Chapter 9. Share your experience with your partner, if desired.

Day 3: Spend the day role-playing the woman partner's pregnancy, observing your emotional reaction to impending parenthood, according to the guidelines in Chapter 9. In the evening, fill in the "First Daily Record Sheet: Imagining Pregnancy." Share the experience and your responses with your mate.

Day 4: Spend another day fantasizing pregnancy, focusing on a second topic. Note fluctuations in your feelings, and record your reactions on the "Second Daily Record Sheet: Imagining Pregnancy." Again, share the day's outcomes with your partner.

Day 5: The last day fantasizing pregnancy and the coming child, this time concentrating on a third general topic area. At the end of the day, complete the "Third Daily Record Sheet: Imagining Pregnancy" as before, and share the results with your partner.

Day 6: Change to imagining a life of permanent nonparenthood, grabbing all the feelings that prospect arouses. In the evening, fill out the "Fourth Daily Record Sheet: Imagining Permanent Nonparenthood." As usual, discuss your feelings and responses, this time to the notion that you and your partner will stay permanently childfree.

Day 7: Return to the questionnaires and information of the first week, and the Daily Record Sheets you completed this week. Summarize your feelings and concerns from both the rational and emotional sides, and compile them as directed in Chapter 9 for the "Final Decision-making Sheet." The "decision alternative" you circle on that sheet becomes your tentative childbearing choice, to be discussed at the final workshop meeting tomorrow. Prepare any questions, comments, or ideas for the final group discussion.

At the Third (Final) Meeting

Activity	Notes to leader
1. Round-the-circle descriptions of last week's at-home activities. State name and experiences imagining pregnancy and permanent nonparenthood.	By now, participants know each other fairly well. Again, encourage all group members to question or provide assistance to each other.
2. After everyone has given a personal overview of the past week's experiences, open up discussion.	Remind participants that the major goal of this meeting is to give and receive feedback on individuals' tentative decisions. This means making an effort to offer constructive suggestions on how each person's inclination can be made to work successfully.
3. Break (10 minutes).	
4. Continue discussion.	Allow at least 25 minutes at the end of the session.
5. Complete "An After Questionnaire," in Chapter 13 independently.	Allow ten minutes for completing this questionnaire.

Activity	Notes to leader
6. Compare responses on "An After Questionnaire" with those on "A Before Questionnaire" in Chapter 6.	Allow five minutes for group members to look back at their earlier forms, noting changes arising from the process.
7. Share "An After Questionnaire" and differences from "before" with partner.	Allow five minutes for couples to talk quietly.
8. Final comments and adjournment.	Sometimes participants express interest in arranging a group "reunion" at a specific point, usually ranging from three months to a year in the future. You may want to pass around a roster to be signed by those who would like to be included, and assign the task of organizing such a gathering to a willing group member. *General note:* Participants often ask my personal childbearing preference. As the leader, I don't want to bias the thinking of any group members, so I usually refrain from discussing my personal situation. If pressed, I do divulge my childbearing decision at the end of the final meeting. If you are going through the childbearing process with workshop members, feel free to fully participate in all discussion.

After the workshop is over, you may want to follow up on the decisions of participants via a postcard to be mailed to you in three to six months. It's helpful to offer a list of local referrals for information on childbearing, parenting, remaining childfree, childcare, and other topics of interest. Usually, several solid friendships are born in the workshops. Evaluations I've done of the process show that, although sometimes the activities and feelings are difficult because they're painful, participants are glad they've participated and feel they've gained a great deal of insight into themselves and their partners.

14

Conclusion

You can see why a method to help couples decide about having a child had to be a *process*. Some counselors provide a useful one-day workshop on this decision, which allows a helpful overview of the issues. But the decision still takes time. A study by Dr. Lucy Scott of the Fielding Institute in Santa Barbara, California found that the decision begins shaping in young minds at about age 12. It swirls around, bumping against every event in your life, every parent or carefree couple you see. After you've established a loving relationship, it comes into focus; but if you stand face-to-face with it and it's still fuzzy, perhaps these materials have helped improve your vision.

You've just completed a focusing process, a microscopic look at something most people never examine. You're as well equipped to make an informed choice as any human can be.

If you've decided *not to decide,* or if you want to evaluate your options for adding a second child to your family, you now have skills you can reuse. You also have in this book a set of resources that can be used repeatedly to organize your feelings, values, and expectations at that later time and provide references for more information.

If you've decided not to decide, or are planning to postpone having a child for a definite period, your reactions to the dilemma this first time will be a guide to your readiness for parenthood. You'll need to *feel or show* on paper a significant difference from the responses you gave this time. You'll need to look for discrepancies between what you say now and your perspective later on. Obviously, if you feel the same then, you won't want to commit yourself to parenthood.

If your anxiety continues, return to your notes and questionnaires in six months. Look at each item and analyze how situations have changed in your life. Look at trends in your career, in your financial situation, in your feelings whenever you see a child on the street. Perhaps when you filled out the questionnaires this time, you were up in the air. Next time you may be jumping less, feeling more solid about certain aspects of your life. Then, a year from now, you'll be more confident about your direction in life and your feelings about children. You've made a change, and you can see it in the way your responses to items and situations change.

Colleen was one person who benefited from repeating the process. "A year ago, I just felt a lot of pressure to make up my mind. Most of my girlfriends were having kids, taking time off to stay home. It seemed somewhat appealing, all that freedom and leisure. I was thinking I might want to have one myself." She shook her head negating the wisdom of that thought.

"I found out that I didn't have to feel pressure—that I had plenty of time left to make up my mind. I also discovered that there were lots of areas of my life I wasn't satisfied with, and that's why escaping to my cocoon of a home with my cuddly infant seemed so appealing." Colleen smiled and squeezed the hand of her husband, seated beside her. "Now things are different. My job has totally changed, to the point where I'm now in charge of 30 other workers. Greg and I bought a new house, and I discovered that I adore my vegetable garden. Last year at this time I was overweight—instead of tackling my problems I'd pig-out on cookies. Because I feel like such a happily different person, I feel I'm much better equipped to have a child—on my own terms."

Indeed, Colleen looked smashing. Her hair was cut shorter, enhancing rather than hiding a slender face. Her questionnaire responses showed that she was less influenced by others and had some direction in her life. She and Greg decided they would have a child in two years, after they'd had time to enjoy some of the pleasures they'd recently recognized.

Probably the most-pondered question doesn't have to do with the process of parenting; it isn't about babies or relationships or careers. Instead, it focuses on *regret.* "Will I wish I'd had kids?" is the nonparents' lament. "Will I wish I'd had the freedom and time to accomplish my dreams?" is the parents' worry.

Professor Linda Beckman of UCLA's Department of Psychiatry did a study of 700 older women, ages 60–75. She asked an equal number of parents and nonparents, married and widowed or divorced women, about how satisfied they were with their lives. Seven aspects of happiness were measured. It turns out that on five of the areas, parents and nonparents were equally satisfied. So for the most part, it doesn't make much difference whether or not you have children.

Childless women were lonelier than their maternal counterparts. They also reported that they were more isolated from the world. But Dr. Beckman also looked at marital status, and those without *anyone* were the unhappy ones; if there was *either* a husband or a child around, life satisfaction remained high. Also remember that this group of women were raised in times when women's major role was homemaking. They were taught to believe their main fulfillment in life would come from mothering and caring for grateful families. Women exposed to other options of more fulfilling jobs, egalitarian marriages, and notions that they're not the "weaker sex" will probably view nonparenthood even more favorably.

Interestingly, both parents and the childless women Dr. Beckman queried would have liked to have had more children. No matter how many offspring mothers had reared, they all wanted one more. Childless women also said that one child would have been welcome.

Dr. Beckman notes that parents can be pleased or agonized by their children, while nonparents can regret missing the experience or be happy with what they've accomplished. Whether you will be remorseful or content as you grow older seems to depend on your attitude toward life and yourself more than whether or not you have children. Adults who develop social skills, have a wide range of friends, and are immersed in rewarding business and leisure pursuits can call upon inner resources for entertainment and support. Those who spend their lives complaining and wishing they had more will never be satisfied, even with a complement of loving children at their feet.

So be pleased with your life; cultivate it carefully, and children will only be a bonus. And if you choose not to have children, you won't be sitting in your rocking chair all alone. The U.S. government's Statistical Abstract of the U.S. for 1978 shows that about 6 percent of married women in their twenties and thirties chose to remain childfree—up from less than 3 percent in 1967. Whether or not to have children is an issue of the 1980s that should continue to be important as long as attractive options for men, women, and children abound.

"An After Questionnaire"

You've huffed, puffed, and blown your mind down completing files, notes, and forms. Perhaps you won't mind just one more. Before you began the decision-making process, you completed "A Before Questionnaire" to assess your conflict, distress, and inclination for or against having a child. Now that you know where you're headed, here's a questionnaire to help you see how far you've come.

Each of you should independently complete "An After Questionnaire" and compare your answers with those on "A Before Questionnaire" in Chapter 4. Notice how far your distress over the decision has reduced and any changes in intensity of negative feelings. Look at the change in inner conflict and conflict between you and your partner. Examine differences in the percentages you and your partner lean for and against having a child. Finally, look at the choices you alone and you with your partner have made to see differences due to the process.

Then share your responses with your partner, looking for similarities and differences between both of your before-and-after sheets. In most cases, the after questionnaire reveals many more similar answers, a result of the discussions and probing process. If you remain undecided, you can use this sheet as a periodic assessment of your status regarding having a child.

Name: _____ Date: _____

"An After Questionnaire"

1. How much is the decision about whether or not to have a child a source of **distress** at this point in time?

   a. For you?   None   A little   Some   A lot

   b. Between you and your partner?   None   A little   Some   A lot

2. If you have any negative feelings at this point in time, are they: (circle one)

   | Very strong (crying, depressed) | Moderately strong (upset, defensive, angry) | Not very strong (nagging worry, a bother) |

3. When you think about having a child right away, how much do you feel each of these at this point in time?

	Most of the time	Some of the time	A small amount of the time	Never
a. Positive (happy, enthusiastic)				
b. Negative (scared, depressed, distressed)				
c. Confused or conflicted (decide back and forth)				

4. How much **conflict** (clash of ideas, uncertainty) is there at this point over the child-bearing decision:

   a. Within yourself?   None   A little   Some   A lot

   b. Within your partner?   None   A little   Some   A lot

   c. Between the two of you?   None   A little   Some   A lot

5. What is the percentage you lean **toward** having a child right away, and the percentage you lean **against** having one?

   a. Within 1 year   **b. In the future** (How long? _____)

   _____% + _____% = 100%   _____% + _____% = 100%

                                                    Toward   Against

                                                    having   having

                                                      one   one

6. What is the percentage **your partner** seems to lean toward having a child right away, and the percentage he or she seems to lean against having one:

a. Within 1 year   **b. In the future**

_____% + _____% = 100%   _____% + _____% = 100%

                                                        Toward   Against

7. Right now, your own preference is to: (check one)

   a. _____ Have a child   b. _____ Postpone a child
                                                              (How long? _____)

   c. _____ Not have any children   d. _____ Not make any decision yet

8. The decision you and your partner have made is to: (check one)

   a. _____ Have a child   b. _____ Postpone a child
                                                              (How long? _____)

   c. _____ Not have any children   d. _____ Not make any decision yet

9. How certain are you that the decision you checked above will hold true?

   a. _____ Very certain   b. _____ Somewhat certain   c. _____ Uncertain

---

When the Decision Is Behind You

Yes, you've read the caveats and misgivings, doubts, ambivalences, and regret. But if you've gone through this evaluation process sincerely and systematically, chances are these bugaboos won't bug you. They'll be a lot smaller than for people who had kids without thinking, because someone "got pregnant," or because it was "the thing to do."

"I'm sure glad I didn't have to make up my mind about having kids," a 50-year old mother of three told me. "I would've been so confused and upset with so many choices. As it was I just went ahead and had them, and never gave it a second thought. It's a lot harder now."

Yes, the decision is a lot harder, because of the many attractive options that we have—and that the mother above lost out on. In many ways, people now in their twenties and thirties are lucky to face this kind of distress. It shows that whatever the outcome, life won't be miserable. It shows that there's hope for happiness, social acceptance, and pleasure no matter which option you choose. Maybe making the choice *is* harder now—but afterwards, life is sure to be rewarding.

Some people ask me what my husband and I ultimately chose. I ask them to guess. Inevitably, each person says that I have made the choice *they* find most appealing for themselves. So I'll leave it at that. Think what you will. I will say that I'm satisfied with the decision. And I become more satisfied with each workshop I conduct and with each couple who leaves knowing they've made the right decision, too.

After all, having a child can be the most exciting task in life—as can pursuing the interests you enjoy, childfree. No matter what you decide, because you took the time and effort to think it through, you'll know how to make the most of it. It's a good feeling.